# Fragmented Women

# Fragmented Women

## Feminist (Sub)versions of Biblical Narratives

J. Cheryl Exum

Trinity Press International
Valley Forge, Pennsylvania

First Edition 1993

Trinity Press International
P.O. Box 851
Valley Forge, PA   19482-0851

Cover art: © Cover design by Brian Preuss
1993 Succession H. Matisse / ARS, New York

Library of Congress Cataloging-in-Publication Data

Exum, J. Cheryl
    Fragmented Women : feminist (sub)versions of biblical narratives
/ J. Cheryl Exum.
        pp.            cm
    Includes bibliographical references and indexes.
    ISBN 1-56338-018-8 :
    1. Women in the Bible.  2. Bible. O.T. Judges—Criticism,
interpretation, etc.  3. Patriarchy—religious aspects.  4. Feminist
theology.  I. Title.
    BS1199.W7E88  1993
    221.6'082——dc20
                                                            93-22674
                                                            CIP

Printed in the United States of America.

93 94 95 96 97 98   6 5 4 3 2 1

*For Detlev Grohn and Francis Landy*

*Chapter 4, which grew out of an essay I was unable to complete for inclusion in his Festschrift, is dedicated to Norman Gottwald*

# CONTENTS

# PREFACE

In the narratives of the Bible, women are usually minor characters in the stories of men. The 'stories' of women examined in this book are parts of the more cohesive stories of their fathers, husbands, and sons—fragments of the 'larger story' that biblical scholarship has traditionally taken as *the* story. So long as we remain within the boundaries of the literary text itself, the study of women in ancient literature cannot become anything other than the study of men's views of women. Thus the first step in constructing versions of women's stories from the submerged strains of their voices in men's stories is to subvert the men's stories. This can only be done, in my opinion, by stepping outside the androcentric ideology of the biblical text.

To construct feminist (sub)versions of biblical narratives and to claim for women a voice denied them by the larger story, the present study draws on contemporary feminist literary theory, in particular certain aspects of deconstruction and psychoanalytic literary theory. This book explores the gender ideology that informs selected biblical narratives in order to reveal strategies by which patriarchal literature excludes, marginalizes, and otherwise operates to subjugate women. By 'gender' I refer to the cultural definition of behavior considered to be appropriate to the sexes in a given society at a given time.[1] In contrast to sex, which is a biological given, gender is culturally created. I use the term 'patriarchal' to refer to both an ideology and a social system in which women are subordinated to men, and younger men to older men.[2] Whereas the biblical text is fundamentally

1. Lerner (1986: 238).
2. With Bal (1987); Fuchs (1985a: 117 n. 2); contra Meyers (1988: 24-26).

patriarchal, it, like patriarchal literature in general, shows traces of the problematic of maintaining patriarchy. In different ways, the chapters of this book seek to expose this problematic by bringing to the surface and problematizing what is suppressed, distorted, and fragmented. For purposes of this study, I wish to set aside the question of who produced these stories, of whether or not, and to what degree, women might be considered responsible for these traditions.[3] In my opinion, that question is secondary to the issue of gender ideology in biblical material. 'Women', as Gerda Lerner points out, 'are and have been central, not marginal, to the making of society and to the building of civilization. Women have also shared with men in preserving collective memory, which shapes the past into cultural tradition, provides the link between generations, and connects past and future.' But whereas men and women share in the making of history and the creation of society, symbolic production has been controlled by men. In the interpretation of civilization, the creation of symbol systems—that is, meaning-giving—women have been marginalized and excluded.[4] Even if the Bible's authors were not all males, the world view that finds expression in the biblical literature is the dominant male world view. As a result, the female perspective is muted, if not altogether excluded.[5] Nor is this exclusion or marginalization of women limited to the biblical literature, it is also repeated in the history of biblical interpretation. Indeed, Lerner well describes the situation with which the feminist critic has to deal when she observes, 'All philosophies and systems of thought in which we are trained have either ignored or marginalized women'.[6]

3. For a different view, see Goitein (1988); and for a promising new approach to this issue that looks at texts in terms of gender-positions and attribution of gender within texts, see Brenner and van Dijk-Hemmes (1993).

4. See Lerner (1986: 4-6, 199-211). The citation is from p. 4.

5. See Lerner (1986: 5-6, 199-211, 231-33 *et passim*). The challenge for feminist analysis is to find women's (sub)texts within these phallocentric texts; cf. the important work of Bal (1988a); Brenner and van Dijk-Hemmes (1993).

6. Lerner (1986: 231-32).

My intention in this book is neither to recover affirmations of women in the Bible nor to attack the Bible as a sexist document. These alternatives marked an earlier generation of feminist criticism, but recently scholars have begun to move beyond this kind of 'either–or' approach to explore new and more suitable methods of feminist critique.[7] The strategy I have adopted here, that of stepping outside the ideology of the text, enables me to disrupt some of the cultural and ideological codes in selected biblical narratives in order to construct feminist (sub)versions of them. I approach the Bible as a cultural artifact, not as a religious object. The Bible, precisely because its ideology has been and continues to be so influential in shaping gender roles and expectations in contemporary society, needs to be approached from a feminist perspective.[8]

I begin with the assumption that the biblical literature was produced by and for an androcentric community. I understand women in the biblical literature as male constructs. They are the creations of androcentric (probably male) narrators, they reflect androcentric ideas about women, and they serve androcentric interests. What Esther Fuchs observes about biblical mothers applies to other female characters as well: they 'reveal more about the wishful thinking, fears, aspirations, and prejudices of their male creators than about women's authentic lives'.[9] Since as long as we remain within the androcentric ideology of the text, we can do no more than describe what ancient men had to say about women, a feminist critique must, of necessity, read against the grain. In androcentric texts like the Bible, women are often made to speak and act against their own interests. This

---

7. See the recent books of Bal (1987, 1988a); Pardes (1992); and Brenner and van Dijk-Hemmes (1993); exceedingly promising also are the directions taken by Newsom (1989) and Bach (1993 and forthcoming).

8. Biblical ideology not only typically privileges male characters, it always privileges the deity, perceived most often in male terms. Questioning the privileged position of the deity, who is, after all, a character in the narrative is, in my opinion, an area of investigation that invites further attention; see Exum (1990, 1992).

9. Fuchs (1985: 118).

being the case, the central organizing question of this book is: what androcentric agenda do these narratives promote? I do not claim exclusivity for the readings of women's stories presented here. To suggest that there is one proper way to read the text results in an authoritarianism characteristic of phallocentric criticism—a position that feminist criticism rejects in its recognition (and celebration) of contradiction and multiplicity. A feminist reading will not be a neutral reading, 'neutral' or 'objective reading' usually being terms for what turn out to be androcentric readings. As a way of underscoring the plurality of interpretive possibilities that feminist reading permits and encourages, and of drawing attention to the role of the reader in determining textual meaning, the chapters of this book employ different reading strategies, and, in so far as it has been possible for me to achieve, reflect a different narrative voice. The chapters are thus autonomous and heterogeneous, moving in different directions and yielding different results, while connected by their common concern with identifying and critiquing the androcentric agenda of the narratives discussed. One of my discoveries in the course of writing this book was that, over and over, that agenda was motivated by male fear and desire in response to women's sexuality and the resultant need of patriarchy to control women.

In Chapters 1 and 6, I break with established notions of literary unity by reading unrelated stories (that is, stories assigned by biblical scholars to different sources and dates) against each other. In both of these chapters I wanted to experiment with reading a text that relies on a particular strategy for controlling women on the level of the plot against a text that uses the same type of strategy at the narratorial level. Chapter 1 deals with murder and its possible motivation in the stories of Jephthah's daughter (Judg. 11) and Michal (2 Sam. 6); Chapter 6, with rape in the stories of Bathsheba and the nameless victim of rape and dismemberment in Judges 19, the Bible's ultimate fragmented woman. Obviously, since they take place in texts, both 'murders' are literary murders, and both 'rapes' literary rapes, but in each case, one is recounted in the story and one takes place by means of the story—the story is the murder weapon or the instrument of rape. Chapter 2 takes another look at Michal, focusing on the fragments of her story not dealt with in Chapter 1, and comparing Michal and her brother Jonathan in order to show how their fates are gender-determined.

In Chapter 3, I am again concerned with comparing the stories of women, but in this case the text itself (the Samson saga of Judg. 13–16) sets up the comparison—between the ideal woman as mother and woman as the seductive and dangerous other—and I set out to undermine it by exposing the problematic of such patriarchal binary thinking.

Chapters 4 and 5 both deal with the matriarchs, but in very different ways. Chapter 4 combines a literary approach with anthropological insights in order to explore the role of the matriarchs in the stories of Israel's origins (Gen. 12–35). Within this larger complex, we encounter a repeated tale, known in the scholarly literature as 'the endangered ancestress' or 'the wife-sister stories' (Genesis 12, 20 and 26). This strange and disturbing tale is the subject of a psycho-analytic literary reading in Chapter 5.

The chapters of this book are not arranged in canonical order. Not only would such an arrangement be impossible, given the juxtaposition of stories from different biblical books in Chapters 1 and 6, but I also find it undesirable, for the very concept of a canon is phallocentric: it tells us, for example, to read in a certain order and to privilege certain texts over others.[10] All the women's stories I examine in this book happen to come from the canon, and a rather limited section of it at that—but my choice of texts was arbitrary, more a reflection of my interests than of my ideological convictions. The narratives I discuss come from the so-called historical books of Genesis to Kings, which tell a purportedly chronological story as a series of stories of men: Abraham, Isaac, Jacob, Joseph, Moses, Joshua, the judges (one of whom is a woman), Samuel, Saul, David, and so on. Because, within this larger story, women's stories are fragmented, one of my strategies is to refuse to read these

10. See Bach (1993).

women's stories in their 'given' (canonical) order, thus symbolically fragmenting the male story-line. Patriarchal texts like the Bible are part of women's cultural heritage. Though in studying the Bible we work with androcentric texts, we are not restricted to phallocentric methodologies for analyzing them. Or, to put it more dramatically by borrowing a comment Mieke Bal once made in a lecture on the rape of Lucretia: 'Thanks for your text, and I'll decide how to read it'. In this book I read biblical women's stories differently, piecing together some of the Bible's fragmented women's stories to create feminist (sub)versions of them. Each chapter of the book is an experiment in counter-reading these stories in ways both that expose the difficulties patriarchy has in justifying its subjugation of women and that uncover traces of women's experience and women's resistance to patriarchal constraints.

Many people have helped this book along its way. Earlier drafts were read by Mieke Bal of the University of Amsterdam, Francis Landy of the University of Alberta, Martha Morrison of Boston College, and Yair Zakovitch of the Hebrew University of Jerusalem. John McDargh of Boston College helped me with psychoanalytic criticism. To all of them I owe both thanks and a word of apology, for this book would be stronger if I had been able to incorporate all of their insights and to respond adequately and creatively to all of their criticisms. Among those who have significantly influenced my thinking and writing, Alice Bach has been a constant source of ideas, inspiration, and support. In David Clines, I found my ideal editor. His unflagging energy and work in seeing this manuscript through to publication can be only inadequately acknowledged. Hal Rast and Laura Barrett of Trinity Press International were a pleasure to work with. Sean Cody, Susan Sweetser, and my research assistant, Karen Howard, also deserve special mention for their help, as does William Carl Ready, who contributed more than he will recognize.

Some parts of this book were read as papers at meetings of the Society of Biblical Literature, and I would like to express my appreciation to members of the audiences who heard them for their comments and suggestions. I also thank members of the 'Feminist Hermeneutics Task Force' of the Catholic Biblical Association for a very helpful discussion of material from Chapter 4. Finally, I am grateful to Boston College for research expense grants and for a sabbatical leave in 1991–1992, during which I completed most of the work on this book.

Portions of this book have appeared previously. Most of the discussion in Chapter 2 is taken from my book, *Tragedy in Biblical Narrative: Arrows of the Almighty* (Cambridge, 1992), and I thank Cambridge University Press for permission to reprint this material. A slightly different version of Chapter 1 originally appeared in *Union Seminary Quarterly Review* 43 (1989), pp. 19-39, and was subsequently published in *The Pleasure of Her Text* (ed. Alice Bach; Philadelphia: Trinity Press International, 1990). Chapter 5 appears also in *The New Literary Criticism and the Hebrew Bible* (ed. J. Cheryl Exum and David J.A. Clines; JSOT Supplements, 143; Sheffield: JSOT Press, 1993).

*About Translations and Transliterations*

Translations from the Hebrew are mine. In many cases, often unintentionally, they are close to the RSV. I have kept reference to Hebrew words at a minimum; transliterations from the Hebrew are not scientific.

Chapter 1

## MURDER THEY WROTE

Nobody seems to go through the agony of the victim...
Agatha Christie

In its implications, the distortion of a text resembles a murder;
the difficulty is not in perpetrating the deed, but in getting rid
of the traces.

Sigmund Freud

Let us begin our investigation by considering two literary murders. One is a sacrifice, which has all the appearances of a murder, except that the victim does not protest. In the other case, the victim does protest, but the murder does not take place in the story, but rather by means of the story. The story is the murder weapon, so to speak. The stories are those of Jephthah's daughter, offered by her father as a sacrifice to the deity, and of Michal, Saul's daughter and David's wife, denied offspring and voice in one fatal stroke, and thus killed off as a narrative presence. One victim is nameless, the other, named; but both are identified in terms of men: one, as a daughter; the other, as 'the daughter of Saul' and 'the wife of David', but never without one or both of these epithets. They thus illustrate the familiar position of women in biblical times, as under the authority of their fathers before marriage and of their husbands after marriage.[1] Neither functions as an independent agent in the sense that, for example, Deborah, Rahab, Delilah, and Jael do. Jephthah's daughter makes no real attempt to act autonomously, whereas Michal asserts herself, with deadly

---

1. For a helpful discussion, see Bird (1974).

consequences.

The 'stories' of these two women are parts of men's stories, part of the 'larger story' that we take as *the* story. David Clines has argued that there is no 'Michal story', that focusing upon a minor character in a story results in a distorted, or at least skewed reading of the whole.[2] He is right, of course, that there is no 'Michal story', nor is there a 'Jephthah's daughter's story', and for feminist criticism of biblical narrative that is precisely the problem. But one can nonetheless discern the submerged strains of Michal's voice and Jephthah's daughter's voice, and the challenge for feminist criticism is to construct a version of their stories from that voice. This can be done at least partially, I think, by de-constructing the dominant (male) voice, or phallogocentric ideology of the narratives.

I do not speak of these women's stories in any absolute sense, as if by de-constructing the male voice we will be closer to the 'truth' or 'the real story'. The relation of reading to truth involves the issue of interests, and our interests determine the questions we ask of a text.[3] In this quest after literary murderers, I am no more capable of telling the whole truth, and nothing but the truth, than the biblical narrators. Rather I shall use my interests to expose and undermine theirs, in the interest of possible truth.

What is the motive for these murders? In other words, what patriarchal function do these narratives serve? In pursuing an answer to this question, I shall endeavor to convict the biblical narrators on the basis of traces of the crime, which they left behind—traces that remain because the female perspective, the female voice, cannot be silenced, even by literary murder. The crime has been committed, the evidence is the text, and the female perspective provides our clue for de-constructing it.

Literary murder is, of course, different from the real thing, and both of our cases can be construed as something else, which may explain why the perpetrators have gotten away

2. Clines (1991: 129-30).
3. Bal (1988d).

with murder for so long.[4] In the case of Jephthah's daughter, the ritual act of sacrifice transforms murder into a socially acceptable act of execution.[5] We do not witness Michal's actual death; there is no need for its description, for, by the end of 2 Samuel 6, she has ceased to play any role in the Davidic house. As we shall see, poetics and ideology conspire to remove Michal as a narrative presence. There is no similar ideological necessity to get rid of Jephthah's daughter. She is the innocent victim of her father's vow. Since by accepting her death at the hands of the father, she poses no threat to the patriarchal system, her memory is allowed to live and to be celebrated within the story. This cannot, for reasons we shall explore below, be the case with Michal.

### The Case of the Dutiful Daughter

The story of Jephthah and his daughter appears in Judges 11. In return for victory over the Ammonites, Jephthah vows to sacrifice to Yhwh 'the one coming forth who comes forth from the doors of my house to meet me when I return in peace from the Ammonites' (11.31). His daughter is the one who meets him, and the alarming similarity in vocabulary brings out the dramatic impact: 'When Jephthah came to Mizpah to his house, behold, his daughter coming forth to meet him . . . ' (11.34). Jephthah's response, rending his garments as a sign of mourning, and his awkwardly expressed agony and consternation make it clear that he had not expected his daughter to be the object of his vow.

4.  An earlier version of this chapter appeared in Exum (1989). In the same year, Fuchs (1989) published a study analyzing how the narrative in Judges 11 subordinates Jephthah's daughter to its androcentric interests in order to make Jephthah a more sympathetic figure. Our analyses overlap in interesting ways, though I find greater ambiguity in the presentation of both the father and the daughter.

5.  This is not to say that we are to condone Jephthah's sacrifice of his daughter, but only that human sacrifice was practiced. No outright condemnation of Jephthah's sacrifice appears in the text, but hints of disapproval appear in the disastrous episode with the Ephraimites that follows the sacrifice; see Exum (1992: 53-54).

> When he saw her, he rent his garments and said, 'Ah, my
> daughter, you have brought me very low and have become the
> source of my trouble. I have opened my mouth to Yhwh and I
> cannot take it back' (11.35).

It has frequently been pointed out that rather than offering
solace, the father accuses his daughter—a classic case of
blaming the victim. But his words also, in my opinion,
express his feeling of not being solely responsible for this
awful turn of events. Just as Oedipus did not intend to kill
his father and marry his mother but does so only because he
does not know their identity, so too Jephthah did not intend
to sacrifice his daughter, but utters his vow without knowing who will be 'the one coming forth'. Both she and he are
caught up in something beyond their control.

The very act of making the vow occurs under ambiguous
circumstances. Jephthah's success in battle against Ammon
and his future as chief over Gilead rest upon divine favor.
His attempt to settle hostilities diplomatically meets with
failure and the battle lines are drawn. The spirit of Yhwh
comes upon Jephthah before he makes the vow, and it is not
clear whether or not he utters his vow under its influence.

> The spirit of Yhwh came upon Jephthah and he passed through
> Gilead and Manasseh, and he passed through Mizpah of
> Gilead, and from Mizpah of Gilead he passed on to the
> Ammonites. And Jephthah vowed a vow to Yhwh. He said, 'If
> you will indeed give the Ammonites into my hand, then the one
> coming forth who comes forth from the doors of my house to
> meet me when I return in peace from the Ammonites shall be
> Yhwh's and I shall offer him [generic] up as a burnt offering'
> (11.29-31).

Is the spirit the driving force behind all of these events, or
only some of them, and if so, which ones? To complicate
matters even further, the next verse tells us, 'Jephthah
passed on to the Ammonites to fight with them and Yhwh
gave them into his hand'. If not a tacit acceptance of Jephthah's terms, this statement at least implicates the deity.
There is otherwise no divine action in the story and, dis-
turbingly, no divine judgment upon Jephthah's act of

human sacrifice. The interposition of the vow between the coming of the spirit of Yhwh upon Jephthah and the victory renders it impossible to determine whether victory comes as the result of the spirit, or the vow, or both.

The problem lies not so much in the making of the vow as in its object. Had Jephthah vowed to build an altar to Yhwh, as Jacob does in Gen. 28.20-22, or to dedicate to Yhwh the spoils of battle, as Israel does in Num. 21.2, it is unlikely that his vow would have elicited much critical commentary. Even the vowing of a person to the deity is not unthinkable, as is seen in Hannah's vow to give Samuel to Yhwh all the days of his life (1 Sam. 1.11). But Jephthah vows the ultimate in order to ensure success, something from his household that will cost him dearly. What is sacrificed must be precious to be meaningful (cf. David's avowal, 'I will not offer burnt offerings to Yhwh my God that cost me nothing', 2 Sam. 24.24). Not until the last two words in the Hebrew (*weha'alitihu 'olah*, 'I will offer him up as a burnt offering') do we discover that Jephthah intends a live sacrifice.[6] By holding us off until the last possible moment, the text alerts us to this unusual aspect of the vow and intimates its horror.

Yet the vow alone does not determine the tragic outcome. Tragedy is assured when Jephthah's daughter, his only child, comes out to meet him. The conjuncture of these two events, the vow and the daughter's appearance, seals two fates: she to die and have no progeny, he to have no progeny and to die.[7] Jephthah takes her life 'according to his vow' (11.39). There is no last-minute intervention by the deity to save the child, no ram in the thicket. In the story Jephthah carries out the murder, and the deity is implicated.[8] And since this is a literary murder, we shall accuse the narrator of complicity in this crime.

How the young woman knows or surmises the terms of

6. On the debate whether Jephthah intended a human or animal sacrifice, see Marcus (1986a: 13-18).

7. His death is reported in Judg. 12.7.

8. There are many parallels where a parent promises to a supernatural figure what turns out to be his or her own child; see Marcus (1986a: 40-43); Exum (1992: 164-65 n. 9).

her father's vow is not stated. Her readiness to accept the inevitable is striking.

> She said to him, 'My father, you have opened your mouth to Yhwh; do to me according to what has gone forth from your mouth now that Yhwh has granted you vindication against your enemies, the Ammonites' (11.36).

The daughter submits to the authority of the father. His word is not to be countermanded but simply postponed: she asks only for a two-month respite before the vow is carried out. After a time of lamentation in the mountains with her companions, she returns to her father, and, the text states, 'he did to her according to his vow that he had vowed' (11.39). We are spared the details, for we could hardly bear them (compare, for example, the piling up of details in the account of Abraham's near-sacrifice of his son Isaac, where a *deus ex machina* assures a happy ending). A young woman's life is snuffed out in its prime. Yet it would be myopic to see what happens as any less Jephthah's tragedy than his daughter's, for his family line comes to an end when he is forced to take his daughter's life.[9] To commemorate Jephthah's daughter, the women of Israel hold a ritual four days each year.

## The Case of the Nagging Wife

Michal's 'story' must be gleaned from scattered references in 1 and 2 Samuel, where she plays a significant but minor role in the events surrounding the fall of Saul's house and David's rise to the throne. For my purposes here, I will focus on Michal's fatal confrontation with David in 2 Samuel 6, though some summary of what happens earlier will be necessary.[10] Michal is King Saul's daughter, who loves David and becomes his wife. Saul and his house have been rejected by Yhwh (1 Sam. 13 and 15), and David has been secretly anointed king by Samuel (1 Sam. 16). David becomes a pop-

---

9. For an analysis of the tragic dimension of the story of Jephthah and his daughter, see Exum (1992: 45-69).
10. See below, Chapter 2, for further discussion of Michal's story.

ular hero after his defeat of Goliath (1 Sam. 17 and 18) and Saul very early realizes the threat David poses to his kingship.

'They have ascribed to David ten thousands, and to me they have ascribed thousands; what more can he have but the kingdom?' And Saul eyed David from that day on (1 Sam. 18.8-9).

When he learns that his daughter Michal loves David, Saul is pleased and uses the opportunity to dangle a desirable prize before his rival, 'Become the king's son-in-law'. He hopes that David will be killed trying to meet the bride price of a hundred Philistine foreskins. But why should it matter to Saul that Michal loves David? What do the woman's feelings have to do with it? Saul had already tempted David with his older daughter Merab—where love is not mentioned—but he gave her to another (1 Sam. 18.17-19). In fact, the reward for killing Goliath was rumored to be marriage to the king's daughter (1 Sam. 17.25). Thus, for the charmed third time, David has a chance at what Saul seems unwilling to let him have.

From Saul's perspective, Michal's love for David may be convenient but it is otherwise largely gratuitous. I think it is largely gratuitous from David's perspective as well. The situation is one in which the men's political considerations are paramount, while, regarding the woman, we hear only that she loves. Already the text perpetuates a familiar stereotype: men are motivated by ambition, whereas women respond on a personal level. It would be much more to Saul's advantage if David loved Michal—but that is precisely what the text leaves unsaid, suggesting that David's motives are as purely political as Saul's. Note that the text tells us 'it pleased David well to be the king's son-in-law', not that it pleased him to have Michal as his wife. Saul even appears to recognize the threat Michal's love for David poses for him—

When Saul saw and knew that Yhwh was with David, and that Michal Saul's daughter loved him, Saul was still more afraid of David—[11]

11. I prefer to follow the Hebrew here; instead of becoming a snare to David, Michal's love becomes a snare to Saul.

and rightly so, for in the next chapter Michal defies her father by helping David escape Saul's attempt on his life (1 Sam. 19.11-17).

In saving David from Saul, Michal loses him, for he leaves his house-within-Saul's-house, his advantageous position as the 'king's son-in-law', never to return. He does return to meet Jonathan and to conspire with him to discover Saul's intentions (1 Sam. 20) and he hides for three days until Jonathan brings him news—but, all this time, he apparently makes no effort to see Michal. David becomes a fugitive and an outlaw, futilely pursued by Saul, and he manages to gain not one, but two wives while roaming about the countryside (1 Sam 25.42-43). At this point we learn that Saul had given Michal to Palti, the son of Laish (1 Sam. 25.44).[12] Saul's political motive seems clear enough, to deny David any claim to the throne through marriage. Time passes, Saul is killed in battle at Gilboa (1 Sam. 31), and David is anointed king over Judah. About Michal we hear nothing until David is offered the opportunity to become king over the northern tribes. (In the meantime David has acquired more wives and many children, 2 Sam. 3.2-5.) Then he does precisely what Saul had sought to prevent: he demands the return of his wife Michal in an apparent move to lay claim to Saul's throne. The description of her grief-stricken husband Paltiel, who follows in tears as Michal is being taken to David, draws attention to the absence of information regarding Michal's feelings. Michal's reunion with David is not reported, a highly significant textual silence that suggests a volatile subtext.

It is little wonder, then, that when Michal has her big scene in 2 Samuel 6 it is a veritable emotional explosion.[13] In the only dialogue that ever takes place between them, Michal accuses David of blatant sexual vulgarity, and he responds with a devastating rebuke. Immediately thereafter the narrator laconically informs us, 'Michal Saul's daughter had no child to the day of her death'.

---

12. Reading the verb tense as past perfect.
13. See the perceptive analysis of Alter (1981: 123-25).

A review of Michal's story reveals that only twice does she appear as an agent in her own right, here and in 1 Samuel 19, where she saves David's life. Elsewhere she neither speaks nor initiates action but is rather the object of the political machinations of the two men, her father and her husband, locked in bitter rivalry over the kingship. The intense nature of the Saulide–Davidic rivalry, however, the exclusiveness of each's claim to the throne, makes it impossible for Michal to belong to both houses at once. She becomes a victim of their prolonged conflict, and her two attempts to act autonomously by choosing her own allegiances result only in her own losses. In 1 Samuel 19, Michal is called 'David's wife', for she allies herself with her husband over against her father. She orchestrates David's escape into freedom by letting him down through the window when Saul seeks to kill him. But she thereby, in effect, loses her husband, who does not come back for her or seek her return to him until it is politically expedient. In 2 Samuel 6, she becomes once again 'Saul's daughter', for she speaks as the representative of her father's house, and, by doing so, forfeits her role in the house of King David.

In 2 Samuel 6, David and 'all the house of Israel' bring the ark of Yhwh to Jerusalem amid great rejoicing. Michal, however, is inside, watching the fanfare through the window. From her perspective we see 'King David leaping and dancing before Yhwh', and for the first time since telling us that Michal loved David (1 Sam. 18.20), the narrator permits us access to her feelings: 'she despised him in her heart' (2 Sam. 6.16). That her love has turned to hatred serves as a pointed indication of her suffering at David's hands. It has been suggested that, as a king's daughter, Michal finds the behavior of the present king beneath the dignity of that office. But her heated exchange with David when she goes out to confront him reveals much more. It doesn't take a psychologist to recognize that David's attire, or lack of it, is not the real issue.

> David returned to bless his house, and Michal the daughter of Saul went out to meet David. She said, 'How the king of Israel has honored himself today, exposing himself today in the eyes

of his subjects' maidservants as one of the worthless fellows
flagrantly exposes himself!' (2 Sam. 6.20).

That nothing less than the kingship is involved can be
seen from Michal's reference to David as the 'king of Israel',
and from David's reply, where he first takes up the subject
of kingship and only then turns to the subject of his
comportment:

> David said to Michal, 'Before Yhwh who chose me over your
> father and over all his house to appoint me king-elect over the
> people of Yhwh, over Israel—I will dance before Yhwh. And I
> shall dishonor myself even more than this and be abased in my
> eyes, but by the maidservants of whom you have spoken—by
> them I shall be held in honor' (2 Sam. 6.21-22).

Notice the pointed references to Saul's rejection—'over your
father', 'over all his house'—and to David's authority 'over
the people of Yhwh', and 'over Israel'. David's response to
Michal touches on a critical issue that the narrative has
repeatedly repressed but never really resolved: David's
taking the kingship from the house of Saul.[14]

With regard to what Michal considers his shameful behavior, David promises to go even further. How will he dis-
honor himself? I suggest the next verse hints at an answer:
by ceasing to have sexual relations with Michal, by putting
aside the woman who once risked her life to save his.[15] The
juxtaposition of David's rebuke and the narrator's statement
that Michal had no children invites us to posit a causal connection. Significantly, however, the text carefully avoids this
connection. Do we have here a case of male solidarity
between the narrator and David? Or should we consider
other possibilities? Since it is Yhwh who opens and closes
the womb (Gen. 20.18; 29.31; 30.2, 22; 1 Sam. 1.5, 6; Isa. 66.9),
perhaps the deity bears responsibility (it has been suggested
that Michal's childlessness is her punishment for speaking

---

14. On the political issues involved, see Rosenberg (1986: 117-18).
15. That Michal's life might have been in danger had Saul discov-
ered her role in David's escape (1 Sam. 19) is suggested by Saul's
response of throwing a javelin at his son Jonathan, when Jonathan
takes David's part (1 Sam. 20.33); see below, Chapter 2.

out against Yhwh's anointed). Perhaps it is Michal who refuses to have sexual relations with David, for such behavior would not be out of character for her. The very ambiguity hints at the text's unease about locating responsibility. The rift between David and Michal is not only inevitable, given the resentment Michal must surely feel toward David; from a narrative point of view it is essential, since any possibility that Michal and David have a child, who would symbolize the uniting of the two royal houses, must be precluded. The transfer of the monarchy from Saul to David is far from smooth and requires justification.[16] To be sure, Saul has been rejected as king by Yhwh and David elected, but Saul has no intention of relinquishing his kingdom without a struggle, and, after Saul's death, 'there was a long war between the house of Saul and the house of David' during which 'David grew stronger and stronger, while the house of Saul became weaker and weaker' (2 Sam. 3.1). One well-established political solution to the rift between the two houses would be their union through marriage and a child, who as a scion of both royal houses might someday reign. Theologically, however, that solution is unacceptable, for Yhwh has declared that no descendant of Saul may sit upon Israel's throne (1 Sam. 13.13-14). Saul's house threatens David politically and Yhwh theologically. Accordingly, Saul's family is systematically eliminated. Jonathan and two of his brothers are killed in battle with their father (1 Sam. 31). Abner and Ishbosheth are treacherously murdered, and the narrator goes to great lengths to declare David's innocence (2 Sam. 3–4).[17] Shortly thereafter, we learn that Michal will remain childless, and the way is thus cleared for 2 Samuel 7, where Yhwh promises David an eternal dynasty, a dynasty in which Saul's house will play no part.

Poetics and ideology work together to remove Michal from the narrative. The rejection of Saul's house requires that Michal have no children. But the narrative goes beyond

16. Jonathan plays a major role in effecting the transition; see Jobling (1978: 4-25); and Chapter 2 below.

17. The so-called 'History of David's Rise' has been seen as an apology for David; see McCarter (1980a: 489-504; 1980b: 27-30).

simply reporting her childlessness; it chronicles in painful detail her humiliation and elimination. The woman provides an opportunity for narratively displacing a strategic and embarrassing problem at the political level onto the domestic level, where it offers less of a threat. The animosity between the houses of Saul and David is then symbolically resolved as a marital conflict. In it David directs toward Michal the hostility one would have expected him to show toward Saul, who sought his life, and toward Jonathan and other members of Saul's family, who to varying degrees stood in his way. Michal, for her part, becomes the spokesperson for Saul's house (she speaks as 'Saul's daughter' not as 'David's wife') and her rebuke of David the king functions as a protest from Saul's house against David's usurpation of royal prerogative. As we proceed to reconstruct Michal's story, we shall seek in her protest another level, one that symbolizes the victim's outcry at being (literarily) murdered.

### Words as Weapons

It is no criminal coincidence that in both our stories words make potent murder weapons. Not only are the words spoken by the male characters deadly instruments of power over women, but the storyteller also uses the women's own words against them. The central role words play in extinguishing the authentic female voice underscores the appropriateness of the term 'phallogocentric' to describe the narrative ideology. The seriousness of words and their power, especially in cases of blessings and curses, oaths and vows, is well documented in ancient Near Eastern literature and assumed in Judges 11.[18] Thus Jephthah makes no

---

18. As Thiselton (1974: 293-96) shows, the power of such utterances is not magical but lies rather in their nature as what J.L. Austin called performative utterances. The blessing, for example, has power insofar as it constitutes the *act* of blessing. Such utterances also have power in that they usually invoke the deity. On the seriousness of vows in Israel and the ancient Near East, see Parker (1979, 1989); on vows not uttered under duress, see Berlinerblau (1991).

attempt to modify the terms of his vow by which he is
bound to sacrifice to God his only child; nor does his
daughter challenge its inviolability.[19] The word kills. The
vow cannot be retracted ('I have opened my mouth to Yhwh
and I cannot take it back', Judg. 11.35), and both Jephthah
and his daughter are caught up in its immutable course
toward fulfillment. But if words can kill, they can also heal.
The destructive power of language is counterbalanced in
this tale by its sustaining capacity.[20] Jephthah's daughter
asks that one thing, *haddabar hazzeh*, 'this word', be done for
her, that she be given two months during which to grieve in
the company of her companions. After her death, the
women of Israel commemorate Jephthah's daughter in a
yearly ritual, understood as a linguistic act, not a silent vigil.
Jephthah's daughter finds life through communal recollec-
tion, though different, to be sure, from the life she might
have had through family and children, the life her father
took away.

I shall return below to the subject of the women's commemoration of Jephthah's daughter and its complex effect
on this story. For now let us consider Jephthah's daughter's
voice. How does she speak against herself? By neither questioning the man who consigned her to death nor holding
him accountable. In encouraging her father to carry out his
vow, she subordinates her life to the communal good. The
seriousness of the vow is upheld, the need for sacrifice is
satisfied,[21] and paternal authority goes unchallenged. It
might be argued that she does not protest her fate because it
would be useless. The futility of protest, however, does not
deter Michal, who thereby lays claim to her own voice.
Michal and David engage in a battle of words in which
David has the last word because he holds the power. These

19. The present story assumes the inviolability of Jephthah's vow,
whereas Lev. 27.1-8 stipulates monetary payment by which a person
vowed to God could be released. In the midrashic literature, one finds
various attempts to explain Jephthah's ignorance of the law in this
case; see Marcus (1986a: 46-47).
20. For fuller discussion of this theme, see Exum (1992: 60-65).
21. See Girard (1977).

are the only words he ever speaks to her, words of rebuke, and they have the effect of critically wounding their victim. Unlike Jephthah's words, however, David's do not kill. Here the narrative serves as the instrument of murder, accomplishing the deed in one blow. Depriving her of children is a symbolic way of killing Michal. Denying her a reply to David kills her off as a narrative presence. By representing her as challenging the king from a position of weakness, the narrator has Michal essentially commit verbal suicide. Notice how negative her portrayal seems at first glance. A king's daughter and a king's wife, Michal appears not as a regal figure, but rather as a jealous, bitter, and, worst of all, nagging woman. She has overstepped her bounds, she dares publicly to criticize the king's behavior, and we should not be surprised to see her put in her place by an angry and dismissive husband. On the surface her criticism sounds petulant and exaggerated—so what if the king makes a fool of himself? But we have seen that her words only barely cloak the real issue, the political problem that the narrator downplays by foregrounding the domestic dispute.

### The Danger of Going Out

> Jephthah came to Mizpah, to his house, and behold, his daughter coming out to meet him... (Judg. 11.34).

> David returned to bless his house, and Michal Saul's daughter came out to meet David... (2 Sam. 6.20).

Both our victims meet untimely 'deaths' when they leave the security of the house to meet the man who will be instrumental in their murder. The house is the woman's domain; here she is safe and can even exercise power, while outside, in the larger world, men wield authority.[22] The men are the

22. Prov. 31 offers a good example. The woman has considerable power over the household, while her husband 'sits among the elders of the land' (v. 23). The distinction between power and authority is helpful; authority is legitimate power, power recognized by society. See Rosaldo (1974: 21-22); Lamphere (1974: 99); see also Hackett (1985: 17-22); Meyers (1988: 40-44); and the discussion of power and authority in Chapter 4 below.

leaders, the heroes whose actions have far-reaching consequences affecting whole peoples. Jephthah has gone to battle, made a vow, and returned victorious; David has consolidated his kingdom and brought the ark to Jerusalem. The men have acted; the women respond and are caught up by forces beyond their control, though somehow apparently still under the control of the men. That is to say, the men are in control in so far as both Jephthah and David could have reacted differently: Jephthah by seeking an alternative to the actual sacrifice; David by treating Michal with respect.

When Jephthah returns victorious from battle, his daughter goes out to meet him dancing and with timbrels. It may have been customary for women to celebrate military success in such a manner. In Exod. 15.20 the women acclaim the victory at the sea with timbrels and dancing. In 1 Sam. 18.6, after David's victory over Goliath, the women of Israel come out singing and dancing, with timbrels and musical instruments. Possibly Jephthah anticipated being met by a woman—more expendable than a man (?)—though, as his response indicates, he did not expect his daughter. The tragedy set in motion by Jephthah's vow is sealed when his daughter comes out to meet him. When David and all Israel bring the ark of Yhwh to Jerusalem, Michal watches from the window. Earlier she had let David down through the window, out of her domain, where he was in danger, to meet his destiny in the man's world of power. Having secured his position as king, David now has no need of Michal. In 2 Samuel 6, Michal occupies the private sphere of the home, safe, but excluded. References to 'all Israel', 'all the people, the whole multitude of Israel, both men and women', and 'all the people' underscore her isolation inside. When she goes outside to confront David in the public arena, she meets rebuke and greater exclusion—losing any role she might have had in the future of David's house.

The men return to their houses, to the domestic order preserved by women. Without the house, there is no 'outside'; the men need what the house represents and what it makes possible for them, the freedom from domestic responsibilities that allows them to concentrate on affairs of state. The house is both place and lineage, shelter and posterity. When the women go outside, houses are cut off. By sacrificing his daughter, Jephthah destroys his house (thus when the Ephraimites later threaten to burn Jephthah's house down over him, the remark is grimly ironic, since his house—his lineage—has already been destroyed by fire). Michal's childlessness brings to an end another branch of Saul's house; in the end only the crippled Mephibosheth and his son Mica will survive. Yet with Michal's removal, the future of David's house is secured. With Saul's house out of the way, David receives from Yhwh the promise of an eternal dynasty.[23]

### Virginity and Childlessness: The Politics of Female Sexuality

> She had not known a man (Judg. 11.39).

> Michal Saul's daughter had no child to the day of her death (2 Sam. 6.23).

What is particularly striking about these statements is that both occur at the end of the story, as a kind of closure sealing the women's fates; both are stated categorically, as if they were entirely neutral observations; and both are necessary. As sacrificial victim, Jephthah's daughter must be a virgin for reasons of sacrificial purity;[24] Michal, as we have seen, cannot have children for ideological reasons. Since one lived on through one's progeny, having offspring—many offspring, especially sons—was important both to men and

23. For very different, but fascinating analyses of the complexity of the symbolism of the house in this material, see Bal (1988a: 169-96); Rosenberg (1986: 113-23).

24. The situation of the sacrificial victim is somewhat more complex, but need not detain us. Married women are not good candidates for sacrifice because a married woman has ties to both her parents' and her husband's families, either of which might consider her sacrifice an act of murder and thus take vengeance; see Girard (1977: 12-13). On the opposition between sacrificial purity and the pollution of childbirth, see Jay (1985). Girard argues that anyone who does not have a champion makes an appropriate sacrifice.

to women (witness, for example, Abraham's concern over his childlessness). Understandably it mattered significantly to women, since women did not have other opportunities, open to men, to leave their mark on the world.[25] That the fates of both Michal and Jephthah's daughter involve childlessness indicates the extent to which patriarchal texts identify women in terms of reproductive function. Without children, the women are somehow incomplete; they have not fulfilled their role as women. If to have no children means to die unfulfilled, it also means that the women have no one to stand up for them, no *go'el* to plead their cases. They can be eliminated without fear of reprisal.[26]

The categorical way in which Michal is denied offspring masks, as I indicated above, a narrative discomfort. Does David put Michal aside so that she, like other of his wives later, will be shut up 'until the day of [her] death [the same phrase as 6.23], living as if in widowhood' (2 Sam. 20.3)? Regarding Jephthah's daughter, the text states, 'She had not known a man'. What is not an issue in patriarchal texts such as these is female sexual pleasure. Indeed, patriarchal literature, and thus the Bible in general, reflects the underlying attitude that woman's sexuality is to be feared and thus carefully regulated.[27] Patriarchy severs the relationship between eroticism and procreation. As Julia Kristeva observes, it affirms motherhood but denies the mother's *jouissance*.[28] Eroticism is not associated with the mother but rather with the whore, the woman whose sexuality is commensurate with her availability. To intensify our critique we need only to acknowledge the importance of sexual fulfillment for women. In our examples, the women are denied not just motherhood, the patriarchal mark of female fulfillment, but

25. Deborah is an important exception who proves the rule.

26. This is crucial according to Girard (1977: 13).

27. Lerner (1986) traces male control of female sexuality from its locus within the patriarchal family to regulation by the state. On woman's sexuality 'not so much as part of her feminine being but, rather, as an exclusive form of male experience', see Aschkenasy (1986: esp. 123-24). Within the Bible, the Song of Songs is the great exception.

28. Kristeva (1986a: 26). On patriarchy's division of eroticism and procreativity, see Lerner (1986), esp. Chapter 7.

also the pleasure of sex, the right of passage into autonomous adulthood that opens the eyes with knowledge (cf.
Gen. 2–3). Jephthah's daughter will know no sexual fulfillment; and whether David refuses to have sex with Michal or
she refuses David, Michal will have only the memory of sex.
As a related point of interest, it is ironic that a women's
ritual (Judg. 11.39-40) serves to honor a virgin. It has been
frequently suggested that the story of Jephthah's daughter is
aetiological, aimed at explaining the women's ritual. There
is, however, no evidence of such a ritual apart from this
story. We shall explore below the androcentric interest
served by the women's commemoration of Jephthah's
daughter. Is this really the kind of ritual women would hold,
or simply a male version of a women's ritual? We do not
know. We can only speculate about what form a genuinely
female ritual might take were free expression of female sexuality possible. Might it be celebration of female eroticism,
of uniquely female power, the power to give birth? (Already
in Genesis 2–3, in a classic illustration of womb envy, the
creative power of women is appropriated by the proto-
typical Man who, like Zeus birthing Athena from his head,
symbolically gives birth to woman with the help of the
creator god—no creator goddess is involved.) Is, then, the
commemoration of the *death of a virgin* an androcentric
inversion of female expression?

*Opportunity and Motive,
Or, Whose Interests Are Being Served?*

The women occupy narratives that, like father or husband,
seek to subordinate, and finally control, them. Jephthah's
daughter accepts her fate with alarming composure. The
vow is carried out, but the unnamed young woman who
leaves behind no children as a legacy is not forgotten. Her
memory is kept alive by the ritual remembrance of women.
Because she does not protest her fate, she offers no threat to
patriarchal authority. And because she voluntarily performs
a daughter's duty, her memory may be preserved:

It became a custom in Israel that the daughters of Israel went year by year to commemorate Jephthah the Gileadite's daughter, four days each year (Judg. 11.39-40).

Patriarchal ideology here coopts a women's ceremony in order to glorify the victim. The phallocentric message of the story of Jephthah's daughter is, I suggest: submit to paternal authority. You may have to sacrifice your autonomy; you may lose your life, and even your name, but your sacrifice will be remembered, indeed celebrated, for generations to come. Herein lies, I believe, the reason Jephthah's daughter's name is not preserved: because she is commemorated not for herself but *as a daughter*. If we translate the difficult *wattehi hoq beyisra'el* at the end of v. 39 as 'she became an example in Israel'[29] rather than 'it became a custom in Israel', her value to the patriarchal system as a model is underscored.

Michal, in contrast, opposes the system that would have her remain inside, in her place, doubly subordinated as subject to her king and as woman to her husband. Here the message is: refusal to submit leads to rebuke and humiliation. Michal speaks out against the figure of authority—the husband/king—and is silenced. Unlike Jephthah's daughter, who participates in the patriarchal system, Michal cannot be honored because she speaks against male authority. I referred earlier to women's identification in terms of their relation to men, as daughters or wives or both. Jephthah's daughter performs her function as a daughter, and is rewarded with commemoration as a daughter by the 'daughters of Israel'. Michal, on the other hand, is punished by being denied her function as a mother. (She also loses her status as 'David's wife'; the narrator calls her 'Saul's daughter', and thus she, too, is reduced to being a daughter.) Submission is rewarded, opposition punished. The women are sacrificed to patriarchal interests in order that the system remain intact and function properly.

---

29. Marcus (1986a: 34); cf. Trible (1984: 106).

## The Speaking Subject:
### De-constructing the Dominant Narrative Voice

To expose the phallogocentric interests served by these stories is to accuse the biblical narrators not of deliberate misogyny but rather of reflecting a culturally inherited and deeply rooted gender bias. Thus the present inquiry seeks to read these stories without censoring them but without being confined to them.[30] The muted female voice provides the means for de-constructing the dominant, male narrative voice. What is repressed resurfaces in another form. In her speech, Jephthah's daughter submits to the authority of the father; in hers, Michal opposes the authority of the husband. If speech confers autonomy, we shall need to look closely at how, and to what extent, these women (re)claim their stories through speech. But first, let us consider the other women in these stories, women who do not speak but who play a key role.

The women of Israel commemorate Jephthah's daughter for four days each year. Exactly what their ritual involves is not clear. The Septuagint and the Vulgate understood the verb to mean 'to lament' or 'to mourn'; however, the only other occurrence of the word, in Judg. 5.11, refers to recounting the victories of Yhwh. This usage suggests that the women recite Jephthah's daughter's story. These women, however, do not actually speak in the narrative. They remember, and their yearly ceremony is used by the narrator to keep alive the memory of the victim (only the narrative bears witness to their witness). Jephthah and the women of Israel represent two poles: he blames his daughter (11.35); they praise her through memorializing her. Praising the victim can, however, be as dangerous as blaming the victim. The problem lies in the victim–victimizer dichotomy, a way of structuring experience that ignores the complicity of the victim in the crime.[31] If we make Jephthah the callous

---

30. I adopt this concept from Kristeva (1980: xi).
31. Cf. Lerner's remarks on the complicity of women in patriarchy (1986: 5-6, 233-35).

victimizer and his daughter the innocent victim, we fall into a patriarchal pattern of thinking. If we allow the women's ceremonial remembrance to encourage glorification of the victim, we perpetuate the crime.[32] How do we reject the concept of honoring the victim without also sacrificing the woman? We must recognize that guilt and innocence are not clear-cut. As I indicated above, Jephthah, like his daughter, is a victim of forces beyond his control; a vow made in ambiguous circumstances and in ignorance of its outcome forces his hand. Nor is the daughter innocent; she did not resist. She speaks on behalf of the sacrificial system and patriarchal authority, absolving it of responsibility. And the women of Israel cooperate in this elevation of the willing victim to honored status.

The role of other women in the account of Michal's rejection is not to immortalize, but to isolate through contrast. Who are 'his (male) servants' women servants' ('*amhot 'abadav*), who, according to Michal, have relished David's sexual display, and by whom David avows he will be held in honor? These women are doubly subordinated—by sex, to all of David's male subjects or servants, and by class, to the royal couple, whose mutual rebukes derive their sting from the imputation of inferior status to these women. Whether or not Michal means to include the '(primary) wives of the free Israelites' in her reproach,[33] by implying that these women are below her dignity, she aims to disgrace the king, who turns her words around ultimately to shame the queen. The issue of social class is raised in the interest of gender politics to set the women over against

32. Thus a reading such as Phyllis Trible's (1984: 93-109), that makes Jephthah all-bad, irredeemably guilty, and wholly responsible for the crime of murder, and his daughter helpless and totally innocent, simply reinforces the victim–victimizer dichotomy. Bal, in contrast, completely reinterprets the daughter's death and the meaning of the women's remembrance; see Bal (1988a: 45-68, 96-113, 119-22, 161-68 *et passim*).

33. The phrase, 'Hauptfrauen der freien Israeliten', is Crüsemann's (1980: 226), who thinks the remark refers only to lower-class women. Cf. McCarter (1984: 187), who believes Michal refers to 'all the young women of Israel, whether slave or free'.

each other, making gender solidarity impossible. Using class to divide women is a fundamental strategy of patriarchal ideology.

> The division of women into 'respectable women', who are protected by their men, and 'disreputable women', who are out in the street unprotected by men and free to sell their services, has been the basic class division for women. It has marked off the limited privileges of upper-class women against the economic and sexual oppression of lower-class women and has divided women one from the other. Historically, it has impeded cross-class alliances among women and obstructed the formation of feminist consciousness.[34]

Despite its possible anachronism, this citation is relevant to our text. Michal's privilege as a king's daughter and a king's wife isolates her from the other women in her story. By having her oppose herself to these women, the narrator leaves her to stand alone against the authority of her husband the king. Moreover, the sexually charged language Michal and David use in connection with these women and *David's* 'disreputable' behavior implies, perhaps, that Michal means to represent the '(male) servants' women servants' as not respectable. That is, the narrator has Michal introduce the distinction between women in a way that makes her appear haughty and elitist, thereby sharpening the unflattering picture of her. The '(male) servants' women servants' have been 'outside' and gotten an eyeful of the king. Yet the 'respectable' woman will not receive society's reward, motherhood.

Michal's going out to confront David is an act of self-assertion. Such boldness on her part cannot be tolerated; the narrator lets her protest but robs her of voice at the critical moment, allowing her no reply to David and no further speech. Whereas the narrator uses Michal's protest to eliminate her, her protest can be used against the narrator to bring to light the crime, to expose the gender bias of the story. By speaking out, Michal lays claim to her own story. She cannot avoid her fate, but she can protest it. She goes to

---

34. Lerner (1986: 139, and Chapter 6 for a fuller argument).

her literary death screaming, as it were. Her protest thus serves as an indictment of the phallogocentric world view represented in and reflected by the narrative.

I have said that, in 2 Samuel 6, Michal is eliminated from the narrative, but this is not quite the case. She reappears in an unexpected context in 2 Sam. 21.8, to contradict the narrator's earlier claim that she had no child.

> The king took the two sons of Rizpah the daughter of Aiah, whom she bore to Saul, Armoni and Mephibosheth; and the five sons of Michal, the daughter of Saul, whom she bore to Adriel the son of Barzillai the Meholathite; and he gave them into the hand of the Gibeonites, and they dismembered them on the mountain before Yhwh (2 Sam. 21.8-9).

What are we to make of this reference to Michal as the mother of five sons? The usual solution is to read 'Merab' instead of 'Michal', with a number of ancient manuscripts, since Michal's sister Merab was the wife of Adriel the Meholathite. But this avoids pressing the embarrassing question of how Michal's name got here in the first place. Is this a simple case of confusion of women (who are notoriously hard to tell apart): Saul's descendants are killed off, so what difference does the mother's identity make? Or is it a kind of Freudian slip that convicts the biblical narrator, an aporia we can read as Michal's refusal to be written out of the narrative? If so, the narrative still has the last, cruel word: it gives her children only to take them away again.

In contrast to Michal, Jephthah's daughter remains within the confines of the patriarchal word. Though she does not lay claim to her story, she makes some motions toward self-assertion. The two parts of her speech pull in different directions. In the first part, she surrenders volition. In the second, within the boundaries set by her father's vow, boundaries she accepts, she attempts to define herself, to lay some claim to her own voice: she asks for a period of two months in which to grieve, accompanied by her female companions.

> She said to him,
> 'My father, you have opened your mouth to Yhwh;
> do to me according to what has gone forth from your mouth,

now that Yhwh has vindicated you against your enemies,
the Ammonites.'

And she said to her father,
'Let this thing be done for me,
let me alone two months
that I may go and wander upon the hills
and bewail my virginity,
I *and my companions*'.

It is likely that the word *betulay* in the phrase usually
translated, 'to bewail my virginity', does not mean
'virginity' but rather refers to a stage in the female life-cycle,
the point of transition from child to marriageable young
woman.[35] In the phrase, which she translates 'to lament in
confrontation with my nubility', Bal finds an allusion to a
rite of passage signifying a young woman's physical
maturity, her preparation for marriage.[36] She finds here the
woman's own point of view, in contrast to the narrator's
androcentric perspective, 'she had not known a man', and
she then proceeds to deconstruct the male concept of virginity via a detour into Freudian theory. Her resultant
(re)reading of the entire story, a counter-reading, challenges
the more traditional interpretations found within biblical
scholarship and illustrates one way to reinscribe a female
perspective.

Another possibility of reading a different meaning into the
phrase 'bewail my virginity' presents itself if we suppose the
young woman's familiarity with the sacrificial system (i.e.
her better knowledge than ours about human sacrifice in the
ancient Near East).[37] She laments not just unfulfillment but
the clear and brutal fact of imminent death, recognizing that
if she were not a virgin daughter, her father could not

35. Tsevat (1975); Wenham (1972); Keukens (1982); Bal (1988a: 46-
48); Day (1989: 59).
36. Bal (1988a: 49). Her argument appears mainly in Chapters 2, 4,
and 5. For a similar argument, see Day (1989).
37. For discussion of this topic, see Green (1975: 199). Green
observes, 'During the formative period of the Federation of Israel,
there is the strong implication that human sacrifice was practiced by
the people as an acceptable aspect of their Yahwistic belief'.

sacrifice her.[38] Such an argument, informed by anthropology and Girardian theory, involves the same kind of retrospective reasoning as the rabbinic objection—what if the 'one coming forth' had been a camel, a donkey, or a dog (*Bereshit Rabbah* 60.3; *Wayyiqra Rabbah* 37.4)—based on purity laws. I have already suggested that narrative necessity determines the outcome. The daughter's tragedy is that she—not another—is the one to come forth to meet Jephthah, and that she is an (I would even say, the) acceptable sacrificial victim. This takes us back to my earlier remarks about the coincidence between the terms of the vow and the daughter's appearance, a conjunction of events apparently beyond human control.

The most interesting feature of the daughter's ceremonial lamentation is her inclusion of other women in the event. Only at the conclusion of her speech does she reveal that, unlike her father, she has companions with whom to share her distress. *Ra'yotay*, 'my companions', is her last spoken word in the narrative; *'abi*, 'my father', was her first. Symbolically, through speech, she journeys from the domain of the father who will quench her life to that of the female companions who will preserve her memory.

Ultimately the text denies autonomy to Jephthah's daughter and confines her voice within patriarchal limits, using it to affirm patriarchal authority. Yet in two ways her speech resists the androcentric interests of a narrator who would sacrifice her to the father's word. First, she shows where responsibility for the crime lies: in paternal authority. When Jephthah returns victorious from battle and is met by his daughter, his words, 'Ah, my daughter, you have brought me very low and have become the source of my trouble', express his feeling of not being responsible for this horrible outcome, as I noted above. They suggest that he expected someone else: his daughter should not have been the one to

38. I thank Ellen M. Ross of Swarthmore College for suggesting this idea. As my discussion above indicates, if Jephthah's daughter were married, her husband, not her father, would have power over her. If she had borne children, she would not be sacrificially pure; see Jay (1985).

fit the terms of his vow. But if Jephthah is somehow subtly
shifting blame to his daughter, in her response she does not
accept blame but places it squarely on him: '*You* have
opened *your* mouth to Yhwh; do to me according to what
has gone forth from *your* mouth... [39] Second, and most
important, her voice transports her to a point of solidarity
with her female friends and with other daughters, the
'daughters of Israel', who refuse to forget (compare Michal's
isolation). The resultant image is too powerful to be fully
controlled by the narrator's androcentric interests. The text
segregates women: the daughter spends two months with
female companions, away from her father and the company
of men; the ritual of remembrance is conducted by women
alone.[40] But, as Gerda Lerner points out, when women are
segregated ('which always has subordination as its
purpose'), they transform such patriarchal restraint into
complementarity and redefine it.[41] We can choose to read
this story differently, to expose its valorization of submission and glorification of the victim as serving phallocentric
interests, and to redefine its images of female solidarity in an
act of feminist symbol-making.

If we approach the stories of Jephthah's daughter and of
Michal as resistant readers, mistrustful of the dominant
(male) voice, or phallogocentric ideology in the narratives,
we can give the victims of literary murder their own voice, a
voice that identifies and protests the crimes against them
and that thereby claims for them a measure of that autonomy denied them by their literary executioners.

---

39. Cartledge (1992: 180 and n. 2).
40. The Israelite women engage in ritual whereas the men are busy
fighting, in the war with Ammon (10.17-33) and among themselves
(12.1-6).
41. Lerner (1986: 242).

Chapter 2

## MICHAL: THE WHOLE STORY

> For a woman silence and discretion are best, and staying
> inside quietly at home.
>
> Euripides, *Heraclidae*

The irony in the title of this Chapter is intentional. By 'the
whole story' I refer to the whole *fragmented* story of Michal.[1]
In the previous Chapter, I dealt with only part of Michal's
story, and to leave it at that would be to perpetuate the
fragmentation of her story. Thus the present Chapter will
consider all of Michal's appearances in the larger stories of
her father Saul and her husband David. Further, it will
expand the argument that gender plays an important role in
determining the ultimate treatment of the character Michal.
Since Michal has a brother and since they have much in
common—they both love David and they both defy Saul to
save David, for example—comparing the way the narrative
removes them from the scene (where in spite of their support of David they nonetheless, as members of the rival
house, represent obstacles to the Davidic monarchy) reveals
the ways in which their fates are gender-specific.

### Narrative Imprisonment

Michal is introduced as Saul's younger daughter in 1 Sam.
14.49: 'The sons of Saul were Jonathan, Ishvi, and
Malchishua, and the names of his two daughters were: the

---

1. For a variety of approaches to Michal and her story, see the
essays in Clines and Eskenazi (1991).

name of the first-born Merab and the name of the younger Michal'. When she is next mentioned, it is with a startling revelation of her point of view: 'Michal Saul's daughter loved David'—a revelation significant for our understanding of Michal not least because it is the only time the Bible tells us that a woman loves a man. By 2 Samuel 6, however, her love has turned to bitterness and rage. For the second time, we learn how she feels: 'Michal Saul's daughter looked down from the window and saw King David leaping and cavorting[2] before Yhwh. And she despised him in her heart' (v. 16). How are we to understand her passage from love to hatred, recounted as it is in snatches and obscured by narrative silences? We can begin to address this question by putting together the pieces of her fragmented story.

| | |
|---|---|
| 1 Sam. 14.49 | Michal is introduced in the list of Saul's children. |
| 1 Samuel 18 | *Saul's daughter Michal* loves David; Saul uses her as a 'trap', in the hope that David will be killed trying to meet the bride price of one hundred Philistine foreskins. She becomes *David's wife*. |
| 1 Samuel 19 | *Michal, David's wife*, allies herself with David against her father, saves David's life by orchestrating his escape through the window, and lies to Saul to conceal her involvement. |
| 1 Sam. 25.44 | Saul had given *Michal, his daughter, David's wife* to Palti. |
| 2 Samuel 3 | David tells Abner he must bring Michal, *Saul's daughter* to him; tells Ishbosheth to return '*my wife Michal*, whom I betrothed at the price of one hundred Philistine foreskins'. Michal is sent to David. |
| 2 Samuel 6 | *Michal, Saul's daughter*, sees, through the window, David and 'all the house of Israel' rejoicing before the ark. She and David quarrel. Michal has no children. |
| 2 Sam. 21.8-9 | David hands over the five sons of *Michal* [or Merab?], *Saul's daughter*, to the Gibeonites for execution. |

2. Usually understood as 'jumping' or 'whirling', but perhaps some activity with his hands such as clapping or snapping his fingers, as an accompaniment to his dance; cf. Avishur (1976); Ahlström (1978); Fokkelman (1990: 379-80); McCarter (1984: 171).

What I observed in the previous Chapter about Michal's appearance only twice as an agent in her own right is apparent from this overview. Michal's two important scenes are 1 Samuel 19, where she allies herself with David over against her father Saul, and 2 Samuel 6, where she takes the part of her father's house over against her husband David. Apart from these scenes, she neither speaks nor initiates action, but rather is the object of the two men's political maneuvering over the kingship. The account in 1 Samuel 19, in which she plays her first active role, demonstrating loyalty to David in defiance of Saul, is framed by occasions where Saul uses her for political purposes at David's expense. Both times he exercises his paternal right of marrying off his daughter, first to David, then to Palti. In the first instance, his motive is stated: 'Saul thought to make David fall by the hand of the Philistines' (1 Sam. 18.25); in the other (1 Sam. 25.44) it is reasonable to assume that he gives Michal to another man to prevent the fugitive David from claiming the throne through her. Michal's other active role, her confrontation with David in which she represents her father's house in 2 Samuel 6, is preceded by the account of David's using her to bolster his title to the throne (2 Sam. 3) and followed by that of David's complicity in the execution of Saul's—Michal's or Merab's?—descendants (2 Sam. 21), a step that removes any remaining Saulide claimant to the throne (his sparing of the lame Mephibosheth has dubious significance). The use of epithets for Michal is especially revealing.[3] When passed back and forth among men for political purposes, she is referred to as both Saul's daughter and David's wife (1 Sam. 18.20, 27, 28; 25.44; 2 Sam. 3.13, 14)—an indication of her political importance to both houses. But as we saw in Chapter 1, Michal cannot belong to both houses at once, given their mutually exclusive claims to the throne.

Michal is 'hemmed in' narratively—the scenes where she is a subject are surrounded by scenes in which she is 'acted upon', first by her father, then by her husband—just as she is

3. See Clines (1972: 269-72).

hemmed in by the men's political machinations. Significantly, the scene in which Michal acts autonomously as 'David's wife' is surrounded by accounts in which she is 'acted upon' by her father Saul; and the scene in which she acts autonomously as 'Saul's daughter' is framed by accounts where she is 'acted upon' by her husband David. This narrative imprisonment underscores the impossibility of autonomy for Michal and represents in the surface structure of the text the confinement we shall explore below in the image of the woman at the window.

As a woman, Michal is not free to choose between conflicting allegiances in an open, political way—in the way, for example, Jonathan is free to align himself with David against his father's will. Her father even exploits her love for David to serve himself. He marries her off to David, but he also takes her back and gives her to another. In the struggle over the kingship, Saul is destined to fail, while David, supported by Yhwh, emerges as the victor. Saul's attempt to block David's access to the throne by giving Michal to another man accomplishes nothing, for, after Saul's death, David's demand for Michal's return indicates his readiness to use her to further his political ambitions. David buttresses his demand by referring to the bride price he paid for Michal, doubtlessly a way of stressing the legitimacy of his claim.[4] The last reference to Michal, if indeed it is a reference to her—some ancient witnesses read 'Merab' for the Masoretic text's 'Michal' in 2 Sam. 21.8—calls her 'Saul's daughter', for the rival claims to the throne have been resolved in favor of David, and Michal has forfeited her role in the Davidic house.

Although she cannot act with political autonomy, in the scenes where she is the subject of action Michal exercises the freedom to take sides denied to her elsewhere, supporting first her husband, but ultimately representing her father's house. Significantly, Michal is called 'David's wife' when

---

4. Alter (1981: 122) observes that the emphasis on the bride price suggests that David wants Michal back for political and not personal reasons. So also Aschkenasy (1986: 142).

she defies her father and orchestrates David's escape, and 'Saul's daughter' when she challenges her husband. Thus it is as rival's wife—not daughter—that Michal confronts her father, the king, in 1 Samuel 19, and as rival's daughter—not wife—that she confronts her husband, the king, in 2 Samuel 6. The tension between Michal's lack of autonomy and her attempts to assert her will draws attention to her impossible position as a woman caught between rival royal houses, a situation fatally resolved in her final attempt.

### *A Woman's Place Is in the House*

In Chapter 1, we examined in detail Michal's final encounter with David and her removal from the scene by means of literary murder in 2 Samuel 6. To appreciate more fully the cruel reversal of Michal's fortunes, replaying the reversal of her feelings for David, let us look more closely at the relationship between that scene, where she represents a voice of protest from her father's house when she criticizes David, and the earlier scene in 1 Samuel 19, where she is disloyal to Saul to save her husband. In 1 Samuel 19, Michal saves David's life by letting him down through the window when Saul's messengers come to kill him. She deceives the messengers, and gains time for David to escape, by disguising an image in his bed and claiming that David is ill. When Saul discovers the ruse and questions her, Michal lies to conceal her accountability, claiming that David threatened her life. Judging from Saul's response to Jonathan in 1 Samuel 20, when he casts his spear at him for abetting David, Michal's life might have been in jeopardy had she not fabricated a clever alibi.[5]

In 1 Samuel 19, David flees his house; in 2 Samuel 6, he comes to bless his house. He has come a long way, from fugitive to king of a united Israel. And what of Michal, whose journey has also been considerable, though of a different nature, from love to hate? Her watching through the

---

5. Fokkelman (1986: 270) diminishes the danger when he suggests Michal averts it by 'making it into a game'.

window as David and the people celebrate the ark's procession recalls her saving David by letting him down through the window, and the recurrence of the phrase, 'through the window' (*be'ad hahallon*), draws attention to Michal's place inside, confined. The text provides our window on Michal, offering us only a glimpse, the kind of view a window gives, limited in range and perspective. We are, as it were, outside, watching her, inside, watching David. The woman at the window is a well-known ancient Near Eastern motif, for which we have both archaeological and textual evidence.[6] The woman looks out upon the world to see what men have accomplished. In 2 Kgs 9.30, for example, Queen Jezebel, having painted her eyes and adorned her head, looks out the window for the insurgent Jehu's arrival, apparently knowing what ferocity to expect from him. And Sisera's mother peers out the window, watching in vain for her son's return from battle laden with spoil (Judg. 5.28).

The house is frequently in literature a metonymical symbol of woman. By letting David out the window—and Michal is the subject of all three verbs, *wattored* ('let [David] down'), *watteshallehi* ('let [my enemy] go'), *shallehini* ('let me go')—Michal figuratively births David into freedom. David, in 1 Samuel 19, passes through the vagina/window into the larger world, so to speak, to meet his destiny. Michal stays behind, inside the house, called 'David's house', attending to domestic matters that appear natural and innocent—making the bed, caring for the sick. She thus manages David's escape from Saul through deception, frequently, though not exclusively, a woman's way of exercising power.[7]

Whereas the window plays an important role in both accounts, the bed, a key term in 1 Samuel 19, is conspicuously absent in 2 Samuel 6. Jan Fokkelman discusses the window and bed in 1 Samuel 19 as indices of movement and

---

6. King (1988: 100, 146-48); Coogan (unpublished paper).
7. See the articles in Exum and Bos (1988); see also Aschkenasy (1986: 161-79), Marcus (1986b), and the discussion of the matriarchs in Chapter 4 below.

standstill, representing life versus death for David.[8] Whereas this symbolism may fit David's (male) perspective, neither image has positive meaning for Michal, for David's escape through the window is his departure from the conjugal bed. Michal's ruse in disguising the image involves the difference between appearance and reality. David was not in his bed, though Saul's messengers believed him to be there. After their angry confrontation does David no longer share Michal's bed? 2 Samuel 6 leaves us with a situation not unlike the illusion created in 1 Samuel 19 for the guards, only this time *we* are the ones who do not know whether David is in his bed or not.

Is the plan that makes possible David's escape Michal's idea, or is she merely an accomplice? Diana Edelman raises this question and argues that the text's ambiguity makes it impossible to tell whether Michal in fact devised the escape plan herself or rather followed orders given to her by David in response to her warning that he is in danger.[9] Edelman believes that Michal's warning puts the burden of managing his escape on David: 'If you do not save your life tonight, tomorrow you will be killed' (19.11).[10] And she questions whether Michal's claim that she let David escape because he threatened her ('He said to me, "Let me go, why should I kill you?"', v. 19) might not be true. She notes, 'Since the audience has not been informed of David's reciprocal love for Michal, his possible threat to her life should she not help him is not inconsistent with any known character trait'.[11]

Edelman's proposals regarding what Michal may or may not have done are an example of gap filling based on close reading. In effect, she is speculating about something *behind the story that isn't told*. While we might argue about any number of ways to fill gaps, I resist, on principle, any gap filling that makes a male character responsible for actions of

---

8. Fokkelman (1986: 267-68).
9. Edelman (1991: 147-49).
10. In my opinion, this is not necessarily the case. I can well imagine a situation in which one person tells another, 'If you don't leave now, you'll be caught. Listen, do this...'
11. Edelman (1991: 149).

which the female character in the story is clearly the subject. Moreover, I am not persuaded that gap filling—no matter how it is done—really does female characters any service. *In the story told to us* Michal is the agent, the active character who executes the plan: she warns David, she lets him down through the window, she puts the teraphim in David's bed and tells her father's messengers that David is sick, and she responds to Saul's accusation that *she let David escape*. David is the active character only when he is outside the house, outside the woman's domain: we are told that David 'fled' and 'escaped' after Michal let him down through the window (v. 12) and the information that 'David fled and escaped' is repeated when Michal's 'scene' is over (v. 18).

Edelman is, of course, aware of Michal's activity in this scene and views it as an indication that the escape plan may be Michal's idea. But whether Michal actively planned David's escape or merely cooperated with it is not the issue. Edelman recognizes what is really at stake here when she refers to the 'double bind [Michal] is in by virtue of her status as royal princess and wife to David: the bind of conflicting loyalty to father and to husband'.[12] Michal, I have argued, cannot show loyalty to both houses at once. Here she is seen acting as 'David's wife' to help her husband and defy her father[13]—in contrast to 2 Samuel 6, where she appears as 'Saul's daughter' to confront David. The female character is a male construct whose narrative entrapment reflects the limitations imposed by gender. In 1 Samuel 19, Michal's ability to help David is limited to her domain, inside the house; once outside, he must, indeed, save his own life.

Michal's defense that David threatened to kill her does, however, contain a proleptic germ of truth. Again, compari-

---

12. Edelman (1991: 147).
13. Michal's use of the image (teraphim) in David's bed to deceive her father is an intertextual reference to Rachel's deception of her father in connection with teraphim. See Alter (1981: 120); Edelman (1991: 148). On the role of the teraphim and on this scene as representing a ceremony for healing the sick, see Edelman (1991: 149-51). On Rachel's theft of the teraphim, see Chapter 4 below.

son of 1 Samuel 19 with 2 Samuel 6 is illuminating. Whereas
Michal was able to exercise power 'inside' in 1 Samuel 19—
warning David, letting him out the window to freedom,
buying him time by deceiving the messengers, and answer-
ing her father's accusation—David, in 2 Samuel 6, has the
power 'outside', in the social and political arena that is the
man's domain. The emotional tension unleashed in 2 Samuel
6, when Michal vents her frustration, makes 1 Samuel 19,
where she remains 'domesticated', almost claustrophobic by
comparison. As a consequence of her bold outspokenness in
criticizing the king in 2 Samuel 6, Michal becomes a victim.
Ironically she had presented herself as a potential victim in
1 Samuel 19, when she claimed that David threatened, 'Why
should I kill you?'[14] The last word of that account is *'amitek*
('should I kill you'), and it reappears hauntingly as the last
word of 2 Samuel 6: 'until the day of her death' *(motah)*.
Michal's literary murder in 2 Samuel 6 at the hands of the
androcentric narrator—by means of David's words and the
hint that David may be responsible for Michal's childlessness—would make it seem that David's threat to kill Michal
has now been carried out.

In the whole of her fragmented story, Michal has only one
dialogue with David. His only words to her are the words of
rebuke we hear in 2 Samuel 6.[15] By alienating David, Michal
forfeits the recognition she might have received as queen.
But the fact that she is inside and does not participate in all
Israel's celebration of the ark reveals her marginalization
and already suggests that she will likely not fill this role. She
might have gained status as mother, and eventually queen
mother, a part resourcefully played by Bathsheba, but after
her confrontation with David, this position also is denied
her.[16] Her losses are many and significant: David, whom she
once loved; Paltiel, who appears to have loved her (2 Sam.

14. Fokkelman (1986: 269).

15. Apart from Nathan, who acts as God's agent, the only other
person to criticize David's behavior to his face is Joab, and he, too,
comes to an unhappy end: immediately afterwards David demotes
him, and on his death bed orders Solomon to execute him.

16. Cf. the important role of the queen mother in Kings.

3.16); royal status and recognition; and, finally, offspring a woman of her time so desperately needed.

### Gender and Destiny: Michal and Jonathan

We can see something of the role played by gender in determining Michal's fate by comparing the narrative treatment of Michal with that of her brother Jonathan. Michal, Saul's younger daughter, and Jonathan, his son and heir, have much in common. After his defeat of Goliath (1 Sam. 18.16), David steals the hearts of 'all Israel and Judah'. Everyone loves David, and Michal and Jonathan are no exception. Twice we are told that Michal loved David (1 Sam. 18.20, 28 [Heb.]), and Jonathan's love for David is repeatedly remarked upon (18.1, 3; 19.1; 20.3, 17). Their love for David leads both Michal and Jonathan to defy their father in order to save David from Saul's plots against him. Michal's deliverance of David by letting him down through the window of his house when the king's messengers come to take him is framed by two interventions by Jonathan on David's behalf, in which he tries—first successfully, then unsuccessfully—to dissuade Saul from seeking David's life (19.1-7; 20.1-34). What makes the love of Michal and Jonathan for David so remarkable is that they represent the house he will eventually—and with their help—displace. But whereas Jonathan's love remains constant, Michal's turns to anger and hatred.

Kingship over Israel is mediated to David through Jonathan, not Michal; that is, through friendship with the king's son, and not the more common means, marriage to the king's daughter. Whereas after his rejection as king (1 Sam. 13 and 15), Saul does everything in his power to hold on to his kingdom, his son and heir apparent is ready to hand it over to David. In structuralist terms, Jonathan is a mediator.[17] His gesture of giving David his robe, armor, bow, and girdle functions as a symbolic giving-over of the

---

17. See the structural analysis of Jobling (1978: 4-25); see also Leach (1966).

kingdom, and he progressively acknowledges David's claim to the throne from early avowals of support (19.3; 20.9, 12-16) to his climactic, 'you shall be king over Israel and I shall be your second-in-command' (1 Sam. 23.17). David refuses to seize the kingship from Saul, but he is granted it generously by Saul's heir. Jonathan thus represents the uncomplicated transfer of kingship from the house of Saul to the house of David.

In contrast to her brother's 'ideal' relationship with David, where no conflict occurs, Michal raises one of the few voices of resistance on the part of Saul's house to David's assumption of royal prerogative after Saul's death. In terms of their meaning for David and his throne, Jonathan is portrayed positively, and Michal negatively. Adele Berlin has observed in the roles of Jonathan and Michal a certain kind of reversal; however, to ascribe to Jonathan feminine characteristics and to Michal masculine ones, as Berlin does,[18] is to look in the wrong direction for the male/female dynamics of the story, as well as to risk reinforcing gender stereotypes. Jonathan and David are alike in many ways. Both are warriors. A comparison of 1 Samuel 14, where Jonathan carries out a surprise attack against the Philistines, and 1 Samuel 17, where David fights the Philistine champion Goliath, shows how deeply the smimilarities between Jonathan and David go: both kill the Philistine enemy against great odds and with bold words of confidence about divine guidance (14.6-12; 17.45-47), and each becomes a popular hero as a result of his bravery (14.45; 18.6-7). The qualities they share make David an appropriate and ideal companion for Jonathan. It is not surprising, then, that Jonanathan should become knit to David (18.1). Or that Jonathan replaces his sister as love object. This 'love' is not eros but *male bonding*, and it explains, I suggest, Jonathan's near absorption into David, what David Jobling aptly describes as his identification with and self-emptying into David.[19] David Damrosch calls this

---

18. Berlin (1983: 24-25).
19. Jobling (1978: 4-25). This is not to exclude political implications of the term 'love'; see J.A. Thompson (1974).

bonding the 'friendship-as-marriage' motif[20] and we see it quite clearly in two classic examples cited by Damrosch: the love between Gilgamesh and Enkidu in the Gilgamesh Epic and between Achilles and Petroclos in the *Iliad*.

Male bonding characteristically excludes and undervalues women.[21] It is Jonathan whom David returns to meet with secretly after fleeing Saul's court (1 Sam. 20). He does not come back to visit his wife Michal nor does he include her when he arranges refuge for his parents with the king of Moab (22.3-4). David's leave-taking from Jonathan in 1 Samuel 20 takes place amid intense emotion and fervent avowals of loyalty, unlike his exit in 1 Samuel 19, where he practically bolts out the window without any parting words to Michal. When David is hiding from Saul in the wilderness, Jonathan goes to meet him to encourage him: 'Do not be afraid, for the hand of Saul my father will not find you; you shall be king over Israel and I shall be your second-in-command—even Saul my father knows this' (1 Sam. 23.16-18). In view of Jonathan's behavior, Saul's accusation of his servants cannot be simply dismissed as the raving of a madman: 'No one discloses to me when my son makes a covenant with the son of Jesse; none of you is sorry for me or discloses to me that my son has stirred up my servant against me, to lie in wait, as at this day' (22.8). When he learns of Jonathan's death, David laments, 'Your love for me was wonderful, more than the love of women' (2 Sam. 1.26). I take the most natural meaning of this statement to be that Jonathan loved David more than women love men.[22]

---

20. Damrosch (1987: 204-206).

21. An important early study of male bonding which elicited a good deal of critical response is Tiger (1984 [1st edn, 1969]). For a recent feminist analysis, see Sedgwick (1985).

22. Nowhere is it unambiguously stated that David loved Jonathan, whereas it is frequently mentioned that Jonathan loved David. In David's lament over Jonathan, it is not entirely clear who loved whom. Freedman (1972: 117, 123) construes the anomalous verb form *npl'th* in 2 Sam. 1.26 as *nipla' 'attah*, and translates, 'You were extraordinary. Loving you, for me, was better than loving women'; see also Cross and Freedman (1975: 47, 50). Such an expression of sentiment suggests that David loved Jonathan more than David loved women, or, that David

In the case of Michal the issue is *male rivalry*, where woman is frequently victim. The rivalry is that between David and Saul, and after Saul's death, its intensity diminished, between David and Ishbosheth, as Saul's successor and king of the northern tribes. Whereas Jonathan functions to mediate the kingship from Saul to David, Michal mediates relations between the two men, Saul and David, who, on the evidence of 1 Samuel 16 and 18, appear in a classical Freudian Oedipal relationship of rivalry and love. Saul intends to use Michal as a 'snare', as a means to rid himself of David (1 Sam. 18.21). Marriage to the king's daughter will bring David closer to the kingship. As we saw in the previous Chapter, the text suggests his political ambitions by stating, 'it pleased David to be the king's son-in-law'; it does not say whether or not it pleased him to have Michal as his wife.[23] The men are motivated by considerations of politics and power; the woman, by love (1 Sam. 18.20). Her desire can find expression only in the context of the men's political machinations, to which she unavoidably falls victim.

After Saul's death, Ishbosheth replaces him as David's rival, though it is a role he is too ineffectual to sustain. In asking for the return of his wife Michal, whom Saul had married to Paltiel apparently to deny David claim to the

---

preferred male bonding to involvement with women—an appropriate commentary on David's less-than-ideal relationships with women. It may also suggest that David gained more from his relationship with Jonathan, though he gained substantially through his liaison with Abigail. If, on the other hand, we take *npl'th* as an archaic form for the sake of assonance, as Holladay (1970: 183) suggests, we may translate, 'Your love for me was wonderful, beyond the love of women', a reading also supported by the Septuagint. Jonathan loved David more than women loved David—or, as I propose above, more than women love men in general. After all, it is a magnanimous gesture to give up a throne for one's friend. Cf. also Shea (1986: 19): 'You were wonderful, (in) your love to me, / more than the love of women'. On the difficulties of the LXX witnesses, see McCarter (1984: 72).

23. We might also take David's concern with a reward in 1 Sam. 17.26, 'What shall be done for the man who kills this Philistine?', as a sign of his political ambitions.

throne, David again appears politically motivated.[24] Paltiel's weeping as Michal is taken away from him (2 Sam. 3.16) draws attention to the textual silence surrounding both David's and Michal's emotions. The rivalry here involves Ishbosheth as much as Paltiel, which is why David asks *Ishbosheth* for her.[25] The Saul–David rivalry reappears in David's and Michal's final confrontation, where, as we have seen, at last it effectively humiliates and eliminates the woman. Connected to the themes of male bonding and male rivalry is the issue of autonomy. Michal expresses autonomy vis-à-vis her father Saul when she defies him by helping David escape and then lying to conceal her involvement. She reveals her autonomy from David when she criticizes his behavior before the ark. The alternating descriptions of Michal as 'David's wife' or 'Saul's daughter' draw attention to Michal's difficult position between the two men. Autonomy proves to be very costly, indeed, ultimately impossible and thus self-destructive, for Michal. The situation is different for Jonathan. As a man, Jonathan is free to support David openly, even to the point of seeming to betray his father (1 Sam. 22.8; 23.16-18), whereas Michal, who could hardly run around the countryside to seek out David, must rely on deception to help him. On more than one occasion Jonathan takes David's part against Saul; he even serves as a kind of surrogate for David when Saul casts his spear at him as he had cast it earlier at David (cf. 20.33 with 18.11 and 19.10).[26] Jonathan's lack of autonomy from David is most clearly attested by the fact that, with two exceptions, Jonathan appears in the narrative only in relation to David.

24. On the importance of Michal to David's claim to Saul's kingdom, see Flanagan (1983: 51-54).
25. Earlier he demanded his wife from Abner, the power behind Ishbosheth's throne. As Clines (1972: 271) observes, from Abner David demands something from *Saul's* house as a sign of Abner's loyalty. From Ishbosheth he demands what is legally his. No man stands in David's way. He can have the wife of another (Michal), the wife of a fool (Abigail), and the wife of a loyal soldier (Bathsheba). Only Yhwh cuts him short.
26. Jobling 1978: 14.

The exceptions are when he is introduced (1 Sam. 14), which takes place before David is introduced, and at his death (31.2). Lack of autonomy from David involves a curious kind of self-preservation through effacement for Jonathan. He gains from David the assurance that David will not destroy his house (20.14-17), yet the degree to which David, after Jonathan's death, remains loyal to his friend's descendants is open to question.[27] Jonathan's identity, however, is not completely submerged into David's; he remains with his father rather than joining David's renegade band, and he fights and dies at Saul's side.

If Jonathan replaces his sister as love object, the converse also holds true: Michal replaces Jonathan as object of David's hostility. Where conflict logically should have taken place—between David and the rightful 'heir' to the throne—there is harmony. The conflict arises between David and his wife from the royal line, where a suitable resolution to the transfer of the monarchy could have occurred: the uniting of the rival royal houses through a child of Michal and David. Such a resolution is impossible theologically, however, in view of Yhwh's rejection of Saul's house. As we saw in Chapter 1, when Michal and David quarrel in 2 Samuel 6, what is actually a political problem (David's accession to the throne and, implicitly, his dealings with Saul's house) becomes an individual, 'family' matter that, in its turn, only thinly disguises the issue of gender and the dynamics of sexual politics. The narrative amalgamates the public and the private, national concerns and individual tensions, and foregrounds conflicts at other levels: relation by blood versus relation by marriage, male versus female. In the handling of these complex issues, the daughter of Saul is sacrificed that the son may be honored.

The fates of Jonathan and Michal are gender-specific. The young prince dies a hero's death. Death on the battlefield preserves his honor and allows Jonathan to remain true both

---

27. Jonathan's son Mephibosheth may eat at David's table (2 Sam. 9), but no trust binds them (see 2 Sam. 16.1-4; 19.24-30) and no place of honor in David's kingdom is held by a descendant of Jonathan (in contrast to the 'second-in-command' expectations of Jonathan).

to Saul and to David. His death at Saul's side, fighting for Israel, demonstrates that he is not a traitor, in spite of the fact that he had supported David against Saul. If he were a real traitor to his father—as, for example, Abner is to Saul's house (2 Sam. 3)—we could not admire him; nor could we approve him if he, like his father, opposed David. Death conveniently removes Jonathan as an obstacle, actual or potential, to David's rise to kingship—for giving David the kingship symbolically is different altogether from achieving the transition in reality, as the opposition of Abner and Ishbosheth and the long war between the house of Saul and the house of David (2 Sam. 3.1) demonstrate. Since Jonathan does not live to become David's 'second-in-command', this vision of his position in the Davidic monarchy is never tested. Jonathan accordingly remains David's friend to the end.

Because he dies early, Jonathan does not have to witness the progressive debasement of his father's house. He mediates the kingship to David on an ideological level, but he does not live to face the actual problem of transition. He is spared, in other words, the indignities Michal must endure. For her there is no graceful exit in honorable death by the sword, death that exalts male courage. A woman's fate is to survive, to remain on the scene, watching as others benefit at the expense of her family.[28] To live in the victor's house as

---

28. The *Iliad* is helpful not only in showing the strength of male bonding but also in revealing gender expectations of male bravery and female victimization, e.g. in man-killing Hector's speech to his wife Andromache:

> All this weighs on my mind too, dear woman.
> But I would die of shame to face the men of Troy
> and the Trojan women trailing their long robes
> if I would shrink from battle now, a coward.
> Nor does the spirit urge me on that way.
> I've learned it all too well. To stand up bravely,
> always to fight in the front ranks of Trojan soldiers,
> winning my father great glory, glory for myself ...
>                                     Even so,
> it is less the pain of the Trojans still to come
> that weighs me down, not even of Hecuba herself

an outsider, as 'Saul's daughter', excluded from celebration that includes 'all the people, the whole multitude of Israel, men and women' is a grievous injury. Michal protests, but as is frequently the case in a protest that issues out of weakness, to no avail, and to her detriment.

Because he has no direct role in Jonathan's death, David can lament it; he is strongly implicated, however, in Michal's bitter fate. Male rivals are honored publicly. David laments the deaths not only of Saul and Jonathan (2 Sam. 1.19-27) but also of Abner (2 Sam. 3.33-34), and he has words of esteem for Ishbosheth, whose death he avenges (2 Sam. 4.10-12). The issue is not whether or not his sentiments are genuine (one can easily posit political motives for David's display of grief over the deaths of members of the rival house, which, no doubt, still had its loyal supporters) but that they are

> or King Priam, or the thought that my own brothers
> in all their numbers, all their gallant courage,
> may tumble in the dust, crushed by enemies—
> That is nothing, nothing beside your agony
> when some brazen Argive hales you off in tears,
> wrenching away your day of light and freedom!
> Then far off in the land of Argos you must live,
> laboring at a loom, at another woman's beck and call,
> fetching water at some spring, Messeis or Hyperia,
> resisting it all the way—
> the rough yoke of necessity at your neck.
> And a man may say, who sees you streaming tears,
> 'There is the wife of Hector, the bravest fighter
> they could field, those stallion-breaking Trojans,
> long ago when the men fought for Troy'. So he will say
> and the fresh grief will swell your heart once more,
> widowed, robbed of the one man strong enough
> to fight off your day of slavery.
>                          *Iliad* 6.534-53, trans. Fagles (1990: 210-11).

For a suggestive analysis of the gender-determined nature of women's deaths in Greek tragedy, see Loraux (1987). The outcome for a woman as spoil of war was often worse; cf. Achilles' speech: 'The girl—I won't give up the girl. Long before that, old age will overtake her in *my* house, in Argos, far from her fatherland, slaving back and forth at the loom, forced to share my bed!' (1.33-37; Fagles 1990: 78). Cf. also the law for treatment of the woman taken in war, Deut. 21.10-14, and Judg. 21, discussed below in Chapter 6.

given public expression. The woman is publicly humiliated, but in a way that makes it seem deserved, for she has disgraced David by criticizing him in public and she cannot be allowed to get away with it.

In conclusion, we might consider the complex relation between autonomy and gender, and between discourse, autonomy, and progeny in this narrative. Jonathan, who as a man could be autonomous without censure, cannot be truly autonomous because of his role as mediator. Michal, as a woman, ought not to act autonomously, and because she dares to try, we should not be surprised to see her put in her place by an angry and dismissive husband. Although Jonathan, like Michal, has only one dialogue with David, he speaks in a number of scenes. His speeches, however, offer no resistance to David: on the one hand, they encourage him; on the other, they seek to ensure the welfare of Jonathan's descendants. Michal's one speech (2 Sam. 6.20) voices resistance and dissatisfaction. Her angry words are a claim for attention, ineffectively challenging David on behalf of her father's house. David's reply abruptly cuts off her protest, and her childlessness cuts off a branch of the Saulide line.

As members of a divinely rejected house, Michal and Jonathan (and other members of Saul's house as well)[29] cannot play a role in the Davidic kingdom and consequently are removed from the scene. In this Chapter, I have sought to show that gender plays an important role in prescribing what conduct is open to them in their dealings with David and in deciding their fates: the king's son is honorably disposed of by the narrator; the king's daughter, dishonorably. Jonathan does not protest his elimination any more than he resisted David's rise to the throne that was rightfully his. Michal resists and, as we saw in the last

---

29. On the treatment of Saul's house, see Exum (1992: 70-119). It will remain for another woman from Saul's house to make an effective protest against David's dealings with Saul's house. Rizpah's silent vigil over the exposed bodies of Saul's descendants in 2 Sam. 21, her appeal beyond the reach of language, achieves for Saul's house what Michal's verbal outburst could not; see Exum (1992: 109-119).

Chapter, we can read her refusal to accept meekly her exclusion from David's story as her way of laying a claim to her own story.

# Chapter 3

## SAMSON'S WOMEN

> The division of women into 'respectable women', who are
> protected by their men, and 'disreputable women', who are
> out in the street unprotected by men and free to sell their
> services, has been the basic class division for women. It has
> marked off the limited privileges of upper-class women
> against the economic and sexual oppression of lower-class
> women and has divided women one from the other. Histori-
> cally, it has impeded cross-class alliances among women and
> obstructed the formation of feminist consciousness.
>
> Gerda Lerner

The story of Samson is a story about women. Just try to
imagine it without them. Four women have a significant role
in a biblical story of only four chapters. This fact alone
invites a feminist response. It seems like a simple story: the
characters have no development, no depth—they are types;
the plot is episodic and repetitious—a variation on traditional folktale motifs; and the narrator breaks frame from
time to time to tell us how to read, lest we decide for ourselves. When Samson expresses his intent to marry a Philistine woman, for example, the narrator informs us, 'His
father and his mother did not know that it was from Yhwh,
for he was seeking an occasion against the Philistines; at that
time the Philistines were ruling over Israel' (14.4). Thus we
are meant to read Samson's folly as the design of Yhwh. Or
we might translate the verse: 'His father and his mother did
not know that she was from Yhwh', a translation that both
fits the context and the story's interest in women.

Appearances are often deceiving, as we all know. This not
only holds true for the woman Samson sees at Timnah and
determines to marry but also for the story itself. Far from

being a simple tale, the Samson saga is a subtle, nuanced, and highly complex narrative with an elaborate literary structure[1] and a sophisticated theological agenda.[2] It also has an ambitious and problematic androcentric agenda that has rarely been called into question.[3] We shall therefore question it in this chapter and inquire how the Samson story functions to reinforce the values of its society. Androcentric values.

In what follows I propose to show how the positive picture of Samson's mother in Judges 13 and the negative pictures of the three 'foreign women'—Samson's Timnite wife, the harlot of Gaza, and Delilah—in Judges 14–16 serve specific gender interests, chief among them, to control women and justify their subjugation. In the process of establishing control, the text shows traces of the problematic of maintaining patriarchy, and these traces will serve as my means for constructing a feminist (sub)version of this story. I shall argue that male fear of women's sexuality lies behind all four images of woman in this story. And I shall attempt to expose a problem in the text's portrayal of women—a problem created by the need to show women as powerful and therefore dangerous *and*, at the same time, to appropriate their power for androcentric purposes. The text has another, related problem that results from its use of binary opposition—a phallocentric way of structuring reality we shall examine shortly—because women belong to both sides of the oppositions the story wants to maintain. In handling these difficulties, the text provides a literary witness to ways by which, historically, patriarchy as a social system has controlled women. If Samson is entrapped by women and they betray him by revealing his secrets, similarly the text is entrapped by its own ideology and betrayed by it.

---

1. See Exum (1981).
2. See Exum (1983).
3. Bal (1987: 37-67) addresses the text's gender ideology.

*Ideology and Reading: The Politics of Motherhood*

Judges 13 is a birth announcement. There are a number of such annunciation type-scenes in the Bible, where, typically, we have the divine promise of the birth of a son to a sterile woman.[4] I have argued elsewhere that Manoah takes a secondary role to his wife and that 'the narrative seems intent on stressing the importance of the woman in the events leading to Samson's birth'.[5] Similarly, Esther Fuchs notes, 'Manoah's wife ... is perspicacious, sensitive, and devout, outshining her inept husband'.[6] Susan Niditch echoes this evaluation: 'Manoah plays the timid uncomprehending fool to his wife, who is featured in the most important scene with the divine messenger and who is more able than her husband to comprehend his message and true identity'.[7] Let us begin, then, with a closer look at this positive portrayal of Samson's mother, after which we shall raise the question, What gender interest does this positive portrayal serve?[8]

The woman is alone when the messenger appears to her with the announcement that she will bear a son and with instructions about him (Judg. 13.3-5). When she hears the news, she runs to tell her husband. Manoah knows only what she tells him about this event, and, interestingly, she leaves out some important details (that their son may not be shaved and that he will begin to deliver Israel from the Philistines). She does, however, pass on the essential information: what she must do (abstain from wine and beer) and

4. See Fuchs (1985a); Alter (1983).
5. Exum (1980: 58).
6. Fuchs (1985a: 125). Unlike my 1980 study, Fuchs's investigation identifies and criticizes the androcentric ideology of the text. My analysis focused on Judges 13; Fuchs deals with the annunciation type-scene in general.
7. Niditch (1990: 611).
8. On the following discussion of the positive portrayal of Manoah's wife, see Exum (1980, 1985). For a different, rather unfavorable view of the portrayal of the woman, see Polzin (1980: 182-84); similarly, Boling (1975: 220-21) sees the woman as rather dull-witted, 'speaking better than she knew' (p. 221).

the boy's destiny as a Nazirite.

After he hears his wife's account of her encounter with the man whose 'appearance was like the appearance of the messenger of God' (v. 6), Manoah prays that the man 'come again to us, and teach us what we are to do with the boy that will be born' (v. 8). His request is strange in view of the fact that his wife has just informed him about the boy's destiny. Can it be that he does not accept his wife's word for it? Perhaps he wants to know more about the child than his Nazirite status. What is apparent from his request that the man come 'to *us*' and 'teach *us*' is that he wants to hear the announcement himself. Significantly, however, though Manoah's prayer that the messenger return is granted, it does not happen as he requested. The messenger appears (v. 9) not 'to us' but again to the woman alone. Lest we miss the point, the text adds, 'and Manoah her husband was not with her'. The messenger does not come to Manoah; rather Manoah must be brought to the messenger by his wife. We might wonder, therefore, whether Manoah would have seen the messenger at all were it not for the woman's intervention. Finally, Manoah gets the audience he wants, but— unlike his wife, who behaves with the proper reserve before such an honored emissary (v. 6)—he has many questions to ask. Ironically, however, for all his efforts, he receives even less information from the messenger than he had from his wife. The messenger merely turns the issue back to the woman: 'Of all that I said to the woman let her beware' (v. 13). By denying Manoah as much knowledge about the child as his wife, the narrative underscores her importance. It also portrays her as more perceptive than Manoah.

Together Manoah and his wife prepare an offering, which provides the occasion for the messenger's divine identity to be revealed. Up to this point, the couple have referred to him as a 'man of God', a title sometimes used for a prophet. The text singles out Manoah's lack of perception ('For Manoah did not know that he was the messenger of Yhwh', v. 16), a situation reversed when he eventually perceives the messenger's identity (v. 21). Nothing is said about the woman's not knowing the messenger's divine status. On the contrary, she senses it from the start. In reporting his initial appearance, she tells Manoah, 'His countenance was like the countenance of the messenger of God—quite awesome' (v. 6). The response of husband and wife to the revelation of the messenger's status (vv. 22-23) further reflects their different comprehension of the situation. Manoah, in keeping with biblical tradition, knows that one cannot see God and live (see Judg. 6.22-23; Gen. 16.13-14; 32.30; Exod. 19.21; 33.20). His wife, however, recognizes the divine purpose behind the theophany. She understands that God would not have promised them a son with a special destiny if he intended to kill them, and she is therefore able to assure her husband that they will not die (in theophanies, it is usually the deity who gives this assurance).

Whereas Manoah seems inept and overanxious, the woman is portrayed as a worthy recipient of divine favor. She receives from the divine emissary more information about the child's destiny than her husband; she senses something otherworldly about the visitor whereas it takes a miracle for Manoah to recognize him; and she understands the divine intention better than Manoah. One can fairly say, I think, that she is more favorably portrayed than her husband. *Cui bono?*

To see how this positive portrayal of the woman nevertheless serves male interests we have to interrogate the ideology that informs and motivates it. Patriarchal literature reflects an underlying attitude toward woman's sexuality as something to be feared and therefore to be carefully regulated. As we saw in Chapter 1, patriarchy severs the relationship between eroticism and procreation, affirming motherhood but denying the mother's *jouissance*, and associating the erotic not with the mother but rather with the whore. Our story vividly illustrates this division between woman as mother and woman as whore.

In a study of biblical mothers, Esther Fuchs observes:

> Male control of female reproductive powers in conjunction with patrilocal and monogamous marriage (for the wife), secures the wife as her husband's exclusive property and ensures the continuity of his name and family possessions through patrinomial

customs and patrilineal inheritance patterns. The institution of
motherhood as defined by the patriarchal system guarantees
that both the wife and her children will increase his property
during his lifetime and perpetuate his achievements and memory after his death.[9]

In conformity with this principle, Judges 13 affirms woman
in her role as mother—motherhood controlled by men;
motherhood without *jouissance*. Our story not only denies
the mother's sexual pleasure; it goes so far as to dissociate
her pregnancy from the sex act, not even acknowledging in
typical biblical fashion, 'Manoah knew his wife and she conceived'. Rather the story begins with the (male) messenger
of Yhwh telling the woman she is pregnant. Indeed, the
woman's sterility draws attention to the fact that the deity
controls her reproductive ability. The absence of sex from
this chapter is even more remarkable and revealing when
viewed against Samson's sexual liaisons in chs. 14–16 and
against the sexual innuendoes and the pervasive sexual
symbolism in these chapters (which we shall consider
shortly).

The wife and mother of Judges 13 can be portrayed more
positively than her husband because she is no threat.
Mothers are not sexually alluring or threatening; they are
nurturing, as when Manoah fears death and the woman
reassures him. She does nothing on her own, and this is a
trait that patriarchy finds desirable in a woman. Unlike the
Timnite and Delilah, who will soon be seeking Samson's
secrets, she does not ask questions: 'I did not ask him from
where he came and he did not tell me his name' (13.6). In
spite of the fact that the messenger appears to her twice
when she is alone, she does not engage him in conversation.
(Every woman's mother teaches her not to speak to
strangers.) Rather she runs off to tell her husband, who will
ask all the questions in this family. The woman is neither
independent nor selfish nor secretive. Imagine Abraham,
when he first hears the promise of numerous descendants,
running off to fetch Sarah so she can hear it too. Or recall

9. Fuchs (1985a: 129).

that Abraham entertains divine emissaries who tell him Sarah will bear a son, while Sarah remains in the tent—that is, inside, in the woman's place—and has to eavesdrop to hear the birth announcement. Manoah's wife may be perceptive, and even more perceptive than her husband in sensing something otherworldly about the messenger, but she does not challenge Manoah's position of authority. The references to Manoah's not knowing and then knowing that the man was the messenger of Yhwh indicate that it is *his* knowledge and not *hers* that is important. For whose benefit is the miraculous disappearance of the messenger anyway?[10]

In contrast to other biblical birth accounts, we are given surprisingly little background information. We are not told the woman's view of her situation or her circumstances or her name. We are not informed that she was old, as Sarah was. Nor does she complain to her husband about childlessness, as does Rachel. She does not try other means of procuring a child, as Sarah and Rachel do, when they give their maids to their husbands. Nor does she turn to aphrodisiacs, as Rachel apparently does. She does not pray for a child, as does Hannah, nor does her husband pray for her, as Isaac prays for Rebekah. Moreover, we do not learn of her reaction to the birth announcement, as we do in the cases of Sarah, Rachel, and Hannah.[11] This suppression of information, I suggest, serves to underscore her role as a *mother*. Like Jephthah's daughter, her importance lies in her fulfillment of a role, and thus she is not even given a name.[12]

Fragmenting women, leaving their stories incomplete so that they are not full characters, is typical of biblical narrative, and readers tend to fill the gaps in the easiest way; that is, according to convention and presuppositions. Patriarchal

10. Cf. how God reveals himself and his plan to destroy Sodom and Gomorrah to *Abraham* (not to Sarah) in Genesis 18.

11. Exum (1980: 47-48). On the birth accounts in the matriarchal stories, see below, Chapter 4.

12. *Contra* Reinhartz (1992), who argues that the woman's anonymity underscores her centrality. I do not question the woman's important role but rather am interested in the gender motivation that informs both her portrayal and the suppression of her name.

ideology represents women as desiring roles that serve its interests: wife and mother. It expects the sterile woman to be overjoyed at birth, especially at the birth of a son (there are no birth accounts of daughters, except the fragmentary one of Dinah). Not surprisingly, some commentators, reading with conventional expectations, reinscribe this ideology by attributing just this reaction of joy to Manoah's wife.[13] Our narrator relies on a simple but effective strategy—offering incomplete portraits and relying on convention to encourage the reader to complete the portraits with stereotypes about women—to shape the portrayal not only of Samson's mother, but also of the other women in the saga: his Timnite wife, the harlot of Gaza, and Delilah.

*The Good Mother and the Whore*

Whereas there is only one good woman in the Samson saga, there are three bad ones. Is this only because—as Prov. 31.10 suggests—a good woman is hard to find? Following the story of the mother in Judges 13, we encounter in Judges 14–16 three important female characters, none of whom is a mother. Rather they are all available and, for Samson, desirable sexual partners. Woman as mother is on a pedestal; in her non-sexual role she is idealized. Woman as object of sexual desire is dangerous. A strategy by which our text seeks to deal with women's threatening yet desired sexuality is to merge the three different women with whom Samson becomes involved (the Timnite, the harlot, and Delilah) into one composite, negative image of the 'foreign woman'. One image of sexual woman is easier to control, and more comfortable, than multiple portraits of women whose sexual attractiveness is acknowledged.

The negative image of the foreign woman is a given in the Bible; it is simply assumed, and exceptions like Ruth only prove the rule. Proverbs warns the young male repeatedly

13. E.g. Blenkinsopp (1963: 69); Boling (1975: 219); Crenshaw (1978: 73, 76-77); Polzin (1980: 182), assuming that 'wonderful news' is not his own point of view.

against her:

> Say to wisdom, 'You are my sister',
> and call understanding your intimate friend,
> to preserve you from the foreign woman
> from the strange woman with her smooth words (Prov. 7.4-5).[14]

The positive image of the mother is also well established. Mother (legitimate wife) was the only positive role available to most women in ancient Israelite society. 'You shall honor your father and your mother', says the decalogue, and Proverbs admonishes the son to heed the teaching of his father and his mother.[15] The Samson saga therefore does not need to establish a contrast between the negative and positive images, the foreign woman and the mother. It assumes it and builds upon it. And it counts on us to accept it and apply it when we read.

Although the text specifically identifies only one of the three women with whom Samson becomes involved as Philistine (Samson's wife from Timnah), most readers assume all three are Philistines. The harlot, because she lives in Gaza, is viewed by all commentators I am aware of as Philistine (but what's to prevent her from being a 'foreign woman' who happens to live in Philistia? an Israelite woman, for example). Only a few commentators raise the possibility that Delilah, who has a Hebrew name and lives on the boundary between Israelite and Philistine territory, might be Israelite. Basically we take her for a Philistine too because we assume the other women are Philistine, and also because she deals with the Philistine lords, and surely an Israelite woman would not betray Samson to his enemies! To follow such reasoning is to be lured into the ideology of the text, into accepting the proposition that Israelite women

---

14. Note that it is 'with her words' that Delilah breaks down Samson's resistance.

15. Proverbs does not offer instructions to daughters, but they must learn somewhere if, when they grow up and have sons, they are to teach them. For compelling analyses that undermine the opposition between the good female figure (Wisdom) and the evil woman, see Camp (1988) and Newsom (1989).

behave respectably, while foreign women are disreputable and treacherous.

The text encourages us to confuse and to conflate the three women by various means.[16] It shows them doing the same things: both the Timnite and Delilah 'entice' (*pittah*) Samson in order to get him to 'tell' (the key word is *higgid*) his secret—in one case, the answer to his riddle; in the other, the source of his strength. In both cases 'he told her' (14.17; 16.17) 'because she harassed him' (14.17; 16.16). Both women pass on the answer to the Philistines.[17] Similar vocabulary is also used to link the Timnite and the harlot. Judges 14 begins:

> Samson went down to Timnah and he saw a woman in Timnah.

Judges 16 begins:

> Samson went to Gaza and he saw there a woman, a harlot...

These women have something in common. The sight of them arouses the desire to possess them.[18] Both are objects of sexual desire: 'I will go in to my wife in the chamber', says Samson (15.1)—the verb used here, *bo'*, is commonly used for sexual intercourse. 'Samson went to Gaza and saw there

---

16. Bal (1987) comments upon the tendency to superimpose the pictures of the women and warns against it; we do it readily, I think, if we (unconsciously) accept the text's ideology.

17. On the extensive parallels between the account of Samson and the Timnite and that of Samson and Delilah, see Exum (1981).

18. The text says that the Timnite was 'right in the eyes of Samson' (14.7; 'right in my eyes', 14.3) and not the more usual 'beautiful in his eyes'. On the significance of the difference, cf. Greenstein (1981: 249), who sees the phrase as referring not to physical attractiveness but rather to proper conduct (indicating Samson's attraction to alien culture) and Sasson (1988: 339 n. 2), who exploits the ambiguity. Gunn (1992: 232, 252 n. 6) concludes that Samson has not just sex but marriage in mind. I see no reason why 'sexual attraction alone would demand at least "beautiful"' (Gunn, p. 232): that men are sexually attracted only to beautiful women is but another gender stereotype. The phrase 'right one in his eyes' echoes an important theme from the end of the book of Judges: in this period without kings, 'every man did what was right in his own eyes'.

a harlot and went in to her', the narrator tells us (16.1), and again the verb is *bo'*.

Another way the text suggests common features among the three women is by juxtaposition: the story of Delilah follows the story of the harlot with only the clause 'and it happened after that' to separate them. It strengthens the associations by way of suggestion. Delilah is not identified as a harlot, but commentators who consider her one—and they are numerous—are reading according to patriarchal ideology and convention. Because she is not identified in terms of her familial relationship to a male—she seems to have her own house, and Samson is apparently her lover though she is not his wife—other possibilities for understanding her position in society are rarely entertained. Incidentally, the text does not say they have sexual relations (as in 16.1-3), only that Samson loved her; the sexual aspect is something, once again, *we* supply, encouraged by the numerous sexual innuendoes and *double entendres* in the story. Even the Timnite, Samson's legal wife (almost: the ceremony is not concluded[19]) is disparaged and cast in the role of a loose woman[20] when Samson charges that his wedding companions 'plowed with my heifer' (14.18), a coarse reference to sexual intercourse.[21]

In a brief sexual interlude described in Judg. 16.1-3, Samson goes to visit a harlot at Gaza and the Philistines learn about it. *How* they get this information is not stated in the text. The placement of this story between accounts in which Samson is betrayed by women encourages the assumption that the harlot was the informant, though, in fact, this story

19. With many scholars, I accept Stade's (1884) famous emendation of 14.18, 'before he went into the chamber'. The point is, I think, that the marriage is not consummated. Samson storms away in anger and the woman is then married off to the best man.

20. The concept of a 'loose woman' is, of course, a patriarchal notion based on the double standard (Samson, for example, is never described as a loose man); see below.

21. Plowing was a common metaphor for sexual intercourse; see the discussions of Levy (1916) and Crenshaw (1974: 493-94).

is different in important ways from the others.[22]
For the identification of all three women as foreign
women and, by implication, disreputable women, the text
relies on its readers to read according to convention.
Encouraging readers to fill gaps with stereotypes about
women enables the narrator on the one hand to give abun-
dant testimony to the dangers of the foreign woman and, on
the other, to provide as little information as possible about
the individual women from which we might construct their
stories.

> *Binary Opposition and the Problem of Woman as Other,*
> *Or, 'Is there no woman among the daughters of your*
> *brothers or among all my people, that you are going to take a*
> *wife from the uncircumcised Philistines?'*

Binary opposition is a way of structuring reality, differentiating it into a hierarchy of opposition, in which one side of
the opposition is always privileged. In binary thought, each
term achieves significance only through its structural relationship to the other.[23] 'Self', for example, acquires meaning
only in terms of and in relation to what is not self; that is, to
'other'. Some feminists consider binary opposition a hall-
mark of phallocentric thinking; in any event, it is
widespread and everywhere observable. Consider some of
the oppositions that figure prominently in the Samson
saga.[24]

  Israelite / Philistine
  own kind / foreign
  male / female

22. Even Bal, while aware of the danger of confusing the women,
succumbs to the temptation when speculating about the identity of the
informant: 'It is plausible to assume that it is the prostitute' (1987: 49).
As I argue below, the Philistines triumph over Samson when a woman
helps them—which suggests that in this case, where they fail to defeat
him, the woman is not involved.
  23. See Moi (1985: 104-105).
  24. Niditch (1990: 609, 614) notes some of these; Bal (1987: 40) discusses other oppositions at work.

circumcised / uncircumcised
nature / culture
endogamy / exogamy
paternal house / women's houses
clean / unclean
self / other
good woman / evil woman

*Israelite / Philistine.* This is the dominant set of oppositions in the story. It is the concrete expression of another opposition, *own kind* versus *foreign.* The Israelite side is the 'right side', the 'us', as opposed to the Philistines who are the 'wrong side'—'them'.

*Male / female.* This opposition is also an expression of *own kind* versus *foreign.* But it does not correspond to the Israelite/Philistine opposition, since some women are Israelite. Hélène Cixous, in a trenchant critique of patriarchal binary thought, suggests that the underlying paradigm for all oppositions is the hidden male/female opposition with its inevitable evaluation of one element as positive and the other as negative.[25]

*Circumcised / uncircumcised.* Circumcision is the mark of participation in the covenant community of Israel, the community by and for whom this text was produced. Religious difference is inscribed in the penis as a physical difference setting Israelite men apart from Philistine men.[26] The Philistines as a people, which includes both men and women, are referred to as 'the uncircumcised' (14.3). Women, who are uncircumcised, are by nature on the Philistine side of this opposition. And Philistine men, who do not bear the distinct mark of covenant relationship on the male organ, are strongly identified with the female, as we shall see.

*Nature / culture.* The best statement of this set of oppositions in the Samson saga is still to be found in the work of

25. Cixous (1986: 63-132).
26. Sexual aggression, fear, and envy are all at work in the account of Saul's demand of one hundred Philistine foreskins as a bride-price for his daughter Michal and David's double payment. For further discussion of circumcision as it relates to gender bias, see Chapter 4 below.

Hermann Gunkel, who characterized Samson as *Natur-mensch* over against the Philistines as *Kulturmenschen*:

> Simson tut alle seine Taten o h n e   e i n   M i t t e l   d e r
> K u l t u r : den Löwen zerreisst er mit der Hand; mit der Hand
> hebt er die Tore von Gazza aus; er zerschneidet nicht, sondern
> er zerriesst seine Bande; an den Haaren reisst er den Aufzug
> des Webstuhls aus dem Boden; mit der Wucht seines Körpers
> stürzt er den Dagon-Tempel um; und nur mit einem Eselskinn-
> backen, wie man ihn auf dem Felde findet, also einem Werk-
> zeug, wie es die Natur bietet, erschlägt er seine Feinde.[27]

> [Samson does all of his deeds without any instrument of cul-
> ture: he tears the lion with his hands; with his hands he lifts up
> the gates of Gaza; he does not cut but rather tears his bonds;
> with his hair he tears the warp of the loom out of the ground;
> with the weight of his body he pulls down the temple of Dagon;
> and with only an ass's jawbone such as one would find on the
> ground—a tool offered by nature—he kills his enemies.]

Ordinarily, one would expect culture to be privileged over nature. Women are usually thought of as closer to nature, while men are identified with culture.[28] The situation is reversed in our text, however, where the privileging of nature over culture reflects the Israelite position as cultur-ally inferior to the Philistines and is a case of the underdog taking pride in the ability to overcome the superior culture.

*Endogamy / exogamy*. This opposition finds expression in the reaction of Samson's parents when he tells them he wants to marry a Philistine: 'Is there no woman among the daughters of your brothers or among all your people,[29] that you are going to take a wife from the uncircumcised Philistines?' (14.3). The book of Deuteronomy insists on Israel's separateness from the surrounding people in the land of Canaan: 'You shall not make marriages with them, giving your daughters to their sons or taking their daughters for your sons. For they would turn away your sons from following me, to serve other gods; then the anger of Yhwh

27. Gunkel (1913: 40; emphasis his).
28. Ortner (1974); Cixous (1986: 63-132).
29. Reading with the Lucianic recension and the Syriac; MT has 'my people'—as if only his father were speaking?

would be kindled against you, and he would destroy you quickly' (7.3-4; notice that even though daughters are not to be given in marriage to foreigners, it is *sons* who the biblical narrator fears will be led astray).

*Paternal house / women's houses.* In my opinion, there is insufficient evidence for the often found reference to Samson's marriage to the Timnite woman as a *tsadiqah* marriage; that is, a marriage in which the wife remains in her parents' house and is visited there by her husband.[30] But the fact remains, Samson does not bring a woman back to his house. Delilah appears to have her own house, and the introduction to her mirrors the introduction to Manoah in such a way as to present her as the negative counterpart to Manoah and the paternal house.

> Now there was a certain man *from Zorah*, from the clan of the Danites, *and his name was Manoah*.
> Now after this he loved a woman *in the valley of Soreq, and her name was Delilah*.

Not only is the narrative style similar but also these are the only characters in the saga who are named, except Samson.

*Clean / unclean.* Samson, even before he is born, is set apart as a Nazirite. He is to eat nothing unclean and drink no wine or strong drink.[31] And his hair is not to be cut. He does not, however, keep these regulations. Scooping honey out of the carcass of the lion exposes him to the unclean; and the description of his wedding feast as a *mishteh* suggests that there is drinking going on and that Samson participates.[32]

---

30. *Tsadiqah* marriage is frequently mentioned in the commentaries in connection with Samson's marriage to the Timnite woman. Samson, however, has left the wedding feast in a fury; the woman's father understands his action as signaling that Samson has renounced his claim to her (cf. Boling 1975: 232, 235); and the woman is married off to another. It is hard to see how she can be understood as still married to Samson. Samson returns later with a gift, but since he is denied access to the woman, it is impossible to know what kind of marriage arrangement, if any, the narrator wished to suggest.

31. These injunctions are actually placed on the mother in Judg. 13.

32. Burney (1970: 344); Gunkel (1913: 40); Blenkinsopp (1963: 66). Though I am not entirely persuaded that the narrator presents Samson

*Self / other.* This is an important opposition for the gender politics of the narrative. In the androcentric symbolic world of our text, 'self' is defined as male; and woman, who most fundamentally represents that which is not self, is 'other'. When Samson surrenders himself to the other, he becomes symbolically the other, as we shall see.

*Good woman / evil woman.* In patriarchal thought, women occupy a marginal position; they are at the boundary of the phallocentric symbolic order, the border between men and chaos. As borderline figures, women can be perceived as either inside or outside male society. When women are viewed as inside the border, they are romantically idealized (the woman on the pedestal; the virgin or the mother); when viewed as outside, they are victimized and cast off (the whore).[33] Motherhood and nurturing characterize the good woman; sexuality and sensuality, the evil one.[34] This opposition also reflects the double standard. Men are not characterized as 'respectable' or 'disreputable' according to their sexual behavior.

In the list of oppositions given above, the categories that appear first are privileged in our story; those in the second position are viewed negatively. Women occupy an ambiguous position in this schema; they belong to both sides of the oppositions. The Philistines are enemies, alien, the other. Women are also enemies, alien, the other. Philistine women are doubly other. But what happens if one is woman and not a Philistine? The text is uneasy about the Israelite woman, for she is good only to the extent that her sexuality (her femaleness, which belongs on the negative side) is controlled. The negative categories are dangerous; they threaten the integrity of the privileged categories. But Samson is

as breaking the Nazirite regulations against contact with what is unclean or drinking wine or strong drink (see Exum 1983: 31-32), I acknowledge the potential for such a reading.

33. See Moi (1985: 163-67); Kristeva (1986b).

34. Reading with the text's ideology, which opposes idealized motherhood to the danger of sexual women, Crenshaw (1974; 1978: 65-98) sees the conflict between filial devotion and erotic attachment as the leitmotif of the story.

attracted to them. He is always crossing boundaries. He does not keep the Nazirite regulations, thus violating the distinction between clean and unclean; he marries a Philistine woman, entering an exogamous relationship; and he prefers foreigners to his own kind. Samson is a limen, a marginal figure who moves between the Israelite and Philistine worlds but does not belong to either of them.[35] He is also a mediating figure between Israelite and Philistine.[36] It is difficult, if not impossible, to remain in a liminal stage, a state of transition marked by ambivalence and ambiguity, and thus of danger. Samson cannot be a successful mediator between the two worlds, the Israelite and the Philistine, because the distinctions between them must be rigorously maintained by our story, even if at the price of the hero's life.

### Knowledge, Power, and Sex

Extensive sexual symbolism in the Samson saga has long been recognized.[37] There is, for example, the association of hair with sexual potency, documented in many cultures,[38] and the connection between cutting the hair and castration established by Freud. At a wedding feast—a suitable setting for banter about sex—Samson asks a riddle: 'From the eater came forth food; from the strong came forth sweet'. Most commentators agree that the present story has made use of existing riddles to produce the present riddle and answer. Whereas Gressmann thought the original answer to this riddle was 'vomit',[39] Eissfeldt opted for the answer

---

35. On the concept of liminality, see van Gennep (1960); Turner (1977). Samson's marginality is further indicated by his lifelong status as a Nazirite, a word meaning 'separate, dedicated', and by his superhuman strength that makes him not 'like other men' (Judg. 16.7, 11, [13], 17).

36. See Niditch (1990: 613-14); Bal (1987: 43-44).

37. Levy (1916).

38. Gaster (1981: 436-38); Leach (1967); Huston (1986: 119-20); Bal (1987: 54-55); Niditch (1990: 616-17).

39. Gressmann (1922: 243).

'semen'.[40] Crenshaw sees in the riddle an allusion to sexual intercourse,[41] and recently Camp and Fontaine have further explored its erotic symbolism.[42] To the riddle's answer, 'What is sweeter than honey, what is stronger than a lion?', Gunkelproposed the solution, 'love'.[43] Lévi-Strauss has explored the sexual symbolism of honey,[44] and Bal observes of Samson's tearing the lion and taking honey from its belly: 'The tearing has positive consequences, a feature it shares with that other kind of tearing that gives pleasure: defloration'.[45] When the Philistines answer his riddle, Samson's repartee, 'If you had not plowed with my heifer you would not have found out my riddle', is a *double entendre* bordering on the obscene.

Samson's attraction to women is a projection of the narrator's own obvious interest in sex. It seems to me that the story of Samson's involvement with the woman from Timnah makes a kind of sexual joke about Samson's not consummating the marriage. The Philistines wait until the last possible moment before giving their answer: 'And the men of the city said to him on the seventh day [of wedding festivities] before he went into the chamber, "What is sweeter than honey and what is stronger than a lion?"' (14.18). The reading, 'before he went into the chamber', for the Masoretic text's 'before the sun had set', rests on a widely accepted textual emendation suggested by Stade.[46] But regardless of whether or not Samson's sexual desire is frustrated here, it clearly is sometime later, when he returns to visit his wife with one thought on his mind: 'I will go in to my wife in the chamber' (15.1). Desire meets with constraint: 'her father would not allow him to go in' (the verb *bo'* here indicates sexual intercourse).

Later, when Samson engages the services of a prostitute,

40.  Eissfeldt (1910: 134).
41.  Crenshaw (1974: 490; 1978: 115).
42.  Camp and Fontaine (1990); see also Bal (1987: 45-46).
43.  Gunkel (1913: 54).
44.  Lévi-Strauss (1973; 1978: 412-13).
45.  Bal (1987: 45).
46.  Stade (1884: 253).

he encounters no opposition: 'he went in to her' (*wayyabo'* *'eleha*, 16.1). The Philistines learn of his presence among them and plan an ambush for the morning, but Samson surprises them by leaving at midnight. He escapes, pulling up the city gates and carrying them off all the way to Hebron. Commentators (mostly men), as much as the biblical narrator, I would say, have relished this story of Samson's prowess. In the middle of a night of sexual activity, his vigor apparently undiminished, he struts off, carrying the Gaza gates on his shoulders, right under the Philistines' noses. Gunkel comments that this is the time when even a strong man needs rest, citing the dictum, *omne animal post coitum triste*.[47] (This is, of course, a male joke.[48])

The narrator's choice of vocabulary reinforces the sexual symbolism. Both the Timnite and Delilah are told to 'entice' Samson. The verb used, *pittah*, also refers to seducing a woman (Exod. 22.16 [Heb. 15]; Hos. 2.14 [Heb. 16]). Delilah asks, 'How might you be bound in order that you might be humbled?' (16.6). The verb here, *'innah*, is elsewhere used of raping a woman (Gen. 34.2; Deut. 21.14; 22.24, 29; Judg. 19.24; 20.5; 2 Sam. 13.12, 14, 22, 32; Ezek. 22.10, 11; Lam. 5.11). I shall return shortly to the significance of applying these terms to Samson. The picture of Samson's sleeping on Delilah's lap, or, as the Greek has it, 'between her knees', is suggestive of love-making. Not only is Samson symbolically castrated when his hair is cut and he is blinded, the labor he is forced to perform, grinding at the mill, has sexual connotations. Grinding seems to be a term for sexual intercourse in Job 31.9-10, for example:

> If my heart has been enticed (the verb is *niptah*) by a woman,
> and I have lain in wait at my neighbor's entrance,[49]
> then let my wife grind for another,
> and let others bow down upon her.

47. Gunkel (1913: 44).
48. Bal (1987: 49), in contrast to most commentators, suggests that Samson 'had to break off prematurely'.
49. Probably also a *double entendre*.

The verb *tsahaq/sahaq*, used of Samson's 'playing' or 'serving as amusement' for the Philistines, also has sexual connotations. It is used of Isaac's fondling of Rebekah, behavior that alerts Abimelech to the true nature of their relationship (Gen. 26.8-9). Finally, there is the image of Samson standing between the two pillars on which Dagon's temple rests, an image Bal likens to correcting the act of birth by breaking the woman's thighs.[50]

What, we might ask, is the significance of this sexual symbolism that is everywhere to be found in the accounts of Samson's encounters with foreign women, but absent in the account of Samson's parents? Sex, knowledge, and power are intimately related.[51] Indeed, the verb 'to know' (*yada'*) also refers sexual intercourse: 'Adam knew his wife Eve, and she conceived and bore a son'. Riddles and riddling have been connected to sexual knowledge. We have seen the sexual symbolism in Samson's famous riddle about the sweet and the strong and its answer, which is itself a riddle. Niditch observes that riddles are a type of power game, in which the one who knows the answer gains status.[52] Bettelheim holds that riddles in fairy tales have to do with sexual knowledge, at least on the unconscious level. The riddle is the mystery of the other sex: 'whoever understands the secret which the other sex presents has gained his [*sic*] maturity'.[53]

Knowledge is elusive in the Samson saga. The line between question and riddle is sometimes thin, as in 13.18: 'Why do you ask my name, seeing that it is wonderful?'[54] Of the many questions—fifteen to be exact[55]—posed in a story

50.  Bal (1987: 62).

51.  For an exploration of their relationship, see Bal (1987: 37-67), whose psychoanalytic reading of the story is a *tour de force*.

52.  Niditch (1990: 620-21).

53.  Bettelheim (1976: 128); I owe the reference to Bal (1987: 43).

54.  On the riddle behind 13.17-19, see Torczyner (Tur Sinai) (1924: 141). LXX[B] writes 14.14 as a question.

55.  Judg. 13.11, 12, 17, 18; 14.3, 15; 15.2, 6, 10, 11 (twice); 16.6, 10, 13, 15. The Hebrew does not supply an interrogative particle in 14.16. In ch. 16, Delilah's inquiries into the source of Samson's strength do not

of only four chapters, it is not only the famous one in ch. 14 that is a riddle; others too take on a riddling cast. Whereas some of these questions are rhetorical (14.3, 15; 15.2, 11), and others are unremarkable in their contexts (e.g. 13.11; 15.6, 10), still others probe more deeply, impinging upon privileged information. In seeking to learn more about the mysterious stranger who has appeared to his wife, Manoah asks three questions: 'Are you the man who spoke to the woman?' (13.11); 'When your word(s) come(s) to pass, what will be the boy's manner of life and what will he do?' (13.12); 'What is your name?' (13.17). Knowledge of the name would give Manoah power over the divine emissary, and the question, like all questions after the divine name, meets with an evasive and ambiguous answer. Similarly, Delilah questions Samson three times about his strength (the fourth time she upbraids him for not telling her), and the correct answer gives her power over Samson.[56] Knowledge is power, and *women* are the ones who succeed in obtaining forbidden information in the story. To be precise, women—the Timnite and Delilah—are the ones who obtain forbidden information directly. Manoah does not succeed, though he tries; and the Philistines gain the information they seek indirectly, through the women: the Timnite tells them the answer to Samson's riddle, and Delilah obtains for them the secret of his strength. The Philistines' use of women to obtain knowledge is significant for the gender ideology of the saga, as we shall see.

necessarily have to be read as questions (cf. LXX, Vulg.), but in any event they serve that function.

56. In ch. 13 we have three questions (vv. 11, 12, 17) and a request (v. 15). Similarly, in ch. 16, Delilah questions Samson three times about his strength (vv. 6, 10, 13), but in v. 15 she upbraids rather than questions him. Both 13.15 and 16.15 imply a question (Will the messenger stay? Wherein is Samson's strength great?) and both call for and receive an answer. Thus if we understand the term 'question' in a broad sense, both Manoah and Delilah ask four questions. On the patterning of the saga and the paralleling of ch. 13 and ch. 16, see Exum (1981).

*What Is Sweeter Than Honey*
*and What is Stronger Than A Lion?*

The answer to Samson's riddle is a riddle whose answer is 'love', whatever other sexual meanings can be found in it. Why does Samson reveal his secrets to a woman? Is he simply stupid or is this a display of hubris?[57] Samson's riddle offers the key. The verb 'to love' ('*ahav*) appears three times in the story. Both women demand of Samson that he prove his love. The Timnite laments, 'You only hate me; you do not love me' (14.16). Delilah complains, 'How can you say "I love you" when your heart is not with me?' (16.15). The narrator informs us in 16.4 that Samson loved Delilah. There is no reason to assume that the narrator wishes to suggest that Samson does not love the Timnite simply because he does mention it explicitly. After all, he has Samson answer her challenge to prove his love by telling her the answer to his riddle. The narrator's statement that Samson loved Delilah is, I think, not a sign that this is the first time Samson has loved, but rather a signal that this time is going to be especially important—a fatal attraction.

The story of Samson and Delilah is a variation of a traditional folktale whose latent meaning discloses male fear of women. There are numerous parallels in world literature. Gunkel cites two Egyptian examples, among others: the tale of the man whose heart is hidden in a tree and who dies when his wife reveals his secret and the tree is cut down; and the myth of Re, who is tricked by Isis into revealing the secret of his name, thereby giving her magic power over him.[58] There is a Greek legend about King Nisus of Megara, who had a purple or golden hair on the middle of his head. When the Cretans besieged Megara, his daughter Scylla fell in love with the enemy king and pulled out the hair from her father's head, so that he died.[59] One can imagine the story of Samson and Delilah as an Israelite folktale that

57. So Niditch (1990: 616).
58. Gunkel (1913: 54-55).
59. Gaster (1981: 436-39) cites this and other examples.

circulated independently before its incorporation into the Samson saga.[60] In my opinion, the story of Samson and the Timnite has been modeled on it by the biblical narrator, who wants to emphasize the moral by repeating it. The first time Samson makes the mistake of entrusting his secret to a woman, the consequences are worse for her than for him (*she* pays with her life). The second time is deadly for *Samson*.

The story expresses the male fear of surrendering himself to a woman, of betraying the self to the other. It also recognizes the temptation the other offers, the male's attraction to her. Samson sees women as desirable but chooses to ignore their danger, even with three chances to learn. Delilah does not betray Samson so much as he betrays himself by telling her 'all his heart' (16.18). She does not use subterfuge or deception. By the fourth time she inquires about Samson's strength, it is clear what she will do with this important information, but Samson reveals it to her anyway. And he tells her because he cannot resist her, because, as the text informs us, he loves her. Samson has to prove his love by surrendering something uniquely his—the answer to his riddle (Judg. 14), the source of his strength (Judg. 16)— something that gives the other power over him. Giving power to the other is always dangerous according to the androcentric ideology of the tale. The text's message to the Israelite male is, 'Don't do it!' (Recall similar advice given to the young man in Proverbs.) Women rob men of their strength. The man who surrenders is emasculated; he loses his potency. At another level, this is the male fear of losing the penis to the woman, an anxiety that finds representation in Samson's symbolic castration that takes place when his hair is cut and he is blinded.

At its psychosexual level, the text's message is about the danger of becoming one with the other. Losing the distinction between self and other in sex is both exhilarating and

---

60. Gunkel (1913: 55) found this 'die eigentliche Simson-Sage'. As he points out, it contains a number of connected motifs that appear individually in other parts of the saga.

threatening. As Samson illustrates, surrendering the self to the other in love is both attractive and dangerous. Too dangerous, according to our story, since it threatens a man's distinctness as male and thus his superior status (women are supposed to surrender to men, not the other way around). Surrendering, making himself vulnerable, is to make himself like the female. This is what happens to Samson. After he makes himself vulnerable by disclosing his secret, he becomes symbolically a woman.

## Identification with the Other

We have already noted the sexual symbolism of the hair and the connection between shaving the hair and the loss of strength and sexual potency. We can now see the significance of the sexual vocabulary applied to Samson: 'entice', 'humble/rape', 'play/serve as amusement', 'grind'. Blinded and shaven, Samson is put to work at the mill, doing the work of women, slaves, or animals. Such punishment of prisoners of war in the ancient Near East had as its object not only to exploit, but also to humiliate them. 'Could a warrior be more ridiculed', asks K. van der Toorn, 'than by making him do the work traditionally assigned to slaves and women?'[61] Having symbolically become woman,[62] Samson must now destroy the other or remain in this emasculated state. Bal, in a brilliant interpretation of the scene in which Samson pulls down the Philistine temple, observes that Samson 'has found a better solution to the birth trauma than anybody else. He takes revenge, breaking the thighs and killing the impure Philistines with it. He outdoes woman, making the gap acceptably large. Not only does he kill the woman and with her, her people; he makes her superfluous, too.'[63] In this act of violence against women, it is interesting to note how Samson topples the pillars. The text says he grasped them and leaned upon them, one with his right

---

61. Van der Toorn (1986: 249).
62. Niditch (1990: 616-17).
63. Bal (1987: 62).

hand and one with his left. Burney points out that 'if he pushed the pillars apart, he would hardly have *grasped* them'.[64] Samson's act of destruction is thus an act that requires holding on. This dual aspect reflects the male view of women as object of both aggression and desire. Might grasping the pillars, in effect pulling them together rather than pushing them apart, represent a refusal of sex—Samson's solution to being taken in by women? The impossibility of refusal as a solution is witnessed by the fact that with it comes death (this is the commonplace that sex is necessary for life to continue).

After he has symbolically destroyed woman, Samson is reincorporated into the male domain of Israelite society, symbolized by the retrieval of his body from the wreckage of the female by 'his brothers and all his father's house' and by his burial in the tomb of Manoah his father (16.31). The ending has a moral: this male setting is where he should have stayed instead of going off to live with women. If the ending is unsatisfying (after all, the hero dies), it is because there is no satisfactory solution to the problem of the other within patriarchal binary thought. The other is both necessary to define the self—to be held onto—and threatening to the self's identity—to be destroyed.

Whereas Samson is temporarily identified with the other, the Philistines are permanently identified with otherness. They are on the negative side of the binary oppositions the text maintains, and they appear more negatively in the story because women are their representatives in their most important dealings with Samson. Women do their dirty work for them, and, in the process, get labeled treacherous and deceptive. The ideology works through circularity; treachery and deception then become identified as *women's* ways of behaving.[65] The (female-identified) Philistines cannot overcome Samson so long as they fight him in the male

64. Burney (1970: 390).
65. On women and deception, see the essays in Exum and Bos (1988).

way, in physical combat; they have to become the other, to resort to the female way.

## The Other Controlled

In popular notions of the tale, women are the cause of Samson's downfall. In the actual story, however, neither the Timnite nor Delilah acts on her own initiative to harm Samson. Their motivation for disclosing his secrets is supplied by others. The Philistine guests at Samson's wedding threaten his bride in order to get her to find out the answer to Samson's riddle: if she does not tell it to them they will burn her and her father's house with fire (14.15). The Philistine lords bribe Delilah, offering her eleven hundred pieces of silver from each of them in return for discovering (uncovering) the source of Samson's great strength and the means to bind him (16.5). Without a woman's help, the Philistines cannot get the better of Samson; this is made clear in the episode with the harlot at Gaza. Only in this case, where a woman is not part of the Philistine plot to trap him, does Samson escape their trap without incurring any losses. There is a paradox here: without women the Philistines are impotent, but for all their power over Samson, the Timnite and Delilah are the pawns of men.

Women, according to the text's gender ideology, are powerful and dangerous. Samson can fight off Philistines by the thousand (15.14-16), but the strong man is powerless against a woman's charms. Now interestingly, the text does not say that the women used sexual favors to get the answers out of Samson. In both cases 'he told her' (14.17; 16.17) 'because she harassed him' (14.17; 16.16). The Timnite uses tears; Delilah presses Samson 'with her words' (16.16). How do convention and stereotyping come into play here to produce a negative picture of women? When commentators suggest that the women used sexual wiles to obtain the answers, are they simply reading in accordance with the ideology of the text, picking up on the latent message about the danger of women's sexuality? Or do they create this association from their own biases, which they project onto the text?[66] Fear of women's power engenders the need to render women powerless. How is this done? In showing us how, the story in which women betray Samson's secrets betrays its own patriarchal agenda. It exposes patriarchy's reliance on two highly effective strategies to assert its control over women: You can threaten them, and they'll give in. You can bribe them, and they'll give in.

The androcentric agenda of the story requires some complicated textual maneuvers to mask its intentions. Women are portrayed as powerful and dangerous and yet subject to control by men. Through literary legerdemain, the biblical narrator manages to attach the blame for Samson's downfall to the women, who are themselves actually victims of exploitation. When it comes to the concept of betrayal, commentators have frequently outdone the text in blaming the women. They are sometimes willing to consider extenuating circumstances in the Timnite's case, because she acts to avert a threat to herself and her father's house. Also, the consequences of her betrayal are not so grave for Samson: he does not fall into Philistine hands, whereas she does. Unlike Delilah's betrayal, which leads to Samson's death, the Timnite's betrayal of Samson brings about her own death: the Philistines burn her and her father after all (so she gets what she deserves).[67] Men, and in fact his fellow Israelites, also betray Samson. Though the Judahites, like Delilah, bind Samson and give him over to the Philistines, they are not generally said to 'betray' him, for they not only tell Samson what they are going to do, they also promise not to harm him themselves. The brunt of the blame is reserved for Delilah—which is really not fair since Samson is complicit.[68]

---

66. On this point, see Bal's reading (1987: 37-67).
67. The Philistines threaten the woman and her father's *house* with destruction in Judg. 14.15, but, according to the MT of 15.6, not the father's *house* but only the woman and her father are burned.
68. Bal's psychoanalytical reading (1987: 37-67) shows this quite clearly.

Like the Judahites, Delilah makes no secret of her intentions to bind Samson; three times she binds him in the manner he has described as able to render him 'like other men', and there is no question she will do so again. Once they have used the women to gain mastery over Samson, the Philistines do not need them any more. They kill the Timnite. And they credit their god, and not Delilah, for their victory over their enemy (16.23, 24). Having served her purpose for males, Delilah is written out of the story (she is not even present among the spectators at Samson's final performance). The only motivation the text suggests for her is greed: other possible motives for aiding the Philistines—patriotism, for example—are suppressed.[69] She is not allowed to become the Philistine equivalent of Jael, for unlike Deborah's victory song (Judg. 5), which praises human agents along with Yhwh, the Philistine victory songs (Judg. 16.23, 24) give Dagon all the credit for giving Samson into their hands. And in the Greek text, Delilah even loses her role as subject of all four attempts to subdue Samson; the Greek supplies a barber and has him, not Delilah, cut Samson's hair.[70]

Women are frequently the locus of the competition between male rivals, and all too often they become the victims of male rivalry. The man who controls the woman's power can gain control over other men. The Philistines exploit women's power, and with it reduce Samson figuratively to the position of a woman under their control. He grinds for them and serves as their amusement. In the end, of course, Samson destroys Philistines, but this requires a *deus ex machina*. Samson is rescued from his emasculated

---

69. See Fuchs (1988) on suppression of motivation as a patriarchal literary strategy for portraying women as deceptive.

70. LXX[A] and the Vulgate have a barber shave Samson. The Hebrew is third-person feminine singular, indicating that Delilah does the shaving, just as she is the agent in the other accounts of binding (16.8, 12) and weaving (vv. 13-14). A problem, however, is created by the phrase *wattiqra' la'ish* in v. 19. Sasson (1988) convincingly argues that the man is Samson and that Delilah calls to him to make sure he is soundly asleep.

state by his god, who, as Judg. 14.4 intimates, may have been controlling everything that has happened.[71] Male superiority is reasserted when Samson, empowered by a god who is *de facto* male-identified, symbolically destroys woman.

## The Androcentric Agenda

At its most obvious, the text teaches the Israelite male a lesson about the dangers of foreign women (cf. Proverbs). Nationalism reinforces the gender ideology of the text. Philistines are by definition bad. The reader identifying with the ideology of the text is predisposed to think the worst of women who are allied with them. As we have seen, the women do not have to be specifically identified as foreign women. They have only to behave like foreign women to be foreign women and therefore dangerous, capable of robbing a man of his vitality. The text complicates the nature of the male–female relationship by casting it in terms of Israel's relation to foreigners. The only good woman is an Israelite woman, and the only Israelite woman in the story appears in her role as mother. Beneath the apparent, surface distinction between Israelite and foreigner lies the gender issue of nonsexual (and thereby non-threatening) woman versus sexual (and threatening) woman.

Women's sexuality must be controlled. In order to reduce its threat, women's behavior must be regulated. Both the Timnite and Delilah are manipulated by the Philistines; their power over Samson ultimately is appropriated by an androcentric agenda to serve male interests. Samson's miraculous birth to a sterile woman shows that the deity, not woman, controls fertility. In teaching its lesson about the danger of women, the text illustrates the strategies that patriarchy has historically relied upon to control women. One is reliance on female fear of male aggression; in other words, by threat, as

---

71. We might say that women's power is appropriated by the Philistine men, whose power, in turn, is controlled by Yhwh who is the guarantor of the patriarchal status quo.

in the case of the Timnite. The threat of physical harm has traditionally been an effective means by which men control women. But it is not always the most desirable. Often a better way to regulate female behavior is by reward, as Delilah's example indicates. Women 'sell out' all the time in patriarchy. To gain an advantage for themselves they cooperate with the oppressor. A third way patriarchy controls women is by dividing women into respectable women and disreputable women, and thus, as we saw in Chapter 1, making gender solidarity impossible. (What might have happened if Samson had brought his wife from Timnah to his parents' house and she had met his mother?) We can now see why Samson is not endangered by the harlot as he is by his wife and by Delilah. The harlot is no threat to the patriarchal system; she already appears in an inferior, subordinate, and carefully regulated role in society. The women to whom men are inclined to make a commitment are the ones they must beware of; Samson gave in because he loved.

Women are not to be trusted; this, in turn, justifies patriarchy's control of them. Women, as the account of the Timnite shows, are easily intimidated and manipulated, and, as Delilah shows, morally deficient. Even Manoah's wife, who is portrayed more favorably than her husband, is shown not to be trustworthy. She, after all, does not tell Manoah the whole message concerning Samson's future. Nor does Manoah really trust her, since he is not content with her account of the visitation but prays that the messenger come 'to us'. Even though Manoah never gets as much information as the woman about his son's future, he does get confirmation of the woman's story from the (male) messenger.

In the series of binary oppositions listed above, one of the story's central oppositions was omitted. It is the one the narrator wants to have reversed. The Samson saga deals with the struggle of the oppressed against their oppressors.[72]

---

72. On the stories about Samson as resistance stories told by the underdog Israelites to poke fun at the superior Philistines, see Wharton (1973) and Niditch (1990).

These are 'resistance stories' told by the underdog Israelites unable to get the better of the militarily superior Philistines—stories in which their hero single-handedly triumphs over their enemies. We may consider, then, another set of oppositions:

oppressors / oppressed
strong / weak
Philistine / Israelite

Keeping in mind the basic male/female hierarchy, we can view the categories on the left as male-identified and those on the right as female-identified except in the case of the Philistine/Israelite opposition. It is this Philistine/Israelite opposition—the oppression of Israel by the Philistines—that the text wishes to see reversed. The powerful Philistine oppressors are represented by women; the weaker, oppressed Israelites are represented by Samson. As we have seen, the Philistines are strongly female-identified. Samson, who also becomes female-identified when his hair is cut and he is blinded and made to grind at the mill, reclaims his male-identified status when he pulls down the Philistine temple. Samson provides a model for Israel. Just as Samson moves from his humbled (female) position to reclaim his 'rightful' superior status, so too Israel will eventually, under David, make the transition from the weak and oppressed nation to the powerful oppressor of its enemies, beginning with the Philistines.

Whereas our story expresses the desire that Israel's situation of oppression be reversed, the oppression of women is taken for granted. Women's subordination to men is, after all, considered to be the natural state of things. For our text, it is not binary thinking, with its inevitable reinforcing of a hierarchy in which one side of the opposition is always privileged, that is problematic, but only the relative positions of Israelite and Philistine that are in need of reversal. But the recognition in the story that something is wrong with the structure of power relations opens the possibility that other relations may be imbalanced. In order to deny that this is the case with the position of women and to justify patriarchy, the text relies on a variety of means to portray women as deserving their inferior status. That Samson loses his life in the process of establishing his superior position over the other betrays an implicit awareness of how costly the struggle to maintain supremacy is, and perhaps even of its ultimate futility.

If the text teaches men a lesson about the dangers of women and justifies patriarchy's control of women's sexuality, its lesson to women depends upon women's accepting its distinction between respectable and disreputable women. The story encourages women to become lawful and loyal mothers. This is the only role in which they can achieve status. As Esther Fuchs observes, this message constitutes a powerful ideological strategy:

> By projecting onto woman what man desires most, the biblical narrative creates a powerful role model for women. The image of the childless woman (barren wife or widow) who evolves from vulnerability and emptiness to security and pride by giving birth to sons offers a lesson for all women. It should be ascribed to the imaginative and artistic ingenuity of the biblical narrator that one of the most vital patriarchal concerns is repeatedly presented not as an imposition on woman but as something she herself desires more than anything else.[73]

We have seen that the text idealizes Samson's mother and relies on convention to encourage its readers to supply the maternal desire. As in the portrayals of the three foreign women, suppressing details prevents the woman from becoming a full personality. The only alternatives this text offers to the image of mother is that of the disreputable woman, and it relies on nationalism to bolster its gender ideology.[74] Given these choices, what Israelite woman

73. Fuchs (1985a: 130).

74. Interestingly, in Proverbs the negative female figure is identified as the 'foreign woman' and the 'strange woman'. The combination of terms suggests that behavior is what is really at stake in defining the 'bad' woman, and not simply, or even necessarily, nationality. Indeed, the same kind of ideology is at work here as in the Samson saga, where whatever is outside the androcentric symbolic order is

would opt to behave like 'one of those *foreign* women'?

described as dangerous, other, strange, and foreign.

# Chapter 4

## THE (M)OTHER'S PLACE

> There has been a basic contradiction throughout patriarchy: between the laws and sanctions designed to keep women essentially powerless, and the attribution to mothers of almost superhuman power (of control, of influence, of life-support).
>
> Adrienne Rich

> If, in speaking of a *woman*, it is impossible to say what she *is*— for to do so would risk abolishing her difference—might matters not stand differently with respect to the *mother*, motherhood being the sole function of the 'other sex' to which we may confidently attribute existence?
>
> Julia Kristeva

The stories of Genesis are stories of the fathers, patriarchal stories. The first of the patriarchs, Abraham, is introduced in Genesis 11 and becomes in Genesis 12 the personification of Israel and bearer of the promise.[1] To Abraham God promises land (the land of Canaan), numerous descendants (as numerous as the stars of heaven and the sand on the seashore, Gen. 15.5; 22.17), and a blessing that Abraham can confer upon others ('I will bless those who bless you, and those who slight you I will curse', Gen. 12.3). And from

1. In this chapter and the next, I use the names 'Abraham' and 'Sarah' throughout. The biblical text uses 'Abram' and 'Sarai' until ch. 17, where God changes their names to 'Abraham' and 'Sarah'. I deliberately alternate between the singular and plural forms, 'the biblical narrator/s', to indicate recognition of multiple traditions behind the narrative voice of the final form of the text. Since my interest in this analysis is the final form of the text, I do not distinguish documentary sources in this material, an enterprise I consider questionable in any event.

father to son this threefold promise is passed on: God repeats it to Isaac (Gen. 26.3-5) and to Jacob (Gen. 28.13-14; 35.11-12).[2] One of the major themes of the Pentateuch, the 'promises to the fathers' is the axis about which the stories in Genesis 12–35 revolve.[3] In the stories about Abraham, for example, numerous obstacles threaten the fulfillment of the promise: the apparent sterility (Gen. 11.30; 16.1) or potential loss (chs. 12; 20) of Abraham's wife Sarah; the fact that Abraham and Sarah are too old to have children (17.17; 18.12); and the divine command to Abraham to sacrifice his son, 'your son, your only son Isaac, whom you love' (22.2).

In the stories of Jacob, too, the theme of the promised blessing continues to figure prominently.[4] Having stolen the patriarchal blessing, Jacob flees his brother's wrath (and the promised land). Any doubts we might have about the efficacy of a *stolen* blessing are immediately resolved when God appears to Jacob in a theophany at Bethel and gives him the threefold promise (28.13-14). While Jacob is in Paddan-aram (chs. 29–32), the blessing is mediated through him to Laban (30.27), and on his return to Canaan, a mysterious stranger, whom Jacob later recognizes as God, wrestles with him on the banks of the Jabbok and blesses him (32.28-29). As the stories of Jacob's adventures draw to a close, God appears to the patriarch once more to reiterate the promise (35.10-12).

These lively stories of the patriarchs' struggles and trials, in which they inevitably come out on top, were, no doubt, savored by the ancient audience, who, as heirs to the promise, knew the outcome in advance. The ancestral stories were recorded in later times to explain who Israel is and

---

2. As my subject is the matriarchs, I treat here only Genesis 12–35, and not the Joseph story of chs. 37–50, where the matriarchs have no role. The blessing is passed on to Jacob's twelve sons, who are the eponymous ancestors of the twelve tribes of Israel (Gen. 49).

3. The 'promises to the fathers' is the traditional—and, indeed, appropriate—label for what has been identified as one of the major themes of the Pentateuch; see Noth (1972: 54-58); Westermann (1980); Clines (1978: 29-47).

4. For detailed analysis of the role of the blessing in the Jacob cycle, see Fishbane (1979: 40-62).

how it got that way. The issue of their historical reliability, a much debated question in some areas of biblical scholarship, has little relevance for our inquiry into the portrayal of the matriarchs.[5] What *is* relevant for our investigation is the fact that later generations selected these particular events to write about and that they interpreted them to justify their position in the world and to account for what they viewed as their uniqueness among the nations. In the previous Chapter, considerable attention was given to the status of woman as man's other. If the fathers are the significant figures in the patriarchal world of Genesis, and as personifications of Israel represent Israel's 'self', what, we may ask, is the place of the 'other', the mother's place? What role do the biblical writers assign to the matriarchs in the stories of Israel's origins? And, since Genesis is the product of a patriarchal world view, in what ways do these stories of Israel's mothers serve male interests?

Where women do not appear in the narrative is as important as where they do appear. The matriarchs' 'stories' (in the sense I spoke of women's stories in Chapter 1) provide a striking example of the incomplete and fragmented nature of biblical women's stories. They are no more than parts of the larger and more coherent stories of their husbands and sons.[6] The matriarchs' secondary status as characters (not to mention their secondary social status) can be seen from the following synopsis of Genesis 11–35, where references to the matriarchs are indicated in boldface (with occasional comments about places where we might have expected them to be mentioned). Events in the patriarchs' lives are summarized briefly; the biblical text, of course, gives the patriarchs

5. On the vexed question of the historicity of the patriarchal narratives, see the discussions of Van Seters (1975) and T.L. Thompson (1974).

6. It should be noted that Isaac's story is also fragmentary. He is overshadowed by his father and by his son. To state the obvious: secondary characters are secondary precisely because there are no well-developed stories about them. The important question is: why are all the female characters secondary characters? See Fuchs (1988: 77). As Fuchs (1985a: 136) notes, 'The biblical mother-figures attain neither the human nor the literary complexity of their male counterparts'.

much greater attention. The fact that occasionally the matriarchs are given the spotlight and are allowed to emerge as well-defined characters whose actions shape the plot does not mean that the Genesis writers are suddenly interested in them in their own right. Rather the matriarchs step forward in the service of an androcentric agenda, and once they have served their purpose, they disappear until such time, if any, they might again prove useful.

*Genesis 11.* Abram's genealogy is given. **Sarai is introduced as his wife and we are told she is sterile.** Terah, Abram's father, takes Abram, Lot, and **Sarai** from Ur to Haran.

*Genesis 12.* In response to God's call and promise to make of him a great nation, Abram journeys to Canaan. **Sarai is 'taken'** along with Lot and the rest of Abram's household and possessions. Abram travels through the land of Canaan, obviously with his retinue, though **Sarah and the others are not mentioned.** A famine drives him into Egypt, **where he passes Sarai off as his sister. Sarai is taken by the pharaoh as his wife, and consequently Abram prospers from the pharaoh's generosity. When he learns Sarai is Abraham's wife, the pharaoh returns her.**

*Genesis 13.* Abram **'and his wife'**, Lot, and 'all that he had' return to Canaan. Abram and Lot have too many flocks and herds and tents to remain together in one place; their herdsmen quarrel. Abram and Lot separate, with Lot taking the region around Sodom in the Jordan valley and Abraham dwelling in Canaan. Yhwh renews the promise to Abram.

*Genesis 14.* Abram defeats a coalition of kings and rescues Lot, who had been taken captive by them. **Sarai is not mentioned.**

*Genesis 15.* Abram complains of his childlessness, and God renews the promise, assuring him, 'Your own son shall be your heir'. God makes a covenant with Abram, promising the land of Canaan to his descendants. God foretells a time of oppression, and then release, for Abram's descendants, and promises Abram that he will die in peace at a ripe old age. **Nothing is said about Sarai.**

*Genesis 16.* **Sarai speaks for the first time. She gives her maid**

**Hagar to Abram as a wife in order to have a child by her. In
response to Hagar's arrogance after she becomes pregnant,
Sarai treats Hagar harshly.** Hagar flees, but God appears to her
(one of the few theophanies to a woman) and tells her to **return
to her mistress and submit to her.** Hagar gives birth; Abraham
now has a son, whom he names Ishmael.

*Genesis 17.* God appears to Abram and again renews the
promise: 'I will make nations of you and kings shall come forth
from you'. God changes Abram's name to Abraham and **Sarai's
to Sarah. Only now do we learn that Abraham's heir will be
his son by Sarah. God promises Abraham that he will bless
Sarah and 'give you a son by her'; 'kings of peoples shall
come from her'.** Abraham laughs at the idea of having a child,
given his and **Sarah's advanced age,** and pleads for Ishmael ('O
that Ishmael might live in your sight!'). God promises to make a
nation of Ishmael but tells Abraham that he will establish his
covenant with Isaac (**'whom Sarah shall bear *to you* at this
season next year'**) and Isaac's descendants. God makes circumcision the sign of this covenant. All the men of Abraham's
household are circumcised that day.

*Genesis 18.* Yhwh/three men appear(s) to Abraham outside his
tent, and Abraham offers them hospitality. **Abraham tells
Sarah to prepare a meal; he serves them outside while Sarah
remains in the tent. The men tell Abraham that Sarah will
have a son. Sarah, who is listening at the tent door, laughs.
When Yhwh asks *Abraham* why Sarah laughed, she denies
having laughed.** The men set out to destroy Sodom and
Gomorrah; Abraham intercedes on behalf of these cities, bar-
gaining with God for the sake of fifty righteous, then forty-five,
then forty, then thirty, then twenty, then ten.

*Genesis 19.* The two divine emissaries destroy Sodom and
Gomorrah, saving Lot's family. Lot's wife is turned into a pillar
or salt. Lot's daughters get their father drunk, become pregnant
by him and give birth to Moab and Ben-ammi, the eponymous
ancestors of the Moabites and the Ammonites.

*Genesis* 20. Abraham journeys to Gerar **where he again passes
his wife off as his sister. Sarah is taken into Abimelech's
harem and returned, untouched, when Abimelech learns she
is Abraham's wife. Abraham prospers on her account.**

*Genesis 21.* **Sarah gives birth to a son** and Abraham names him Isaac. **Sarah expresses amazement that she has borne Abraham a son in his old age.** After Isaac is weaned, Sarah has Hagar and her son Ishmael cast out so that Isaac will not have to share his inheritance with Ishmael. God saves Hagar in the wilderness and promises her that Ishmael will be the father of a great nation. Abraham and Abimelech quarrel over water rights and make a covenant.

*Genesis 22.* God tests Abraham, telling him to go to the land of Moriah and sacrifice his son Isaac as a burnt offering. Abraham obeys, but as he prepares to kill Isaac, a messenger of Yhwh calls to him from heaven and stops him. Abraham sacrifices a ram instead of his son. Because of Abraham's obedience, Yhwh renews the promise. **Sarah's absence is noteworthy.** The chapter concludes with a brief genealogy that introduces **Rebekah as the daughter of Bethuel,** the son of Nahor, Abraham's brother.

*Genesis 23.* **Sarah's death at 127 years is reported. Abraham mourns her death.** From Ephron the Hittite, Abraham purchases the field and the cave of Machpelah; **there he buries Sarah.**

*Genesis 24.* Abraham sends his servant to Mesopotamia to find a wife for Isaac among Abraham's kin. The servant prays for a sign: the woman who responds to his request for water both by giving him water and by offering to water his camels will be the woman Yhwh has chosen for Isaac. **While the servant is still praying, Rebekah appears at the well with her water jar, gives him water, and then waters the camels.** The servant explains his mission to Rebekah's brother Laban and her father Bethuel, and they agree to the marriage. **Rebekah is consulted and agrees to leave for Canaan immediately.** 'So Isaac was comforted after his mother's death.'

*Genesis 25.* Abraham takes another wife, Keturah, who bears him six children. To the sons of his wives (plural)[7] of secondary rank, Abraham gives gifts, but he sends them away, leaving everything he has to Isaac. Abraham dies and is buried by his sons Isaac and Ishmael in the cave of Machpelah **with Sarah his**

7.  Perhaps this refers to Hagar and Keturah; otherwise we know nothing of these wives; cf. Speiser (1964: 187).

**wife.** Ishmael's descendants are listed, and attention turns to Isaac. **Rebekah is sterile, Isaac prays for her, and Yhwh grants the prayer.** Rebekah conceives twins, who struggle within her; she inquires of Yhwh and is told that two nations shall be born of her and the elder will serve the younger. The twins are born, with Jacob grasping his brother's heel. When they grow up, Isaac prefers Esau 'but Rebekah loved Jacob'. Esau is tricked by Jacob into selling him his birthright in exchange for lentil soup.[8]

*Genesis 26.* Isaac goes to Gerar in time of famine (obviously he takes his family but none of them is mentioned). Yhwh appears to him and gives him the threefold promise that he had sworn to Abraham. In Gerar Isaac passes his wife off as his sister. Abimelech sees Isaac engaged in some form of sexual play with Rebekah and upbraids him for his deception. Isaac becomes very wealthy, and Abimelech sends him away. Isaac and the Philistines engage in a series of disputes over wells. Yhwh appears to Isaac and renews the promise. Isaac and Abimelech make a covenant. Esau takes Hittite wives, 'and they made life bitter for Isaac and Rebekah'.

*Genesis 27.* Rebekah orchestrates Jacob's deception of his father and theft of the blessing. When she learns of Esau's plan to kill Jacob, she gets Isaac to send him to Paddan-aram to take one of her brother's daughters as a wife.

*Genesis 28.* Isaac sends Jacob away with the blessing of Abraham. Esau takes another wife, this time an Ishmaelite. On the way to Haran, Jacob has a dream in which God appears to him and gives him the threefold promise. Jacob vows Yhwh will be his god if he protects him and brings him back to the land of Canaan in peace.

*Genesis 29.* Jacob arrives in Haran, where he meets Rachel by the well when she comes to water her father's sheep. Jacob loves Rachel and serves his uncle Laban seven years for her, but Laban deceives Jacob and brings Leah to him on the wedding night. A week later, Jacob gets Rachel as his wife in return for serving Laban another seven years. Yhwh, seeing

8. Von Rad (1961: 261); Westermann (1985: 418). Daube (1969: 194-97) suggests that Esau thought he was getting blood soup, considered to have special powers for reviving a tired body.

that Rachel is preferred over Leah, makes Leah fertile and she bears Jacob four sons (Reuben, Simeon, Levi, and Judah).

*Genesis 30.* **Rachel, who is sterile, gives her maid Bilhah to Jacob in order to have a child through her, and Bilhah bears Dan and Naphtali. Leah gives her maid Zilpah to Jacob and she bears Gad and Asher. Leah bears two more sons, Issachar and Zebulun, and a daughter, Dinah. Finally Rachel gives birth to Joseph.** Jacob wishes to return to Canaan and agrees with Laban that the speckled and spotted sheep and black lambs in Laban's flock will be his wages. Laban tries to cheat Jacob by hiding these animals, but Jacob uses a trick of his own to make the flocks breed striped, speckled, and spotted offspring, thereby increasing his flocks.

*Genesis 31.* In response to the jealousy of Laban's sons and to a command from Yhwh to return 'to the land of your fathers', Jacob decides to return to Canaan. **He consults with Rachel and Leah, and they agree to his plan, accusing their father of selling them and using up their dowry, and claiming the property Jacob got from Laban as theirs and their children's.** Jacob, his sons, and **his wives** depart secretly and **Rachel steals her father's household gods.** Laban pursues, but God tells him in a dream not to harm Jacob. Laban overtakes Jacob and accuses him of stealing his gods; he searches the tents but does not find them **because Rachel sits on them and says she cannot rise because 'the way of women is upon me'.** Laban and Jacob make a covenant, in which **Jacob agrees not to ill-treat Laban's daughters or take other wives (Jacob's wives of secondary rank, Bilhah and Zilpah, are not mentioned).**

*Genesis 32.* Jacob sends messengers to Esau and learns that Esau is coming to meet him. Jacob prays to Yhwh for deliverance. Hoping to appease Esau, he sends a generous present ahead of him. Jacob sends all he has, including **his two wives and his two maids,** across the Jabbok and remains alone, where he wrestles all night with a man, who blesses him and changes his name to Israel. Jacob identifies the mysterious stranger as God.

*Genesis 33.* In preparation for his meeting with Esau, which he fears, Jacob divides his household into four camps, **putting the maids and their children in front, followed by Leah and her children, and then Rachel and Joseph.** The brothers are reconciled; Jacob agrees to follow Esau to Seir, but instead settles in

Shechem.

*Genesis 34.* Dinah, **'the daughter of Leah'**, is raped by Shechem when she goes out to visit the women of the land. The She-chemites make a treaty with Jacob, but two of Jacob's sons avenge the rape by killing the men of Shechem and plundering the city.

*Genesis 35.* God tells Jacob to go to Bethel and build an altar there. Jacob and his household put away their foreign gods. God appears to Jacob again, changes his name to Israel, and repeats the promise of land and descendants. **Rachel dies in childbirth. She names the child Ben-oni ('son of my sorrow') but Jacob changes the name to Benjamin ('son of the right hand'). Reuben has sexual relations with Bilhah, and Jacob learns of it (but *we* hear nothing more of it).** The chapter ends with a list of Jacob's twelve sons and an account of Isaac's death.

## The Absent Matriarch

Although the matriarchs are not actually absent from the narrative, they regularly drop out of view at critical points in the family's history.[9] When the threefold promise of land, descendants, and Israel as a sign or mediator of blessing is addressed to the patriarchs, Abraham, Isaac, and Jacob, there are no matriarchs in sight. When Abraham is called by God and Israel's unique relationship to God is thereby established (Gen. 12), Sarah is invisible. Abraham follows the divine call to the promised land and Sarah is simply 'taken' with him (12.5). When Abraham undergoes his criti-cal test of faith and is willing to sacrifice Isaac at God's command (Gen. 22), Sarah is not mentioned.[10] It is *his* test just as it was *his* call in Gen. 12.1-3, and everything depends

9. To be sure, the text acknowledges the presence of women: Abraham 'took' Sarah to Canaan (12.5); Jacob returns to Canaan with his wives (31.17). Elsewhere, however, the patriarch, as the key figure in the narrative, stands for his entire company; e.g. 12.6, 8, 9, 10, where only Abraham is mentioned as traveling through Canaan to Egypt, and 26.1, where Isaac 'went to Gerar'.

10. For a compelling discussion of the Akedah, focusing on the stakes for God as well as Abraham, see Landy (1989).

upon his trust in the divine promises, not hers. And when, in Genesis 32, Jacob becomes 'Israel' as a result of his wrestling match with God, the matriarchs are actually and symbolically nowhere to be seen. They are on the other side of the Jabbok, a convenient distance from the patriarch's solitary struggle:

> The same night he arose and took his two wives, his two maid-servants, and his eleven children, and crossed the ford of the Jabbok. He took them and sent them across the stream, and likewise everything that he had. And Jacob was left alone... (Gen. 32.23-25).

In all these events not just the family's future, but that of the nation Israel, hangs in the balance. The matriarchs' absence at these crucial junctures reflects the fact that Israel is personified in its fathers, not its mothers.

The matriarchs are absent not only from these pivotal scenes but also from many other segments of the narrative. Equally revealing of the narrators' lack of interest in the matriarchs is the absence of their point of view even when they are present. How does Sarah react to Abraham's telling foreigners she is his sister, and to being taken into a foreigner's harem? What is the suspense like for Rebekah while Jacob executes her plan for stealing the blessing? Does Leah meekly accept being used by her father to deceive Jacob, and have no reservations about the fact that Jacob, who prefers her sister, is tricked into marrying her? And how do Bilhah and Zilpah, whose point of view is never shown, react to being given to Jacob by their mistresses?

There are scenes where the matriarchs are actually given center stage in the Genesis narratives. But despite the attention they receive, their actions are allowed to advance the plot only insofar as they have important consequences for their sons, the future patriarchs: either to ensure that the 'right' son become the bearer of the promise, i.e. become 'Israel' (as Sarah and Rebekah do), or to increase Israel (as Rachel, Leah, and their maids do by bearing Jacob twelve sons—the twelve tribes of Israel). The matriarchs appear in the narrative as the wives, or suitable wives-to-be (as in Gen. 24; 29.4-20), who will bear the sons of the promise to the fathers, but never as characters in their own right. The repeated story in Genesis 12, 20, and 26, in which the patriarch passes his wife off as his sister, is no exception, for although the matriarchs provide the occasion for the story, the protagonists are men. And the story reflects the narrator's interest in the matriarchs' role as mothers, for if the patriarch loses his wife to a foreign ruler, how can he have descendants? Moreover, by posing a threat to the exclusive rights to a woman by her husband, these accounts reveal their concern with the issue of the proper lineage of the chosen people. And that issue, as we shall see, lies at the heart of the patriarchal narratives. Even a story that on the surface might seem to acknowledge a greater role for the matriarchs, one less directly focused on offspring—Jacob's consultation with Rachel and Leah about leaving Paddan-aram (Gen. 31.4-16)—serves a patriarchal agenda connected to the theme of proper lineage, which we shall explore below.

It is, of course, understandable that Genesis portrays the matriarchs' lives as revolving around their sons, for it was through bearing children that women achieved status and gained some security for themselves in the patriarchal society of ancient Israel.[11] Having sons who will bear the promise is, of course, crucial for the patriarchs too. The promise of numerous descendants is made to them no less than eight times (Gen. 13.16; 15.5; 17.2-21; 22.17; 26.3-4, 24; 28.13-14; 35.11; see also 46.3).[12] In contrast, there is no birth announcement to any of the matriarchs in Genesis.[13] The

11. See Bird (1974: 51-55, 61-71).

12. There are actually more references than these to the promise of descendants, depending on what references one counts; see the helpful chart in Clines (1978: 32-33).

13. In contrast to the matriarchs, the non-Israelite mother, Hagar, is the recipient of a birth announcement, Gen. 16.10-12. In the absence of a male figure (Abraham's lineage is to be reckoned elsewhere), she takes on a role comparable to Abraham's; but note that the promise to her in Gen. 21 incorporates the woman into a promise for the son's descendants. Both Hagar and Sarah suffer losses; cf. Exum (1985: 77): 'One is cast out, becoming the mother of a great nation excluded from the covenant; the other stays within the patriarchal hearth and almost

crucial birth announcement for which we are forced to wait so long in narrative time, and the protagonists, in chronological time—that Sarah will bear a son—is made to Abraham alone on two different occasions (17.15-16; 18.10). The second time the announcement is made, Sarah *overhears* it.[14] Peter Miscall observes that Sarah's surprised response in Genesis 18 indicates that Abraham had not informed her of the birth announcement the first time it is made.[15] In other words, the narrator has no interest in including her at all the first time and includes her only indirectly the second time.

The matriarchs are never more absent from the narrative—even when they are mentioned by name—than at the moment of their deaths. By contrast, the patriarchs' deaths are grand occasions, fitting conclusions to their important lives. Abraham dies 'at a ripe old age, an old man and full of years', and is buried by his sons, Isaac and Ishmael, who are united in family solidarity for the first time since Ishmael's expulsion from Abraham's household (Gen. 25.8-9). This pattern is repeated for Isaac; he, too, is 'old and full of days' when he dies, and he is buried by his reconciled sons, Jacob and Esau (Gen. 35.29). Jacob dies in Egypt, surrounded by his twelve sons, the family once again united after threatened dissolution, and his sons and their households form a large company to take his body back to Canaan for burial (Gen. 49.33–50.14). The patriarchs die peacefully, surrounded by their sons in a grand show of unity and harmony that somehow belies the deep filial discord that has characterized each generation.

loses her only child to the father'. For a woman as the recipient of a birth announcement, see also Judg. 13, discussed in Chapter 3 above.

14. In Gen. 18, the announcement is made to Abraham alone even though Sarah, and not Abraham, is the subject of it. Unlike Gen. 17.16, where God says, 'I will give you [Abraham] a son *by her*', Gen. 18.10 speaks only of Sarah, 'Sarah your wife shall have a son', without making it a son 'to [*le*] Abraham'.

15. Miscall (1983: 32). In Gen. 18, the narrator uses their new names, Abraham and Sarah, but he does not tell us at what point and under what circumstances Sarah learns about the name change and its meaning (she refers to herself as Sarah in 21.7)—another indication of his lack of interest in the woman's point of view.

It is different with the matriarchs. For Sarah, there is only the briefest of notices, the first we hear of her since she had Hagar and Ishmael sent away, just after Isaac was weaned. The placement of her death notice immediately after the near-sacrifice of Isaac (Gen. 23.1-2) barely hints at a connection—though a later midrash interpreted the juxtaposition to mean that Sarah dropped dead upon hearing what Abraham was prepared to do (Tanhuma, *Par. Vayira* 23). Sarah never sees Isaac again after his father takes him away for the sacrifice—a cruel fate for both mother and son. Isaac is later 'consoled' for the loss of his mother (24.67) when he marries Rebekah, but Sarah is not comforted after her son's brush with death. We are not told that Isaac is present at her death, as he is at Abraham's. We are told that Abraham mourned Sarah. Yet more attention is given to Abraham's negotiations to buy a burial place from the Hittites, which involves a claim to the promised land, than to Sarah's death.

Of Leah's death we hear nothing. All we ever learn is that she was buried in the cave at Machpelah, along with Abraham, Sarah, Isaac, and Rebekah (Gen. 49.31). The narrative neglect of her death is reminiscent of the neglect Leah suffered at the hands of her husband Jacob during her life. The circumstances of Rebekah's death are not recorded either, but, in her case, this appears to be less a case of narrative neglect than of narrative punishment for her role in securing the blessing for Jacob, her favorite son. When she sends Jacob away to her brother Laban in Haran, she expects the separation from her favorite son to be temporary: 'Stay with him a while until your brother's fury turns away ... then I will send and fetch you from there' (27.44-45). But she never sends for him and she never sees him again. When Jacob returns to Canaan and eventually goes 'to his father Isaac at Mamre' (35.27), there is no mention of his mother. Whether she is dead or alive makes no difference.

Rachel, Jacob's beloved wife, dies in childbirth (35.16-20). Are we to regard this as her punishment for stealing her father's household gods (teraphim, Gen. 31.19, 32)? In protesting his innocence of the theft to Laban, Jacob had said, 'Anyone with whom you find your gods shall not live'

(31.32). Upon whom could his pronouncement fall if not on Rachel? Strictly speaking, of course, Rachel's death cannot result from Jacob's declaration because Laban *did not find* his gods.[16] But regardless of whether or not it serves as a kind of punishment, when Rachel's death is reported, it is by no means the central concern of the narrative but merely a marginal note to the birth of Benjamin.[17] Whereas the patriarchs die surrounded by their sons, the matriarchs, whose lives are lived for virtually nothing else but their sons, are not accorded peaceful deaths in their sons' company. Rebekah's and Leah's deaths are not reported (nor are Bilhah's and Zilpah's, their maids). Only Sarah dies in ripe old age, but we do not learn whether she dies with a sense of fulfillment—'full of days' like Abraham—or of loss. And Rachel dies in her prime, her child-bearing years, bemoaning her lot. In contrast to the honor the narrative accords the patriarchs at their deaths, there is no sense of harmonious closure to the matriarchs' lives. For their lives, and thus their deaths, hold little interest for the biblical narrators.

## The Right Wife and the Right Mother

What *is* the importance of the matriarchs for the biblical narrators? To answer this question we need to recognize that, as a major statement of biblical ideology, Genesis offers 'ancestral' justification to two key biblical concepts: Israel's claim to be the chosen people and its claim to the land of Canaan. Abraham (= Israel) is singled out by God as the recipient of the promise that his descendants will inherit the land of Canaan. As this promise will be passed from generation to generation, the crucial question becomes, How is a pure line of descent to be maintained? An obvious answer to this question would appear to be: through endogamous marriage. The marriage of men to women from their own patriline would ensure the offspring's patrilineage membership not simply if descent is figured in the typical biblical

16. Daube (1969: 216-17); Fuchs (1988: 81).
17. Fuchs (1985a: 132).

fashion—through the father—but even if it were figured through the mother.[18] The issue, of course, is no less than the identity of Israel: who belongs to the chosen people and who does not? Ishmael, for example, though he is Abraham's son and a covenant is made with him, is excluded from the line of the promise, for God has decided that Sarah shall be the mother of the chosen people (18.15-19) and that her son will be heir to the promise to Abraham: 'through Isaac your descendants shall be named' (21.12). When it is time for Isaac to marry, Abraham makes his servant swear that he 'will not take a wife for my son from the daughters of the Canaanites among whom I dwell, but will go to my country and to my kindred, and take a wife for my son Isaac' (24.3-4). Similarly Isaac charges his son Jacob, 'You shall not take a wife from the daughters of the Canaanites. Go at once to Paddan-aram to the house of Bethuel your mother's father, and take from there a wife from the daughters of Laban your mother's brother' (28.1-2). These passages make clear that, in the case of Abraham's descendants, the 'right wife' for the patriarch and thus the 'right mother' for his sons cannot be a local woman, a Canaanite, but rather must come from the same family line as the patriarch himself.[19] Thus

---

18. Jay (1992: 98). It might be tempting for us to take the biblical pattern of reckoning descent through fathers for granted, but, as Jay's study shows, patterns of calculating descent have to be established; and establishing the reckoning of descent through fathers is precisely what the Genesis narrators seek to accomplish.

19. Steinberg (1991) argues that the proper wife is a woman from the patrilineage of Terah and thus the proper heir to the promises both belongs to and marries a woman from the patrilineage of Terah. She proposes that Esau, who has both the correct father (Isaac) and the correct mother (Rebekah), is excluded from the Israelite lineage because he married the 'wrong' wives, women from outside the appropriate kinship boundaries (p. 50). It is not entirely clear whether or not Abraham and Sarah's marriage is endogamous. In Genesis 20, Abraham claims Sarah is his half-sister, the daughter of his father but not the daughter of his mother; see the discussion of this issue in Chapter 5 below. It is not essential that the marriage be endogamous since Abraham *begins* the lineage (that is, there is a break between Abraham's line and Terah's); see Eilberg-Schwartz (1990: 167), and the discussion of circumcision below.

Isaac marries Rebekah, the daughter of his father's brother's son,[20] and Jacob marries Leah and Rachel, his mother's brother's daughters.

Anthropological studies have shed considerable light on kinship patterns in the Genesis narratives[21] and contribute to our understanding of the ideological function endogamous marriage serves in this material. That the matriarchs belong to the same patriline as the patriarchs ensures that the patriarchs (= Israel) will not have to share their inheritance of the land of Canaan with the indigenous Canaanites and that their privileged position as the chosen people will not be compromised by intermarriage with 'foreigners'.[22] The situation of patrilineal endogamy in our narrative—that is, the marriage of men to women from their own patriline— enables the biblical narrators to maintain a pure line of descent, tracing descent through fathers while at the same

On the issue of 'correct' marriages, see also Pitt-Rivers (1977: 151-70). Jacob's wives of secondary rank, Bilhah and Zilpah, are not Canaanite, but though they are from Mesopotamia, they do not belong to Jacob's patriline. Although these marriages are not endogamous, Rachel and Leah 'correct' the irregularity in the descent of Dan, Naphtali, Gad, and Asher by accepting the maids' sons as their own (something Sarah did not do for Ishmael). Joseph marries exogamously, but Jacob corrects Joseph's sons' irregular descent by adopting Ephraim and Manasseh (Gen. 48.5); see Jay (1992: 109-10; 1988: 56).

20. So Gen. 24.15, 24, 47; on the basis of Gen. 24.48 and 29.5, one might conclude she is Isaac's father's brother's daughter (i.e. that her father is Nahor). Steinberg (1991: 52) explains the apparent contradiction by suggesting that in Gen. 24.48 and 29.5 the genealogy is traced to the significant ancestor for the text, Nahor, from whom the descent line is traced. Similarly, Wander (1981: 86).

21. See Steinberg (1991); Oden (1983); Andriolo (1973); Donaldson (1981); Prewitt (1981); Wander (1981).

22. As the work of Lévi-Strauss and others who have followed his lead has shown, ideology does not necessarily reflect social reality, and often inverts it; see Lévi-Strauss (1966); Andriolo (1973). The biblical text regards Canaanites as 'other', as 'foreign', though evidence exists that Israel was largely composed of native Canaanites; see Gottwald (1979: esp. 358-75, 464-583). Leach (1966) investigates the contradiction between the promise of the land to Abraham, which, he argues, implies a preference for endogamy, and the fact that the people in the land actually intermarry freely.

time recognizing descent from mothers. But it also, as Nancy Jay points out, 'conceals a conflict: it is unclear about which is the "real" parent through whom unilineal descent flows'.[23] Whose is the child—the mother's or the father's?[24] The text's acknowledgment of the importance of mothers in the line of descent does not mean we are dealing with matrilineal social structure; rather, what is at stake here is an ideological problem. The Genesis narrators are wrestling with a potential complication, an underlying tension that exists because Israel's ancestry is traced not only through its fathers but also through its mothers. Their problem is to demonstrate that it is the male line of descent that determines Israel's identity, while at the same time affirming the importance of descent from the proper mother. That such a contradiction exists is not all that unusual, for irresolvable conflicts and tensions occur in all societies.[25] And that the biblical narrators do not succeed in resolving it is no surprise, since the contradiction is real. Their inability to resolve the contradiction, and their efforts to obscure and evade it, aid us in exposing some of the ways gender politics have shaped Israel's picture of its origins.

The matriarchs' ambivalent status makes them a problem. They are 'other' who are also 'same', outsiders who are part of the family. In discussing the ideological difficulty they pose for a system based on the concept of family as continued through male descendants, Nathaniel Wander observes:

> The advantages of organizing a society along clear lines of descent (in this case, through males) and of reckoning the relations between such descent groups in terms of genealogy tend to be lost when wives are taken from within these groups rather than from 'strangers'. In such circumstances, the lines of descent become obscured as the group of people actually living and working together are all equally related through females as through males. The ideal of unilineality (or descent measured in

23. Jay (1992: 98-99); see also Wander (1981) for a similar argument. Jay, who distinguishes between the pentateuchal sources J, E, and P, makes extremely interesting observations about their differences.
24. Jay (1992: 100).
25. See Douglas (1966: 140-58); Turner (1967: 22-39); as this applies specifically to Genesis, see Wander (1981); Leach (1969: 7-23).

a single line) is falsified and the use of genealogy to order relationships of power, authority, succession, inheritance is called
into question by a contrary reality.[26]

Acknowledging descent through mothers not only makes
mothers extremely important—in itself problematic for
patriarchy—it also competes with the recognition of descent
from fathers; for whereas motherhood is biologically
verifiable, fatherhood must be established. Patriarchy relies
on a number of strategies to affirm the paternal claim to offspring, all of which entail suppression or denial of the
woman's importance. Here I shall consider four of them and
their role in Genesis, reserving a fifth for discussion in
conjunction with the motif of the sterile matriarch below.

1. *Omitting women's names in genealogical lists.* An
extremely effective strategy by which the Genesis narrators
establish the paternal claim to offspring is by omitting wom-
en's names in genealogical lists. Genealogies serve to order
social relations among groups, whether in the domestic or
political spheres, or even in religious matters. In the Bible,
these groups always have males as their eponymous ancestors. A man begets a son, who in turn begets his son, and so
on down the line. A man may, of course, have more than
one child, but because genealogies include only the portion
of the family tree that is of interest to those who preserve
them, descent is usually traced through the son or (as in
Jacob's case) sons considered to be the ancestor of the group
responsible for the genealogy.[27] To read the genealogical
lists in the Bible, one would think the men did not need
wives to reproduce. Women's names do not appear apart
from exceptional cases, for which an explanation is usually
to be found in the surrounding narrative. In Genesis 11, for

---

26. Wander (1981: 81).
27. See Wilson (1977: esp. 183-202). Wilson notes (p. 198) that
whereas the Israelite genealogies may have once functioned in social
or political spheres, they do not have this function in their present literary context. He proposes that only in oral form can genealogy function successfully in these areas because of the need for genealogies to
change in order to reflect changing relations among the people
involved.

example, Sarai appears because her apparent sterility poses a problem for the continuity of Abraham's line. That not only Sarah but all the matriarchs are, in fact, exceptional cases is hardly fortuitous. They cannot be omitted from the genealogies because of the narrative insistence on descent from the proper mother.[28] Rebekah is mentioned at the beginning of Isaac's genealogy (*toledot*, 25.19-20), and she disrupts genealogical stability by effecting the substitution of Jacob for Esau as his father's rightful heir.[29] Not surprisingly, in view of their role as the mothers of the twelve tribes of Israel, the greatest attention of a genealogical nature is given to Rachel, Leah, Bilhah, and Zilpah. They are the subjects of a genealogical narrative (29.31–30.24; 35.16-20) and their names appear in the genealogical lists of Gen. 35.22-26 and Gen. 46.8-27, where they account for the division of Jacob's twelve sons into subgroups of different status.[30] Since Israel obviously has many more maternal ancestors than Sarah, Rebekah, Leah, Rachel, Bilhah, and Zilpah, we can say that, in general, the strategy of suppressing women's names in genealogical lists in Genesis succeeds in confirming the paternal claim to the lineage. That the matriarchs stand out among the few women who make their way into the genealogical lists attests to their ambiguous status and their problematic presence for the narrator. They resist any simple narrative resolution that would confine them entirely to the mother's place, which in the case of the genealogies means being absent, not being remembered.

2. *Insistence on exclusive sexual rights to a woman by her husband.* Establishing the paternal claim to offspring also lies

28. On the narrative structure of Gen. 12–50 as representing movement from equilibrium (represented by genealogy) to disequilibrium (represented by the problems each of the patriarchs has in obtaining the proper heir—all of which involve the matriarchs) back to equilibrium, see Steinberg (1989: 41-50; 1984: 175-88).

29. Cf. Furman (1985: 114): 'Rebekah's deceitful action ultimately disturbs the exclusively male genealogical lineage'.

30. For a discussion of these texts, see Wilson (1977: 184-88); Wilson distinguishes between genealogical list and genealogical narrative (p. 9).

behind patriarchy's insistence on the exclusive sexual rights to the woman by her husband.[31] The possibility that the matriarch might have sexual relations with a man other than the patriarch, which can be regarded as a threat to the purity of the line, is raised three times in Genesis. In all three accounts, the patriarch fears for his life at the hands of foreign men because of his beautiful wife. In order to prevent their killing him in order to have her, he passes her off as his sister. In Genesis 12 and 20, Sarah is taken into the harem of a foreign ruler. Whereas Genesis 12 does not explicitly deny that sexual relations took place between Sarah and the pharaoh, in Genesis 20 we hear that Abimelech did not touch Sarah. That Abraham's exclusive right to Sarah is not violated is important at this particular point in the story, since, immediately after the encounter with Abimelech, Sarah gives birth to Isaac, and the narrative can permit no doubt that Isaac is Abraham's son. In Genesis 26, Rebekah is not taken into Abimelech's harem. Unlike Sarah, she is not, *even potentially*, dispensable to the patriarch, for she has secured her place in the patriarchal household by having already borne Isaac two sons.[32] It is peculiar that the issue of exclusive sexual rights to the matriarch is raised three times in a manner so similar and yet with such curious differences. These accounts are so unusual and unconventional, and traditional interpretations of them so unsatisfying, that I shall return to them in the next chapter and attempt an unconventional interpretation.

3. *Resolving the issue of descent and residence in favor of the husband.* One way the paternal claim to the lineage is reinforced in Genesis is by resolving the issue of descent and residence in favor of the husband. Lineage plays a crucial role in determining the inheritance of property and the

---

31. See the discussions in Lerner (1986: 101-22); Bird (1974: 51-53).

32. See Steinberg (1984: 180; 1988: 8); Clines (1990: 70, 72-77). I am not convinced by Steinberg's and Clines's proposals about the matriarch's dispensability in Gen. 12 and 20; it might make sense in Gen. 12, but it is hard to see how, in Gen. 20, Abraham could consider Sarah dispensable since God has told him in Gen. 17 that Sarah would be the mother of his heir. See the discussion below, Chapter 5.

proper lines of authority as well as for structuring relationships between groups. In establishing the proper identity for
Israel, two important issues are involved, and they are inter-
related—descent and residence.[33] The proper wife and
mother must be related to Abraham (which means she must
come from Haran), but Isaac and Jacob may not marry uxo-
rilocally (which means the 'right wife' must be brought back
to Canaan from Haran). Uxorilocal marriage, in which the
husband lives with the wife's family, is a threat not only
because it would take the rightful heir out of the land
promised to his lineage (loss of residence) but also because
such an arrangement could result in Abraham's lineage
being swallowed up by the woman's family (loss of
descent). Abraham twice instructs his servant not to take
Isaac back to Mesopotamia to find a wife (Gen. 24.6, 8). On
the symbolic level, Canaan, as the residence of the
patriarchs, and Haran, as the home of the matriarchs,
function in the story as metonyms for the father's place and
the mother's place respectively.[34] In Haran, in Rebekah's
'mother's household' (Gen. 24.28), the father's role is

33. Bal stresses the importance of the 'house' as 'the shifter where
residence and descendance meet' (1988a: 85). Leach (1966) examines
the biblical preoccupation with endogamy and land rights.
34. My point has to do with ideology and does not imply that
descent was reckoned matrilineally in ancient Mesopotamia, for which
there is no evidence. Nevertheless, the tension these narratives reflect
regarding marriage and descent patterns is real. Jay's discussion of
these narratives in terms of the conflict between descent through
fathers and descent through mothers illuminates many of the
difficulties the stories present; see also the similar observations of
Wander (1981). The conflict between Jacob and Laban (discussed
below) corresponds to what Bal (1988a: 84-86) identifies as a conflict
between patrilocal and virilocal marriage in the book of Judges.
Primarily for the sake of clarity, but also because in Genesis the
conflict is brought to the fore by the insistence on descent through
mothers, I use the terms 'uxorilocal' (marriage in which the husband
resides with the wife's family) and 'patrilocal' (marriage in which the
couple resides with the husband's family). It is, however, the case in
Genesis that the movement is toward virilocal marriage: Isaac and
Jacob establish their own households rather than living in the households of their fathers; thus I also refer to their situations as patrilineal
virilocal marriage.

minimal—so minimal, in fact, that some scholars argue that he is dead, in spite of the fact that he appears in the narrative in v. 50.[35] Whereas Rebekah's brother and father (not insignificantly, the name of Laban, the brother, is first) agree to let Rebekah become Isaac's wife (v. 50), gifts—apparently representing the bride-price—are given to Rebekah, to her brother, and to her mother. Her brother and her mother request that Rebekah be allowed to remain with them for a brief time before leaving for Canaan, and Rebekah is the one who decides to depart immediately (24.55, 58). The blessing she receives as she departs mother-identified Haran for father-identified Canaan affirms descent through mothers: 'May *your descendants* possess the gate of those who hate them' (v. 60).

The story of how Isaac acquired the correct wife serves to affirm patrilocal marriage over uxorilocal marriage and, by uprooting the woman from her family, privileges the husband's line of descent, or Abraham's side of the family, into whose genealogy the woman will be absorbed. The story of how Jacob acquired his wives serves the same purpose, but here the threat is represented as more serious. Jacob flees Canaan, the father's place, and settles in Haran, the mother's place, with his mother's brother, Laban. He marries his mother's brother's daughters[36] and lives and serves in his maternal uncle's household for twenty years. Laban's position as head of the household is witnessed by the fact that Jacob must ask his permission to return to Canaan with his wives and children: 'Send me away that I may go to my

---

35. E.g. Skinner (1910: 344); Speiser (1964: 184); Vawter (1977: 272); Westermann (1985: 388). Jay (1988: 61-62; 1992: 103-104) finds the social structure described in Genesis 24 consistent with matriliny; however, Abraham's servant speaks of 'the house of my master's brothers/kinsmen' (24.27, 48) and 'the daughter of my master's brother/kinsman' (24.48). On the 'mother's house' and 'father's house' as alternate designations for the same social unit, see Meyers (1991).

36. This is, interestingly, a marriage pattern characteristic of matrilineal societies; cf. Steinberg (1991: 48); Jay (1988: 63-64); Wander (1981: 83). In actual matrilineages, the mother's brother is the head of the family. On the unique relationship of a man to his maternal uncle, see Oden (1983: 199-203).

place and my country. Give me my wives and my children for whom I have served you that I may go, for you know the service I have done for you' (30.25-26).

For the promises to Abraham to be fulfilled through him, Jacob must return to Canaan to claim his patrimony, and his descendants who will possess the land must be reckoned through the male line back to Abraham. This is already stipulated and prefigured in the blessing Jacob receives from his father when he leaves Canaan.

> May he [God] give the blessing of Abraham to you and to your descendants with you that you may take possession of the land of your sojournings which God gave to Abraham (Gen. 28.4).

Consequently, Yhwh commands Jacob to 'return to the land of your *fathers*' (31.3).

The narrative resolves the descent conflict—are the children of Rachel, Leah, and their maids to be reckoned to Jacob's household, or to Laban's (cf. 31.43)?—and 'rescues' Jacob from his uxorilocal situation in Haran in two stages. First Jacob consults with Rachel and Leah about leaving Haran for Canaan. We are now in a position to see why this consultation is not so egalitarian as it might have seemed at first glance. Since their father Laban, and not Jacob as their husband, holds authority over the household, Jacob needs his wives' support to make his move from a uxorilocal setting in Haran to Canaan, where he will establish his own household. Otherwise he would be guilty of having 'abducted my daughters like captives of the sword', as Laban later accuses him (v. 26). He makes therefore a long plea in his defense (vv. 5-13), and his success in turning his wives against their father (vv. 14-15) marks a victory for descent through fathers over descent through mothers. The women respond: 'Do we any longer have a portion or an inheritance in our father's house? Are we not regarded by him as foreign women? For he has sold us and moreover he has used up our dowry (literally, 'eaten up our money').'[37]

---

37. Whether this is their dowry or the bride-price (the equivalent of the wages for Jacob's labor, which was sometimes used to provide for the woman's dowry), it is money the sisters consider theirs to pass on

Their description of themselves as 'foreign women' (*nokriyyot*) in their father's eyes is noteworthy. Their response can be taken as hyperbole designed to show their strong support of their husband. If we understand the women to be speaking in the interest of the patriarchal text, then their characterization of themselves as foreign women symbolically places them in the position of outsiders. To be regarded as foreign women by their father is to be cut off from their line of descent, the line of descent they share with Jacob. The conflict caused by having mothers from the same patriline as fathers would thus be symbolically eliminated and the ideal of unilineal descent from fathers could be more easily maintained. The text projects onto the women a denial of the importance of descent through mothers (a double move, since they project it onto Laban) and, because they cast their lot with Jacob, an affirmation that descent will be reckoned through the father. In this case, what is in the text's interest—that the women and their children pass from the father's control to that of the husband—is also in the women's interest, as suggested by the next verse, where they lay claim to their dowry as theirs to pass on to their children: 'All the property that God has taken away from our father *belongs to us and to our children*; so do whatever God has told you' (v. 16). It bears noting that the motivation attributed to them is not loyalty to Jacob but maternal concern to preserve their sons' inheritance. It is in their interest to secure their sons' futures, for their own future well-being depends upon their sons.

The victory of patrilocal marriage and descent from fathers over uxorilocal marriage and descent from mothers is confirmed in the confrontation between Laban and Jacob, when Laban overtakes his son-in-law en route to Canaan. Laban, as the head of the household, lays claim to the lineage: 'The daughters are my daughters, the children are my children' (Gen. 31.43). The children, Jacob's children, are his because the daughters, Jacob's wives, are his; Laban's claim depends on recognition of descent through mothers. There

to their children; see Morrison (1983: 160-61); Westbrook (1991: 150).

is, however, nothing Laban can do to prevent Jacob's departure for his paternal home, for 'the God of your [Jacob's] father' (v. 29) is on the side of descent from fathers and in a dream has warned Laban not to oppose Jacob. Only divine intervention prevents Laban from doing what Jacob feared, taking his property by force (vv. 29, 31). The two men resolve the conflict by making a covenant, after which they go their separate ways, but not before Laban has reintroduced the issue of Israel's descent from the proper mother(s) by stipulating that Jacob not 'take wives besides my daughters' (31.50).[38] Not insignificantly at this point of triumph of patrilineal virilocal marriage, the covenant is made in the name of the God of the *fathers*, a further affirmation of descent reckoned through fathers. Laban calls upon 'the God of Abraham and the God of Nahor, the God of their father', and Jacob swears by 'the Fear of his father Isaac'.

4. *Constructing male relationships through blood sacrifice.* In a recent cross-cultural study of societies in which blood sacrifice has been practiced, Jay argues that the institution of sacrifice serves as a means for men in patrilineal descent groups to affirm their kinship bonds. She takes as her point of departure the widespread exclusion of childbearing women from sacrificial rites and proposes a view of sacrifice as a 'remedy for having been born of woman'.[39] Focusing on the symbolic opposition between sacrifice and childbirth, Jay examines how sacrifice, by socially and religiously establishing lines of descent reckoned solely through males, enables males to transcend their dependence on women's reproductive powers.

> When membership in patrilineal descent groups is identified by rights of participation in sacrifices, evidence of 'paternity' is created which is as certain as evidence of maternity, but far more flexible. Kinship relations can be restructured, individuals adopted, and even subsidiary lineages incorporated into a descent group by participation in sacrifice. Conversely, it is

38. Jacob already has two other wives of secondary rank, Bilhah and Zilpah, whose sons have been accepted into 'Israel' through symbolic adoption by Rachel and Leah.

39. Jay (1992); see also Jay (1985, 1988).

extremely important to exclude improper persons because partaking may constitute recognized alliance by descent.[40]

Although there are problems with the application of Jay's theory to the biblical material (Samson's mother, for example, participates in a sacrifice), her thesis nonetheless merits consideration for the insight it provides into the nature of the conflict in Genesis between descent reckoned through fathers and descent reckoned through mothers. Among other things, it allows us to recognize that Sarah's absence from the account of Abraham's near-sacrifice of the young Isaac is no accident but rather the suppression of the maternal claim on the son in favor of the paternal one. Jay remarks, 'By this act, Isaac, on the edge of death, received his life not by birth from his mother but from the hand of his father as directed by God (Elohim), and Abraham received assurance of countless descendants'.[41] (The concern of this story with the proper lineage also explains why Ishmael is ignored in the command to sacrifice 'your only son': Abraham has already been told that his descendants will be reckoned through Isaac in 21.12.)

The covenant between Jacob and Laban (Gen. 31.44-54) is accompanied by sacrifice. Jay interprets the sacrifice as a redefinition of their relationship in terms of patrilineal descent. By invoking 'the God of Abraham, the God of Nahor, the God of their father', Laban appeals first to Jacob's patrilineal grandfather, then to his own patrilineal grandfather, and finally to their common great-grandfather (Terah), who represents the point of patrilineal alliance between Laban and his nephew. In the context of this sacrifice, Laban ceases to be Jacob's mother's brother (a relationship defined through a woman) and becomes his patrilineal classificatory brother. In other words, the two men become members of the same patrilineal descent group sacrificing together.[42]

40. Jay (1988: 54-55).
41. Jay (1988: 60); similarly Jay (1992: 102).
42. Jay (1992: 108; 1988: 67). That Laban is now reckoned as Jacob's kinsman explains why, in Jay's view, it is not said that Laban shared the meal: he is included in the 'kinsmen' Jacob invited to eat (31.54).

The examples discussed above illustrate patriarchy's reliance upon a range of strategies to establish the father's claim to progeny in response to the biologically evident claim of the mother. In the course of the next section, we shall consider how circumcision might also be seen as a strategy for privileging fatherhood over motherhood, in addition to its obvious privileging of males over females. Like sacrifice, circumcision provides a means of establishing and maintaining the intergenerational link between father and son.

## The Sterile Matriarch

Given the high mortality rate for women and children in ancient times, it is understandable that great value would be placed upon women's reproductive ability.[43] How does patriarchy respond to the obvious importance of women's reproductive power and to its dependence on that power? Our narrative, which displays an overriding concern with offspring, insists that the 'right mother' is important, but it also tells us that the 'right mother' is sterile—three of them, anyway, and the most important three at that.[44] In other words, the Genesis narrators undermine the chosen mothers' importance by denying the very thing for which they are so highly valued, their reproductive ability. Sarah's sterility is mentioned within the genealogy of Terah in Genesis 11, a clue that it will be significant as the plot develops. Not only is she sterile at the beginning of the narrative, before the plot gets underway, but she remains sterile for an exceedingly long time. Rebekah, too, is sterile (Gen. 25.21), and Rachel endures years of apparent sterility during which her sister is fruitful (30.1-21). Sterility is the women's problem, as it is elsewhere in the Bible, where the

43. See Meyers (1988: 64-71, 95-121, 183).
44. The birth of a hero to a barren mother is a well-represented biblical type-scene; see Alter (1981: 47-62; 1983). On its features, see Brenner (1985: 95; 1986); Williams (1982: 52-55). Our question here is what social (and phallocentric) function this type-scene serves; see Fuchs (1985a).

male's role in the couple's inability to conceive is never at issue: Abraham and Jacob already have sons when their sterile wives, Sarah and Rachel, finally conceive. As testimony to his potency, Abraham begets Ishmael when he is 86, and he has more sons later. That women needed children to give them status in patriarchal society is evident. Conversely, it is in the interest of patriarchal ideology not only that women bear children but also that they desire to do so.[45] Thus these narratives represent the matriarchs as desiring children, especially sons (Hebrew *banim* can mean both), at all costs. Indeed, Sarah's first speech, addressed to Abraham, is an acknowledgment of the problem of childlessness and an attempt to resolve it: 'See, Yhwh has prevented me from bearing children. Go in to my maid; perhaps I shall be built up through her' (16.2). Similarly Rachel's first words, also addressed to her husband, express her desperation: 'Give me children/sons, otherwise I am dead' (30.1). Sarah and Rachel are presented as so eager for offspring that they give their maids to their husbands in an attempt to have children through them. Does this reflect an actual custom in Israel according to which children born to a woman's maidservant would be considered hers, or is it a male fantasy that would like to imagine women behaving in this manner—a fantasy projected onto the ancestral figures?[46] The narrator presents this particular means of obtaining children as something that is done for the woman's sake and not the man's, as is clear in both cases: Abraham could take other wives to bear him children (he does take another wife and have children by her, but only after Sarah is dead, Gen. 25.1) and Jacob already has sons by his other 'correct' (i.e. from the same

45. See Fuchs (1985a: 130-33). See also the discussion of Samson's mother in Chapter 3 above.
46. Ancient Near Eastern evidence is often adduced for such a custom; see Frymer-Kensky (1981: 211-12). See also von Rad (1961: 186); Westermann (1985: 239); Bird (1974: 53). Since I take women in the biblical narrative as male constructs and because I believe this material was composed in a period of Israelite history for which we have no evidence of such a custom, I assume male fantasy may well be involved in these narratives.

patriline) wife Leah. Indeed, by having Leah also give her maid to Jacob, although she has already borne him sons, the biblical narrator reinforces the stereotype that women will go to any lengths to have children. Presenting the matriarchs as sterile is one way of undermining their significance; having them offer their maids to the patriarchs as surrogates is another. The replacement of the matriarch by her maid implies a denial of the matriarch's uniqueness as the 'right' wife.[47] And such a denial of the mother's uniqueness contradicts the narrative claim that the proper wife is critical for continuing the Abrahamic line. Not only does the substitution motif threaten the matriarchs' position as the 'right' wives, it also allows another patriarchal strategy to come into play. By dividing women into upper and lower class women, patriarchy prevents women from gaining power by forming alliances. Women of lower status (Hagar, Bilhah, Zilpah) are exploited for the sake of higher class women, which is really for the sake of patriarchy. Patriarchy relies upon women's cooperation, and one of its rewards for cooperation is status. Using their servants as surrogates is presented as the matriarchs' idea—not as something imposed upon them. The matriarchs consent to the exploitation of other women because from it they gain status as mothers and can thereby realize the patriarchal ideal of fulfillment through motherhood. In one case, that of Sarah and Hagar, the narrative dramatizes the conflict between women over status. Hagar's change in status when she becomes pregnant and her change of attitude that results pose a challenge to Sarah's superior status as primary wife that Sarah will not tolerate. Hagar is, of course, doubly exploited: by Sarah, who uses her to obtain a child, and by the androcentric narrators, who use her to endorse androcentric values. Her arrogance shows pregnancy and motherhood to be a source of pride. Patriarchal ideology can imagine it as nothing else; it cannot imagine motherhood as

47. On barrenness as a threat to the matriarchs' role as mothers, and substitution as a threat to their position as wives, see Wander (1981: 92-96).

unwanted.

The most important use to which the repeated theme of the sterile matriarch is put, as a patriarchal strategy, is to transfer the control over their procreative power from the women to the deity.[48] Sarah acknowledges God's role, 'Yhwh has prevented me from bearing children', and she conceives only because 'Yhwh visited Sarah as he had said and Yhwh did to Sarah as he had promised' (21.1). Her own attempt to resolve the problem of her sterility by having a child through Hagar backfires. And her own knowledge about herself—that having ceased to menstruate (18.11) she cannot conceive—is contradicted by the deity (in the form of three men), who responds to her incredulity by asserting his power over her body: 'Is anything too miraculous for Yhwh?' (18.14). In Rebekah's case, conception comes from God as the result of patriarchal intervention: she becomes pregnant when her husband Isaac prays on her behalf and the deity grants the patriarch's request: 'Yhwh granted his prayer, and Rebekah his wife conceived' (25.21). Although Yhwh is sympathetic to Leah and 'opens her womb' to compensate for Jacob's preference for his other wife (29.31), it is apparently he who is also responsible for keeping Rachel sterile. Jacob, at any rate, regards it as God's doing: when Rachel complains to him about being childless, he replies, 'Am I in the place of God, who has withheld from you the fruit of the womb?'

Leah acknowledges God's responsibility for conception (29.32, 33, 35; 30.18, 20), and Rachel likewise attributes her maid's fecundity to God (30.6). It is true that, in an effort to conceive, Rachel turns to aphrodisiacs (30.14-16), but apparently they play no role in her conception, for in the time before she conceives Leah gives birth to two sons and a daughter.[49] And in any case, the narrator attributes nothing

48. Fuchs (1985a: 129). It also heightens the suspense surrounding the birth of the promised offspring and offers an opportunity for the deity to intervene; see Exum (1985: 76).

49. Mandrakes were considered aphrodisiacs, promoting fertility (Speiser 1964: 231; von Rad 1961: 290; Westermann 1985: 475), but we cannot attribute to them any role in Rachel's conception unless we

to the mandrakes, but regards female fecundity as due solely to divine intervention: 'God remembered Rachel and God heard her and opened her womb' (30.22). Rachel, for her part, in acknowledging God for removing her sterility, at the same time testifies (on behalf of all the sterile matriarchs) to the stigma of childlessness and to the craving for sons imposed on women in the patriarchal world: 'She said, "God has taken away my reproach", and she called his name Joseph, saying, "May Yhwh add to me another son"' (30.23-24). If permitting conception is the prerogative of God, impregnating women is the work of males. The counterpart to the sterile matriarch is the fertile patriarch, whose procreative role is enhanced through an implicit association of reproduction with circumcision, the mark of the covenant. In Genesis 17, when God promises to make Abraham the 'father of a multitude of nations', circumcision is the symbol of their covenant:

> I will make you exceedingly fruitful and I will make nations of you and kings shall come forth from you. I will establish my covenant between me and you and your descendants after you throughout their generations... I will give to you and to your descendants after you the land of your sojournings, all the land of Canaan, for an everlasting possession... As for you, you shall keep my covenant, you and your descendants after you throughout their generations. This is my covenant, which you shall keep, between me and you and your descendants after you: every male among you shall be circumcised. You shall be circumcised in the flesh of your foreskins, and it shall be a symbol of the covenant between me and you. He that is eight days old among you shall be circumcised; every male throughout your generations... (17.6-12).

Now why, if some physical mark is to symbolize the covenant, is that mark to be made upon the penis and not on a part of the body where it could be readily seen? It seems self-evident that some connection with virility and procreation is implied, at least on a symbolic level. The symbolic connection between circumcision and fertility has been

assume that she kept them for some time before using them.

argued at length by Howard Eilberg-Schwartz, who cites ethnographic studies to demonstrate the association of circumcision with notions of fertility, virility, maturity, and genealogy, in cultures where circumcision is practiced as a puberty rite.[50] Even though in Israel circumcision was performed soon after birth rather than at puberty (and thus was not a symbol of virility and maturity), in Eilberg-Schwartz's view a connection between the practice of circumcision and two of these themes, fertility and genealogy, is suggested in the biblical literature. The biblical writers, he argues, view circumcision as symbolically preparing the male organ to perform its future task of impregnating women and producing offspring. Analogies can be found in the metaphoric use of circumcision in reference both to other organs and to fruit trees.

> Israelite writers equated the lack of circumcision with the improper functioning of a human organ. Uncircumcised hearts, ears, and lips are organs that cannot do what God intended them to do. By extension, the removal of a man's foreskin symbolically enables the penis to more effectively discharge its divinely allotted task. That task, as suggested by the content of the covenant, is to impregnate women and produce offspring.[51]

Citing the widespread application of horticultural metaphors to human sexuality and fertility in general, and the reference to 'uncircumcised' fruit trees in Lev. 19.23-25, in particular, Eilberg-Schwartz argues for an implicit connection between circumcising the penis and pruning fruit trees.

> [T]he priestly writings suggest an analogy between an uncircumcised male organ and an immature fruit tree. They thus associate the circumcision of the male with pruning juvenile fruit

---

50. Eilberg-Schwartz (1990: 141-76); see also Lerner (1986: 191-93). As Eilberg-Schwartz concedes, the connection between circumcision and fertility is not explicit in Gen. 17. The circumcision of Ishmael, recounted in Gen. 17, is used by Eilberg-Schwartz to support his theory of circumcision as a symbol of fertility and not just a sign of the covenant: Ishmael will be the progenitor of multitudes, but he is excluded from the covenantal promise (17.18-21).
51. Eilberg-Schwartz (1990: 149).

trees; like the latter, circumcision symbolically readies the stem for producing fruit.[52]

In the verses quoted above from Genesis 17, three important themes appear together—the fruitfulness of the patriarch, the intergenerational continuity between males, and circumcision as symbol of the covenant—creating a symbolic link between reproduction, genealogy, and masculinity.[53] Circumcision distinguishes Abraham as the founder of a new lineage and establishes a line of descent traced through males who bear this distinctive mark in their flesh. Circumcision provides physical evidence of kinship ties between men. Like sacrifice, it establishes intergenerational continuity between males (as the emphasis on 'descendants' and 'throughout your/their generations' in Gen. 17 makes clear). As a symbol of male fertility, and as a sign of membership in a community from which women, who do not bear the mark of membership, are excluded, circumcision functions to privilege the father and suppress the mother. The effect is particularly powerful in our narrative because the repeated theme of the sterile matriarch already casts doubt on the matriarchs' reproductive role.

As if the association of circumcision and fertility were not sufficient to secure the father's position, a concomitant move, the designation of menstrual blood and the blood of parturition as unclean and polluting, further undermines women's importance in procreation and provides a rationale for isolating them from the privileged society of males. Taboos regarding menstrual blood and the blood of childbirth are widespread. Jay examines from an anthropological perspective the opposition between the purifying power of sacrifice and the pollution of childbirth and menstruation.[54] Julia Kristeva proposes that pollution rites serve as protection against the generative power of women and that circumcision separates the son from maternal, female impurity

---

52. Eilberg-Schwartz (1991: 8; 1990: 149-54).
53. Eilberg-Schwartz (1991: 9).
54. Jay (1992, 1988, 1985).

and defilement.[55] Eilberg-Schwartz also argues for a view of circumcision as a ritual for separating the male child from the impurity of his mother, and he suggests that circumcision and sacrifice have overlapping functions: to create and to demonstrate patrilineal kinship ties among men.[56] In their different ways, these interpretations all point to patriarchy's fear of women's reproductive power, its need to suppress it, and its equally strong desire to appropriate it—as, for example, in Genesis 2, where the first man gives birth to woman, aided by the creator god and in the absence of a creator goddess or goddesses.[57]

Both Kristeva and Eilberg-Schwartz comment on the mention of circumcision in the middle of the discussion of a woman's ritual impurity after childbirth in Lev. 12.2-4:

> If a woman conceives and bears a male child, then she shall be unclean seven days; as at the time of her menstruation she shall be unclean. On the eighth day the flesh of his foreskin shall be circumcised. For thirty-three days she shall continue in the blood of her purification; she must not touch anything consecrated nor come into the sanctuary until the days of her purification are completed.

To purify herself after childbirth, a woman offers a burnt offering and a sin offering. Kristeva proposes that the son's circumcision is, for him, the equivalent of sacrifice, a purifying rite that 'does away with the need for sacrifice, of which it nevertheless bears the trace'.[58] In a similar vein, Eilberg-Schwartz believes we can infer a connection between the mother's impurity for seven days and the infant's, which would account for the delay of circumcision until the eighth day after birth. Circumcision thus becomes, in Eilberg-Schwartz's words, 'a rite that marks the passage from the impurity of being born of woman to the purity of life in a

55. Kristeva (1982: 77-79, 99-101).
56. Eilberg-Schwartz (1990: 174-86).
57. On this theme, and the woman's attempt to claim creator status in Gen. 2, see Pardes (1992: 40-58).
58. Kristeva (1982: 99-100). Kristeva goes on to say that 'what the male is separated from, the other that circumcision carves out on his very sex is the other sex, impure, defiled' (p. 100).

community of men'.[59]

Perhaps in this context we can better appreciate the significance of Rachel's theft of her father's household gods (teraphim) and its association with menstrual blood in Gen. 31.35. The text does not give Rachel's reason for stealing the teraphim, but it is reasonable to conclude that her motive has something to do with concern with the family line, which the teraphim must in some way represent.[60] Jay argues that what is at stake here is control over the line of descent reckoned through mothers, and that Rachel's possession of the teraphim signifies her claim to her son Joseph as the one through whom the proper line of descent should be reckoned.[61] If Rachel is indeed menstruating, sitting on the teraphim would be a scandalous way of defiling them—and whether or not this is the case is left open.[62] By insinuating that Rachel profanes the teraphim, the story discredits both the woman and her implicit claim on the family line,

---

59. Eilberg-Schwartz (1990: 175). Eilberg-Schwartz seems to regard the new-born infant as unclean, and he conveniently ignores the father's position: either the father would not touch the infant for seven days, which is hard to imagine (and if that were the case it is even harder to imagine why it would not be stipulated in the law). Alternatively, the father is repeatedly in a state of uncleanness. I do not think this problem invalidates Eilberg-Schwartz's more general observations about the impurity of being born of woman, since, as he frequently points out, cultures are not perfectly logical systems. On the symbolic association of menstrual blood with death, see Eilberg-Schwartz (1990: 177-89); Wenham (1983: 432-35).

60. See Morrison (1983: 161-62); cf. Greenberg (1962); Huehnergard (1985); Jay (1988: 65-66); and for a summary of various views, Sherwood (1990: 308-11). To argue, as Jeansonne (1990: 136 n. 44) does against Fuchs (1988), that Rachel was motivated by revenge against her father (here Jeansonne follows a number of commentators) ignores the complexity of the issue: what could she hope to achieve? Is she simply spiteful?

61. Jay (1992: 106-107; 1988: 65-66). Jay views Rachel's theft as the reverse of Jacob's theft from Isaac and Esau, for, whereas Jacob steals a patrilineal line, Rachel steals a matrilineal line.

62. A number of features conspire to make Rachel look bad, as Fuchs (1988) shows: she steals; her reasons for robbing her own father of his sacred property are not made clear; she lies (possibly) to conceal her theft.

symbolically demonstrating that the matriarch cannot control the line of descent (recall that Rebekah upset the male line of descent by enabling Jacob to displace Esau as Isaac's 'true heir'). Jacob can steal from Esau the place of privilege in the Abrahamic line of descent and still legitimately receive it, but Rachel cannot displace her sister.[63] Nor would her efforts matter in the larger scheme of things, since descent reckoned through mothers will not ultimately decide the offspring's status.

In Gen. 35.2 members of Jacob's household are told to put away their foreign gods, which suggests that Rachel may not have been the only one to bring such objects with her. The significant point about the gods Rachel takes with her is that they are *stolen*: they belong to her father. This fact lends credence to Mieke Bal's proposal that possession of the teraphim represents Rachel's transfer of the child from her father to her husband. Bal reads the account in the larger social context of the transition from patrilocal to virilocal marriage; that is, from marriage in which the wife remains in her father's house and her father—not her husband—has authority over her and her offspring, to marriage in which the husband takes his wife to his own clan.[64] Jacob's exodus from his wives' father's household and his move to establish his own household is precisely the issue in the conflict between Jacob and Laban. In the narrative resolution of the conflict in favor of Jacob, Rachel's transfer of the child from her father to her husband not only supports virilocal marriage; it also undermines descent through mothers, for it symbolically removes the child from Rachel's side of the lineage (Laban's house where descent from mothers is recognized) and assigns it to Jacob's (where the ideal is to establish descent unilineally from fathers).

Whatever meaning we ascribe to Rachel's act, we are interpreting the text's silences. Precisely because we do not know *why* Rachel stole the teraphim, we cannot know what

---

63. On this aspect of the Rachel–Leah conflict, see Pardes (1992: 63-78).

64. Bal (1988b: 151-52); see also Bal (1988a: 84-86 *et passim*.).

possession of them might mean. The difficulty is symptomatic of the contradiction that has occupied the narrator all along: how to affirm the importance of having the correct mother while ignoring the implications of such an affirmation for tracing descent. In the case of the theft of the teraphim, explaining Rachel's action would involve tacit recognition of its meaning for descent from mothers—thus the need to discredit it indirectly, which the association with stealing, deception, and, especially, menstrual blood (even if fictitious) accomplishes forcefully.

## The Matriarchs and the Plot,
## and the Plot against the Matriarchs

Israel traces its origins from Abraham through Isaac and Jacob, and the writers who preserved these stories knew this is as it should be. But as the plot of Genesis unfolds, the promises to Abraham do not pass automatically from Abraham to Isaac, and from Isaac to Jacob; rather it is the matriarchs who see to it that the promise is passed on to the 'right son' (that is, the rightful heir): it must be Isaac and not Ishmael, Jacob and not Esau. Sarah has Hagar and Ishmael cast out of Abraham's household so that Isaac will not have to share his inheritance with his half-brother (Gen. 21). It is Rebekah's idea to have Jacob pretend to be Esau and steal his father's blessing while Esau hunts game for Isaac to eat (Gen. 27). When Jacob hesitates, fearing that his father might discover the ruse and curse him rather than bless him, Rebekah boldly assumes the risk: 'Upon me be your curse, my son' (v. 13). She arranges everything; Jacob has only to follow her instructions, to 'obey me' (27.8, 13). She prepares the food for Jacob to take to Isaac, and she dresses Jacob in Esau's clothes so that his blind father will think he is Esau and bless him. Jacob has nothing to lose in this scheme, and he gains everything. When Rebekah learns that Esau plans to kill Jacob for his deception, she instructs Jacob (again, 'obey me', v. 43) to leave Canaan for Haran. And it is at her urging that Isaac sends Jacob to Haran, with the 'blessing of Abraham' (28.4), to take a wife from his mother's family (thus ensuring that he will obtain the 'right wife').

Rachel and Leah act on behalf of their sons when they agree to leave Haran for Canaan. They are motivated, as we saw above, by maternal concern to preserve their sons' inheritance. And, of course, it is necessary to get the family to Canaan, since only in Canaan can the twelve sons become Israel. Only when it serves the text's androcentric interest do Rachel and Leah cooperate; otherwise it is competition (also in the text's androcentric interest) that motivates them. Their rivalry results not so much in a victory for either of the women (both are unhappy) as a victory for patriarchy: numerous sons are born to Jacob, ensuring that Israel will increase. The competition is not between women of different rank, as in the case of Sarah and Hagar, but between co-wives of equal status, and sisters at that. Nor are the sisters in conflict with the other wives of Jacob, who are of lower status, for Bilhah and Zilpah are needed to bring the number of Jacob's sons to twelve. Unlike Sarah, who does not acknowledge Ishmael as her son, Rachel and Leah accept the sons of Bilhah and Zilpah as their own, thereby 'correcting' the irregularity of their descent from women who are not of the proper lineage, and enabling the sons of the servant women to share in the promises to Abraham.[65] The status of their mothers, however, which corresponds to the patriarch's preferences, does play a role in deciding the relative ranking of the twelve sons/tribes, who are not treated entirely equally in the tradition (see, e.g., Gen. 49, where Jacob's blessing of his sons reflects their different valuation). The only attempt by one of Jacob's wives to claim special privilege for her son—if that is what Rachel's theft of her father's teraphim means—fails.

The biblical narrators give the mothers credit for their

---

65. No doubt the repetition of *leya'aqov* (to Jacob) in connection with the births of sons to the wives of secondary rank serves to reinforce the theoretically equal status of the twelve sons/tribes. The fact that Hagar and Ishmael pose a problem and are not acceptable into the Israelite lineage, whereas Jacob's wives of secondary rank are, may also reflect different valuations of Israel's relationship with Mesopotamia and with Egypt in the tradition.

sons' successes, but, in the process, they make the women look bad. In having Hagar and Ishmael 'cast out', Sarah appears cruel and unfeeling. The picture of a harsh and vindictive Sarah was already prepared for in Genesis 16, where, to defend her position as primary wife, Sarah has Hagar, who is pregnant, cast out because 'I became slight in her eyes' (v. 5). When, in Genesis 21, Sarah once again defends her position against her rival, she objectifies Hagar and Ishmael by avoiding use of their names. Speaking of them impersonally makes it easier to dispose of them: 'Cast out *this slave woman* with *her son*'—as if Ishmael were Hagar's son alone and not Abraham's also—'for *the son of this slave woman* shall not be heir with my son Isaac'. Indeed, Abraham, in his role as father, reacts negatively to Sarah's prompting: 'The thing was very displeasing to Abraham *on account of his son*'. With Sarah to do the 'dirty work', Isaac need play no role in the conflict and can remain innocent of any animosity toward his brother. The sons do not see themselves as rivals or enemies; and, according to the Greek text, they are 'playing' together when Sarah decides that Hagar and Ishmael must go.[66]

Just as Sarah ensures her son Isaac's inheritance, so Rebekah ensures that of her son Jacob. To have Isaac favor his younger son Jacob over Esau, the elder, would be damaging to the patriarchal status quo, where the oldest son is the primary recipient of his father's estate. Thus the narrator makes the matriarch responsible for disrupting the natural line of inheritance. And Jacob, the son who usurps the blessing, is less culpable than if he had devised everything himself. Rebekah is cast as cunning and deceptive, while Jacob simply, and even reluctantly (though only out of fear of discovery), carries out her orders when he deludes his father into believing he is Esau. To be sure, Jacob had earlier tricked Esau into selling his birthright. But, in that scene (Gen. 25.29-34), Esau was portrayed as foolish, thinking only

66. The verb in 21.9 is *tsahaq*, a pun on Isaac's name, and the Hebrew lacks 'with Isaac her son'; cf. LXX, Vulg. The exact nature of the play is debated; see Exum and Whedbee (1984: 13); Landy (1984: 137).

of his stomach, and thus unworthy of the birthright. In contrast, Esau and Isaac are portrayed sympathetically in Genesis 27, and so their deception cannot be so easily dismissed as fitting. On the contrary, Isaac is deluded not because he deserves it but because he is old and blind. He is overwhelmed with anguish upon discovering the ruse, as is Esau, whose bitter cries cannot but arouse our pity.[67] Though Jacob is guilty of deceiving them ('Is it because his name is Jacob that he has supplanted me these two times?', v. 36), the blame does not attach to him primarily. It was, after all, his mother's idea.

The matriarchs' depiction reflects a male view both of the way mothers behave—maternal instinct leads them to protect their sons and promote their interests—and of the way women in general behave—they are jealous, manipulative, and untrustworthy.[68] If Sarah is callous and Rebekah deceptive, Rachel and Leah are envious and competitive. Women, even sisters, cannot get along, the text tells us; they cannot form bonds that transcend their own narrow interests and cannot cooperate except on rare occasions.[69] In a poly-

67. See the discussion of this scene in Exum and Whedbee (1984: 17-18).

68. To be sure, the patriarchs are also deceptive and untrustworthy: Abraham deceives the foreign ruler about his wife's status (Gen. 12 and 20) and Jacob's entire career is marked by episodes of deception and counter-deception. Jacob is punished in kind for his deceptive behavior: Laban substitutes Leah for Rachel on the wedding night, echoing Jacob's deception of Isaac; Leah trades her son's mandrakes to Rachel in exchange for a night with Jacob, echoing Esau's exchange of the birthright for Jacob's lentil soup; in his old age Jacob is deceived by his sons with a garment, as he deceived his father by wearing Esau's clothes. On the many parallels, see, *inter alios*, Cassuto (1964); Fokkelman (1975); Fishbane (1979); Sherwood (1990). The matriarchs are also narratively punished for their deeds; see below. Nevertheless, gender plays an important role in the way character traits are evaluated; consider only how differently our society evaluates ambition or competition on the part of men and on the part of women. On gender bias in the different handling of the motivation behind deception and therefore of its resolution, see Fuchs (1988).

69. See Brenner (1985: 93-96); Fuchs (1985a: 131-32). Leah and Rachel cooperate twice: when they agree to leave Haran and when they trade mandrakes for Jacob's sexual services (see below). Both

gamous household, co-wives depend on their offspring to improve their social status.[70] The competition between the sisters to produce sons takes on life and death proportions ('give me children, otherwise I may as well be dead', 30.1). It is so single-minded as to become almost ludicrous, as each sister tries to outdo the other, even to the point of giving their maids to Jacob to acquire more sons. Whereas Jacob wrestles with God in face-to-face combat (Gen. 32), Rachel's olympian struggle (*naphtuley 'elohim*, literally, 'wrestlings of God', 30.8) is with her sister.[71] He becomes a nation; she becomes a mother. Far from discouraging envy on the part of co-wives, patriarchy exploits it as a means of keeping women divided against one another and therefore powerless. As we have seen, patriarchal ideology rewards women for competitiveness. Jacob encourages the competition between his wives by preferring one over the other. Moreover, God encourages the competition by making one fruitful and the other sterile.

As if being envious and competitive were not enough to discredit the favored wife, Rachel is also a thief, who deceives both her father and her husband. Yet another possible interpretation of the teraphim is that they were used for divination.[72] If Rachel took the teraphim so that Laban

times they decide issues of residence and descent in favor of patriarchy: the result in the first case is settlement of Jacob's family in Canaan (residence); and, in the second case, more children for Jacob/Israel (descent).

70. See Lamphere (1974: 105-108). The sibling rivalry between Rachel and Leah, of course, mirrors that between Jacob and Esau. The men are the rivals for the blessing of Abraham; the women, for the privilege of bearing Israel's descendants. Only one man can win (that is, can father the lineage); both women become Israel's mothers; see the discussion below under Unity and Difference.

71. The outcomes of both struggles are important for the future of Israel, but the woman's victory typically takes place in a domestic setting, on the home front, while the man's occurs against a larger backdrop, on the banks of the Jabbok, a symbolically charged point of crossing/transition. On the symbolism of the Jabbok crossing, see Fokkelman (1975: 208-22).

72. This interpretation is supported by the similarities between the account of the theft of the teraphim and the later story of the 'theft' of

could not divine the location of Jacob's entourage and thus overtake them, she fails, for Laban does overtake them. But her theft of the teraphim does have the effect of making Jacob look better. That Jacob is a thief we know: the narrator tells us that 'Jacob stole the heart of [deceived] Laban the Aramean in that he did not tell him that he intended to flee' (Gen. 31.20). But whereas Laban accuses Jacob of stealing his heart *and* stealing his gods (vv. 26-30), we know that Jacob is innocent of the latter charge: true, he stole Laban's heart by departing secretly (which he justifies by adducing his fear that Laban would reclaim his daughters by force)—but he did not steal the teraphim (about which he is righteously indignant). Rachel's crime overshadows his.

The scenes in which the matriarchs initiate the action show them to be impatient: they do not wait for the divine promises to be fulfilled but take steps to bring them about. And they are narratively punished for their 'intervention'. Sarah uses Hagar and suffers as a result. Rebekah is told the elder son will serve the younger; rather than waiting for it to come to pass, she brings it about—and, as we have seen, she never sees her beloved son again. Rachel uses aphrodisiacs in an effort to obtain children, but without success; instead Leah has two more sons.

In giving the matriarchs an active role in achieving its ends, the androcentric narrative conveys an ambivalent message about mothers. It acknowledges Israel's mothers for the part they played in determining Israel's fortunes, thereby providing models with whom women might have wished to identify. But, in the process, it offers a picture of women as mean-spirited, deceptive, and untrustworthy—

Joseph's cup (Gen. 44.1-13). In the case of the cup, which was used for divination, the stolen object is found where Joseph had it hidden, in the sack belonging to Benjamin, *Rachel's* son. In the case of the teraphim, Rachel *is* a thief but the stolen objects, hidden under Rachel's saddle bag, are not found. The sin of the mother, whose crime is not found out, is visited upon the child, who is not a thief but found guilty of stealing. I owe this observation to Yair Zakovitch; on such intertextual echoes, what he calls 'reflection stories', see Zakovitch (1993).

and for these reasons, a threat to the patriarchal social order. Because the matriarchs are determined and enterprising and able to get their way, they are dangerous. They must be kept in their place, the mother's place, the place for the other where patriarchy can control them.

## Power and Authority

The stories about the matriarchs reflect androcentric views of women, either what men think women are like or what they wish them to be. They also mirror social reality, in addition to helping to shape it. The picture the text gives of the matriarchs corresponds in a number of ways to what we know from anthropological studies about women's position and behavior in traditional patricentered societies.[73] In such societies, the subordinate position of women does not make them into helpless victims. We have already seen examples of ways in which women cooperate with patriarchy to better their lives. Various avenues are open to women for getting what they want, avenues we can identify more precisely in our text by adopting the anthropological distinction between power and authority. Power is the ability to gain compliance with one's wishes and to achieve one's ends. Authority is culturally legitimated power, power recognized by society and distributed according to a hierarchical chain of command and control.[74] The matriarchs do not have authority; they are subordinate to their husbands. But they are not powerless.

One of the most important strategies available to women for achieving their goals is influence.[75] Sarah uses influence to get what she wants where Hagar and Ishmael are concerned. She takes her complaint about Hagar's rude behavior to Abraham, making it an issue between her and her husband ('May Yhwh judge between *me* and *you*', Gen. 16.5), and only when Abraham puts Hagar in her power ('See,

73. See Lamphere (1974); Rosaldo (1974).
74. Lamphere (1974: 99); Rosaldo (1974: 21-22); see also Hackett (1985: 17-22); Meyers (1988: 40-44, 181-87).
75. Lamphere (1974: 99-100).

your maid is in your power; do to her as you please'), does Sarah acquire the authority to mistreat her rival ('then Sarai afflicted her, and she fled from her'). Similarly, in Genesis 21, Sarah cannot expel Hagar and Ishmael from Abraham's household on her own authority. Once again she must depend on her ability to influence her husband, since he alone has the authority to send them away (21.14). Rebekah relies on another strategy to get what she wants. She resorts to deception to circumvent her husband's authority and obtain the blessing for her favorite son Jacob (Gen. 27). On more than one occasion, the narrative shows women eavesdropping in order to learn what was going on, as when Sarah overhears the announcement that she will bear a son (18.10) and Rebekah overhears Isaac inform Esau of his intention to give him the blessing (27.5). Rebekah also has informants (27.42). On the basis of the instructions she has overheard Isaac give to Esau, Rebekah sets in motion a plan which successfully dupes Isaac into blessing Jacob. Later, when she is told of Esau's plan to kill Jacob, she uses her influence to get her way. Although she tells Jacob to flee to Haran (v. 43), the authority to send him away with the patriarchal blessing rests with Isaac. By complaining about the Canaanite women and raising the specter of Jacob's marrying one of them, Rebekah influences Isaac to send Jacob to Haran to take a wife (27.46–28.5).

Sarah and Rebekah illustrate how women can have power in areas not normally accorded them by working through those in authority. One place where women sometimes have authority of their own is in the domestic sphere. On one occasion, we see Rachel and Leah exercising such authority, when they decide between themselves with which of them the patriarch must sleep. Jacob's sexual services are traded for some mandrakes in what Rachel and Leah consider a mutually beneficial exchange, and the patriarch apparently has no say in the matter (30.14-16).

Women sometimes acquire power as a result of male fears. Ideas of purity and pollution, for example, which generally serve to circumscribe women's activities, can be turned against men and used by women to their own advantage.

M.Z. Rosaldo gives an example from New Guinea, where a man will acquiesce to his wife's wishes out of fear that in anger she might serve him food while she is menstruating, or step over him while he sleeps so that blood drops on him.[76] This is the kind of power we see Rachel relying upon when she hides the teraphim from Laban by sitting upon them and claiming she cannot rise because she is menstruating. We cannot, of course, assume that Rachel is telling the truth—and this is the point. As Bal points out, the taboo of menstrual blood is a male problem. The taboo is semiotic in nature: it interprets blood as a symptom of bodily impurity, which, in turn, is interpreted as a symptom of female inferiority. In Rachel's case, menstruation, the sign of female inferiority, becomes a sign of male inferiority; that is, of male fright. Is Rachel lying to Laban? 'A woman would simply have checked, a man would not dream of trying.'[77]

We might keep in mind that, due primarily to dietary factors in ancient times, menstruation was probably infrequent (we should thus not assume that women were regarded as ritually impure as often as once a month).[78] It may even be that 'the way of women' in Gen. 31.35 refers to pregnancy: thus, Rachel appeals to a difficult or advanced pregnancy as the reason she cannot rise before Laban.[79] The issue, however, is not so much Rachel's actual condition but rather the fact that she uses male fear or respect for a uniquely female condition to gain power over a man. The issue, in other words, is the testimony of a woman, the power of a woman's *word*.

These examples reveal ways in which women both co-operate with and resist patriarchal control. The fact that, even within the confines of patriarchy, women can exercise power poses a threat, for what happens if they use their power to undermine their husbands' authority? This is, in

76. Rosaldo (1974: 38).
77. Bal (1988b: 151).
78. See Hare-Mustin and Marecek (1990: 3). I thank my colleague Patricia DeLeeuw for drawing this fact to my attention.
79. For discussion of this possibility, see Sherwood (1990: 328-29, 368-69 nn. 164-65).

fact, exactly what Sarah and Rebekah do when they secure the promise for Isaac and for Jacob. Abraham would have been content to have Ishmael as his heir: 'O that Ishmael might live in your sight', he implores God, when God announces that Sarah will bear him a son (17.18). And Isaac prefers Esau and intends to give him the patriarchal blessing (25.28; 27.2-4). The matriarchs' ability to achieve ends that are not in harmony with their husbands' wishes is dangerous; such power threatens to destabilize patriarchy. In particular, Rebekah's use of deception to get Isaac to bless Jacob instead of Esau shows how subversive a woman could be. It also shows how women are trapped in a vicious circle, where lack of authority forces them to resort to indirect and often underhanded means to achieve their ends. Their subversive exercise of power, in turn, provides patriarchy with justification for its need to control them. In response to the threat of women's power, patriarchy seeks to recuperate and appropriate that power for its own purposes.

The Genesis narrators treat women's power in the patriarchal family and its threat in much the same way they handle women's reproductive power. The matriarchs owe their success in achieving their aims, no less than their fertility, to God; that is, Sarah and Rebekah succeed in influencing or circumventing their husbands because it was God's will. God, who has *already* rejected Ishmael as Abraham's heir and informed Abraham that his line will be reckoned through Isaac (17.19-21), supports Sarah when she tells Abraham to cast out Hagar and Ishmael: 'Whatever Sarah says to you, obey her, for through Isaac shall your descendants be named' (21.12). According to the narrator, Sarah's demand displeased Abraham, and it is apparently only because God is in favor of their expulsion that Abraham agrees to send Hagar and Ishmael away. When Rebekah orchestrates Jacob's theft of the blessing, she is also represented as serving God's plan. Before Jacob and Esau were born, Yhwh had informed her, 'Two nations are in your womb; two peoples, born of you, shall be divided. One people shall be stronger than the other, and the elder shall serve the younger' (25.23). Like Abraham, who does not tell

Sarah about God's promise that she would bear a son (chs. 17–18), Rebekah does not tell Isaac about this oracle. Isaac must be kept in the dark about Jacob's prophesied future even before Rebekah and Jacob rely on his blindness in stealing the blessing, for how could a patriarchal text portray a father preferring his younger son over the firstborn?[80] With Rebekah to intercede on Jacob's behalf, Esau can safely be his father's favorite (25.28). Because of its serious consequences for patriarchal authority and succession, Rebekah's act requires nothing less than a divine oracle to justify it (and here a woman receives an oracle from God without an intermediary).

In addition to portraying the matriarchs as the instruments through whom God works to achieve his ends (the narrators' ends being identified with God's ends), the narrators emphasize the matriarchs' maternal motives. Their power is somehow less threatening and their behavior more acceptable if they can be seen as acting not selfishly, but rather for their sons.[81] Whereas acting on behalf of their sons may reflect the actual behavior of women in traditional polygamous households, where a woman's only hope of bettering her lot is to secure a strong position for her son(s),[82] as a narrative strategy it also reinforces the patriarchal ideal of the self-sacrificing mother. In a society where curses bear serious weight,[83] Rebekah's 'upon me be the curse, my son' shows just how much the narrator expects a mother to risk for her son.

### The Mother's Voice

We saw in Chapter 1 a dramatic illustration of the manner in which women characters in androcentric texts are made to

80. Jacob prefers Joseph over his older brothers, but Joseph is his first-born son by his favorite wife. And, of course, the preference creates problems for both father and son.
81. See Fuchs (1985a: 132-34).
82. Lamphere (1974: 100, 105-108).
83. Like the vow, discussed above in Chapter 1, the curse has power insofar as it constitutes the *act* of cursing and in that it invokes the power of the deity; see Thiselton (1974: 293-96).

speak and act against their own interests. As part of our investigation of the mother's place, we could examine all the speeches of the matriarchs to see to what extent and in what ways they speak against themselves. Such an investigation, however, would be repetitious since we have already looked at many of their speeches in other contexts. I propose rather to focus here on a few utterances of the matriarchs and to read them in a deconstructive vein, as places where, in spite of themselves, the narrators let the truth of women's experience of subjugation slip through. The women's experience is, of course, displaced and distorted as a result of the textual ideology that assumes and is uncritical of patriarchy. As characters created by androcentric narrators, the matriarchs share in an androcentric world-view. Thus they cannot name the source of their oppression as the patriarchal system itself and their responses to patriarchal domination are displaced. However subdued their protest may now appear in the text, each of the matriarchs at some point says something particularly revealing of the evil effects patriarchal constraints have on women. In these submerged strains of women's voices we can uncover evidence of patriarchy's uneasiness and guilt with regard to its treatment of women.

When Sarah's plan to have children through Hagar backfires, her angry words to Abraham, 'May the wrong to me be upon you!' or 'The wrong done to me is your fault!' (16.5),[84] provide an indictment of a system that encourages competition among women and values women in terms of the offspring they produce. Rachel's frustration is similarly represented in her complaint to Jacob, 'Give me children or I am as dead'. In these instances, the women's dissatisfaction with their lot receives recognition, but the real source of the problem—the patriarchal system itself—remains unacknowledged, and the matriarchs can only vent their anger at the patriarchs rather than at the true cause of their distress.

In the mouths of both Leah and Rachel, who are portrayed as fiercely competitive for the honor of bearing children to Jacob, we find speeches that belie the patriarchal ideal of

84. See the discussion of this verse by Westermann (1985: 241).

motherhood as bringing fulfillment and satisfaction in life. In contrast to Sarah's and Rachel's displaced anger at their husbands, Leah's anger has no object, and anger without an object becomes despair and hopelessness. For Leah, the way open to women of improving their position—bearing children—is her only means of fulfillment, and though she is quite successful at it, she remains unhappy with her lot. Initially she believes that by bearing Jacob's firstborn son, she will gain his affection: 'Surely now my husband will love me' (29.32). But by the time she bears her sixth and last son, she seems to have abandoned her hope of winning Jacob's love in favor of the more modest goal of earning his respect: 'Now at last my husband will honor me because I have borne him six sons' (30.20).[85] As for her sister Rachel, the woman who exclaimed, 'Give me children or I am as dead', dies in childbirth. The androcentric narrator speaks through the midwife to console her, disregarding her intense pain and anguish and affirming the patriarchal valuation of children:[86] 'Do not be afraid, for now you have another son'. Rachel's point of view, reflected in the name she gives her son, Ben-oni ('son of my sorrow'), is overwritten (overridden) by her husband, who changes the name to Benjamin ('son of the right hand' or 'son of the south'). But it is not erased; a trace of the woman's voice remains. In the name, 'son of my sorrow', we hear the woman's regret. Her complaint draws attention to the risk childbearing presented to women, who had little choice in the matter.

In Rebekah's memorable words, 'upon me be the curse, my son', we find a powerful testimony to the desperation that results from lack of authority. As Fuchs observes, 'Had Rebekah been able to express her love for Jacob through maternal blessings, she would not have needed to use deception. She would have in all probability blessed Jacob by herself.'[87] As it is, Rebekah must play one man off against another: she must both circumvent her husband and

85. See Exum (1985: 79).
86. Fuchs (1985a: 132).
87. Fuchs (1985b: 138).

4. The (M)other's Place 143

manipulate her son if she is to accomplish her plan. If, to convince her son to cooperate, she must risk bringing down a curse upon herself, so be it. And is dying (disappearing from the narrative) without seeing her beloved son again not a kind of curse?

. In giving us some access to women's anger, frustration, and despair at their place in patriarchal society, these few utterances condemn patriarchy's subjugation and oppression of women. Even though patriarchy may claim the last word, they stand as traces of women's resistance. Ridicule can also be a form of resistance, as when Leah informs Jacob, 'I have hired you with my son's mandrakes' (30.16). When women cooperate in spite of patriarchal pressures, as Rachel and Leah do in negotiating the exchange of Jacob's sexual services for the mandrakes, they gain strength. Only once in the entire patriarchal story, are women allowed to engage in conversation, and the result is surprising. This moment of cooperation between Rachel and Leah makes the patriarch the butt of a woman's joke. Sarah's laughter is another case of ridicule, but here the woman is humiliated. In forcing her to deny her laughter the narrator forces her to deny her knowledge about her body.

In the previous chapters, we observed that patriarchy affirms motherhood but denies the mother's sexual pleasure. Interestingly, however, in Gen. 18.12, the biblical narrator indirectly acknowledges female pleasure in Sarah's words to herself, 'Now that I am dried up, shall I have pleasure?— and my husband is old!' If, by this remark, the narrator means to deny that an old woman could be sexually aroused, he thereby recognizes the fact of female sexual pleasure. The slip has serious repercussions, for acknowledging that women experience sexual pleasure raises the issue of men's ability to satisfy women sexually, a fundamental source of male anxiety. In this case, Sarah's words suggest some doubt about Abraham's ability to please her; after all, he *is* old. As if the androcentric narrator senses the problem, he takes it all back, by having the deity paraphrase Sarah's comment in non-threatening, patriarchally acceptable terms.

Sarah's speech can be understood as having solely to do with sex and nothing to do with the announced conception. The verb she applies to herself, *balah*, can mean 'worn out' (as of old clothes, Deut. 8.4; Josh. 9.13) or 'dried up' (as of bones, Ps. 32.3).[88] If we allow for the possibility that here it refers to the vaginal dryness that results from menopause, then Sarah's question deals with whether or not intercourse could be pleasurable for her. But the primary question comes last, as the punch line: will intercourse be possible at all, given her old husband's questionable ability to maintain an erection? Whereas Sarah soliloquizes about sex, when Yhwh repeats what Sarah has said in order to challenge her, his version of her speech is about reproduction. And significantly, it questions only the *woman's* ability to have a child: 'Shall I really bear a child now that I am old?' (v. 13). On behalf of patriarchy, God interprets the mention of pleasure as a reference to giving birth. In addition, any doubt that may have been cast on Abraham's virility is removed by compressing two parts of Sarah's comment into one. 'I am old' does double duty, replacing 'I am dried up' and 'my husband is old'.[89] This substitution eliminates any sexual overtones and shifts the issue from the man's advanced age to the woman's, whose age represents, in this version, not an impediment to performance, but only Sarah's inability to have a child. Thus by the time the androcentric narrator has finished revising the woman's speech, there is no reference to sexual pleasure, no hint of male inability to satisfy a

---

88. See Westermann (1985: 281).

89. Most English translations (e.g. RSV, NRSV, JB) reinforce the androcentric reading by (1) rendering *balah* as a reference to Sarah's age, and (2) reversing the word order in Sarah's original speech: 'After I have grown old, and my husband is old, shall I have pleasure?' (18.12 RSV, NRSV). In these translations it is no longer apparent that 'I am old' in v. 13 is a replacement for 'my husband is old' in v. 12. In the Hebrew, however, Sarah's speech ends with, 'my husband is old', and Yhwh's version of it with, 'I am old'. The Jewish Publication Society version best captures the original: 'Now that I am withered, am I to have enjoyment—with my husband so old?' (v. 12); 'Shall I in truth bear a child, old as I am?' (v. 13). The balance between the clauses calls attention to the substitution that has taken place.

woman, and no question of Abraham's age as an obstacle. All that remains in the new version is doubt on the part of the matriarch about her ability to conceive.

Sarah is rebuked by Yhwh, but not directly at first: God asks Abraham why Sarah laughed and why she said what she said (in its revised version). When Sarah responds in self-defense, she is put in her place by the narrator, who portrays her as afraid, and, moreover, has her lie to God: 'I did not laugh'. And, of course, he cannot let her have the last word: 'No, but you did laugh'. The deity's final word is a displacement. His rebuke seizes on Sarah's laughter as the reason for reproaching her, and not on the content of her remark, with its potential for exposing male insecurity about female sexuality.

### Unity and Difference

I began this chapter by observing that the book of Genesis deals with the issue of Israel's identity: who qualifies to be a member of Israel and who does not. Connected to this issue is the question of Israel's relationship to its neighbors, to the larger world outside Israel. The biblical tradition describes Israel's relation to its neighbors in terms of complex family relationships. How is it that Israel alone receives the special promises of God, while its relatives—the Ishmaelites, the Edomites, the Ammonites, the Moabites, the Midianites, the Arameans—are excluded? Abraham is the father of Israel, Ishmael, the Midianites and other Arab tribes of the east (Gen. 25.1-6), and Edom is his direct descendant through Isaac. The father is a source of unity; in him various peoples have a common ancestry. At the same time, he can have only one true heir. Enter the matriarch.

The mother, the other, is the source of difference. Disunity is located in divisions among women. The (m)other's place in Genesis is to differentiate Israel from (some of) the surrounding peoples. The polygamous family, with its squabbles among co-wives and its divisions based on conflicts of interest, is a microcosm of Israel's view of itself in its environment. In these stories, issues of national (male) conflict

and dominance are resolved through the women, who are
seen as the source of the discord and division. Females
become the locus of conflict, when, in reality, male rivalry
constructs stories in which women are assigned the role of
disrupting familial integrity: Ishmael's exclusion is due to
Sarah; Edom's to Rebekah.

The matriarchs provide internal as well as external distinctions. In addition to differentiating Israel from its neighbors, the matriarchs determine Israel's internal diversity.
The ranking among the tribes, a hierarchy among equals, is
based on the status of their mothers and corresponds to the
patriarch's preferences.[90] The order in which Jacob arranges
his wives and children when he goes to meet Esau reveals
their relative standing: first come the maids and their children, then Leah and hers, and finally Rachel and Joseph.
Tribal rivalry, says the text, like the rivalry among nations,
has its roots in maternal rivalry. But it is different. Where the
mothers undermine their husband's authority, disunity
results. Sarah and Rebekah use their power to ensure the
future of the 'proper'/favorite son and to exclude the rival
son. When, however, the father's preferences influence the
ranking of the sons, as in Jacob's case, other sons are not
excluded. Tribal unity prevails, for Israel is one despite its
subdivision into twelve parts. The father, who is one, stands
for unity; the mother, for difference, which is multiple—thus
four mothers.

A kind of primal unity is associated with the father, and
its enduring appeal despite centrifugal forces is illustrated
by the display of unity on the part of their sons at the patriarchs' deaths. The unity of the father is the unity of peoples
and the unity of the tribes. To resolve issues of difference
and differentiation, Israel relies upon its mothers. The ideal
of unity co-exists with the necessity of differentiation. Israel
cannot be defined solely in terms of itself. It needs the other,
the mother, to help it define its position in the world, as dis-

90. It is not necessary for us to be able to resolve the nature of tribal
relations reflected here (see Gottwald 1979) to appreciate the fact that
the status of the mothers is used to indicate the status of the tribes (see
Wilson 1977: 184-88).

tinct from other peoples, and to clarify its identity, as an association of tribes distinct from one another.[91] Difference thus has positive meaning, and the matriarchs, as the origin of difference, play an indispensable role. Their importance cannot be underestimated, but it cannot be fully acknowledged by a text in which the significant figures are the fathers. Precisely because the matriarchs are so important for establishing Israel's separateness and identity as a people, the (m)other's place in these stories of origins must be undermined. Otherwise patriarchal hegemony over women based on the opposition between self and other would be challenged, and patriarchy would have to acknowledge the value of multiplicity and difference.

---

91. For development of this argument, see Andriolo (1973); Oden (1983: 196).

# Chapter 5

## WHO'S AFRAID OF 'THE ENDANGERED ANCESTRESS'?

> Who's afraid of the big bad wolf, the big bad wolf, the big bad wolf?
>
> The three little pigs

> Let's take a look: we shall find illumination in what at first seems to obscure matters ...
>
> Jacques Lacan

### A Thrice-told Tale

Three times in Genesis the patriarch, the eponymous ancestor of Israel, travels to a foreign country, where he passes his beautiful wife off as his sister because he fears the locals will kill him on her account if they know he is her husband. Abraham and Sarah are the ancestral couple in the primal scene (Gen. 12, where their names are Abram and Sarai) and in the first repetition (Gen. 20, by which time their names have been changed to Abraham and Sarah). Sarah is taken to be the wife of the foreign ruler (the pharaoh of Egypt in Gen. 12, and Abimelech of Gerar in Gen. 20) and then returned to Abraham when the ruler learns of the ruse. The third version (Gen. 26) concerns Isaac and Rebekah; the foreign ruler is again Abimelech of Gerar; and the matriarch is *not* taken. In all three cases, the patriarch prospers, the foreign ruler is (understandably) upset, and the matriarch has no voice in the affair.

It is generally agreed that the tales are variants on the same theme. The characters change and details vary, but the fabula remains the same. Within biblical scholarship, this thrice-told tale is often referred to as 'the Endangered

Ancestress' or 'the Ancestress of Israel in Danger'.[1] The widespread use of this label raises the question, What kind of danger do scholars think the matriarch is in? If, as is generally accepted, these stories represent in some way a threat to the threefold promise to Abraham of land, descendants, and blessing, then the threat is to the promise, and it follows that the patriarch, not the matriarch, is in danger. The promise, after all, was made to him—not to her or to the two of them (see Gen. 12.1-3)—and without his wife how can he have descendants?

Or is the danger faced by the matriarch the loss of honor? This could be said to be an issue in Genesis 20, where the narrative is at pains to assure us that nothing of a sexual nature took place between Abimelech and Sarah. Here the omniscient narrator tells the audience:

> Now Abimelech had not approached her (Gen. 20.4).

He then gives the statement divine authority by placing it in the mouth of God, who speaks to Abimelech in a dream:

> Therefore I did not let you touch her (Gen. 20.6).

Finally, by having Abimelech publicly justify Sarah's reputation, he ensures that all the characters in the story share in this knowledge.

> To Sarah he said, 'Look, I have given a thousand pieces of silver to your brother; it is your vindication in the eyes of all who are with you; and before everyone you are righted'[2] (Gen. 20.16).

It is not so clear that nothing of a sexual nature happened in the primal scene, Genesis 12, where we hear that 'the woman was taken into the pharaoh's house' (v. 15) and the pharaoh says, 'I took her for my wife' (v. 19). Interestingly, what did or did not happen to Sarah in the royal harem receives more attention from scholars than it does from

---

1. E.g. Keller (1954); von Rad (1961: 162-65, 221-25, 266); Koch (1969: 111-32); Polzin (1975); Westermann (1985: 159); Coats (1983: 109, 149, 188); Biddle (1990).
2. Following the RSV. The translation of the obscure Hebrew is problematic, but this seems to be the sense; see Westermann (1985: 328); von Rad (1961: 224); Skinner (1910: 319).

Abraham. Bernhard Anderson, in his annotations to the Revised Standard Version, would apparently have us believe that the story is less explicit and shocking than it actually is, for he explains that Sarah 'was *almost* taken into Pharaoh's harem' (italics mine). (Does this mean she got only to the door?) Koch, Polzin, Miscall, and Coats, in contrast, assume that Sarah did have sexual relations with the pharaoh.[3] Koch's judgment, incidentally, is as ethnocentric as it is androcentric: 'There is one feature of the story missing which would be natural to us: there is no reluctance to surrender the woman's honour'. To support his conclusion that the earliest form of the story did have Sarah committing adultery, Koch appeals to what he believes other women would do: '... it seems obvious that the Bedouin women are so devoted to their menfolk that to protect a husband's life they would willingly lose their honour'.[4]

What is this honor anyway but a male construct based on the double standard, with its insistence on the exclusive sexual rights to the woman by one man? The scene in Genesis 16, where the situation is reversed, is comparable and illuminating. Genesis 12 and Genesis 16 raise the issue of the matriarch or the patriarch having sexual relations with someone else. In Genesis 12, Abraham tells Sarah to let herself be taken by another man 'in order that it will go well with me because of you and I may live on your account' (v. 13). In Gen. 16.2, Sarah tells Abraham to have sexual intercourse with Hagar ('go in to my maid') so that she may obtain a child through Hagar. Neither Abraham nor Sarah is concerned with what this intimate encounter might mean for the other parties involved, but only with what he or she stands to gain. In Genesis 16, we are told specifically that Abraham had sexual intercourse with Hagar ('he went in to Hagar and she conceived', v. 4), but such specific detail is omitted from Genesis 12 (we shall return to this point

---

3. Koch (1969: 125); Polzin (1975: 83); Miscall (1983: 35); Coats (1983: 111).
4. Koch (1969: 127); cf. Abou-Zeid (1966: 253-54, 256-57). For discussion of honor and its relationship to the politics of sex, see Pitt-Rivers (1977: esp. 113-70).

below). Significantly, no one speaks of Abraham's loss of honor in Genesis 16, nor is there much concern for Hagar's honor—an indication that 'honor' is not only a male construct but also a class construct. Abraham, who as a man is not required to be monogamous, cannot be dishonored by having sex with Hagar at Sarah's urging. Neither can Hagar be dishonored, since a slave has no honor to lose.

It is not the woman's honor so much as the husband's property rights that are at stake. Still, we might expect the patriarch to show some concern for his wife's well-being. It is thus curious that in all three cases the patriarch does not consider that the matriarch might be in danger. On the contrary, he thinks *he* is in danger:[5]

> I know that you are a beautiful woman. When the Egyptians see you, they will say, 'This is his wife'; and they will kill me and let you live (Gen. 12.11-12).

> It was because I thought, There is surely no fear of God in this place, and they will kill me because of my wife (Gen. 20.11).

> When the men of the place asked about his wife, he said, 'She is my sister', for he feared to say 'my wife', thinking, 'lest the men of the place kill me because of Rebekah, for she is beautiful' (Gen. 26.7).

Whether or not the patriarch's fear is justified—whether or not he really is in danger or whether his fear is simply displaced—is a question we shall explore. If the patriarch does not suppose that the matriarch is in danger, neither is there any evidence that the *matriarch* thinks she is in danger. In fact, we do not know what she thinks about *anything*, which is a very good indication that the story is not really about the matriarch at all. She neither acts nor speaks in any of the versions, though in the second version speech is indirectly attributed to her: Abimelech tells God that Sarah told him that Abraham was her brother (Gen. 20.5). If her only speech is one reported by another character in the narrative, the matriarch can hardly be said to become a narrative presence in any real sense. She is merely the object in a story about

---

5.   Clines (1990: 67-68).

male relations (and we shall inquire below how the two men respond in relation to the object). What, then, is the danger, and to whom? More important, why do we hear about it three times?

Most studies of Genesis 12, 20, and 26 are concerned with the relationship between the three stories: how are they alike and different, and how are the differences to be accounted for (which often means, how can the repetition be explained away)? Now what happens in Genesis 12, 20, and 26 is very disturbing. A man practically throws his wife into another man's harem in order to save his skin. Yet the questions one most often encounters about this text are generally along the lines of: What is the oldest form of this story?[6] Or, Are the three accounts oral or written variants?[7] Are Genesis 20 and 26 more ethical than Genesis 12?[8] The disturbing issues raised by the story are sometimes deplored[9] but then set aside in favor of disengaged discussion of the growth of the tradition, the relative dates of the versions, and such historical questions as whether or not the stories reflect customs of 2000 to 1500 BCE (the so-called patriarchal period), or whether a man could or should marry his half-sister (the controversial evidence of Nuzi).

A few scholars have inquired into the role of these stories in the context of the larger narrative.[10] A sustained contextual reading of the three stories is offered by David Clines,

6. See Van Seters (1975: 167-91); Koch (1969: 111-32); Noth (1972: 102-109); Westermann (1985: 161-62).

7. On the issue of literary dependency, see Van Seters (1975: 167-91); Westermann (1985: 161-62); cf. Alexander (1992). For an argument that the pentateuchal sources use the same (wife-sister) motif to develop different themes, see Petersen (1973). For discussions of the stories as oral variants, see Culley (1976: 33-41); and the more recent folkloristic approach of Niditch (1987: 23-66).

8. Most commentators agree with Koch (1969: 126), who thinks that 'moral sensitivity becomes gradually stronger'; Polzin (1975: 84) argues that Gen. 12 is as sensitive to ethical issues as are chs. 20 and 26.

9. Von Rad (1961: 162) calls Gen. 12 'offensive', and speaks of the 'betrayed matriarch' (p. 164); see also Vawter (1977: 181).

10. Clines (1990: 67-84); Fox (1989); Rosenberg (1986: 70-98); Steinberg (1984); to a lesser degree, Polzin (1975); Miscall (1983: 11-46).

who concludes that the patriarch is more of a danger to foreigners than they are to him.[11] But reading the three tales in their context also exposes problems. For example, in Genesis 20 Sarah would be over ninety years old, and we might wonder why Abraham thinks other men would take such an interest in her. Moreover, Abraham has now been told by God that Sarah will be the mother of his heir, which makes it even harder to understand why he would let another man take her (it may even be the case that Sarah is already pregnant with Isaac).[12] In Genesis 25, Esau and Jacob are born to Isaac and Rebekah, and by the end of the chapter they are already hunting and stealing birthrights respectively. Thus in Genesis 26, when Isaac says of Rebekah, 'She is my sister', we might wonder, what has become of the twins? These are only some of the difficulties a contextual reading must engage. I mention them not because I intend to offer a contextual reading here, but rather to underscore how puzzling and uncanny the tale is both in context and in isolation. We encounter one set of problems when the three versions are read in their larger context and other problems when they are considered in their own right. In fact, one might say that this tale in its three forms calls attention to itself by virtue of the surplus of problems it poses to interpretation. I propose that a different kind of approach to the repeated tale in Genesis 12, 20, and 26 could provide new insights into some recurrent difficulties. Specifically I want to offer a psychoanalytical alternative to previous, largely form and tradition-historical, approaches.

By proposing a psychoanalytic-literary reading as an alternative, I am not claiming that this approach will 'solve' the problems posed by these chapters whereas other approaches do not. On the contrary, I maintain that posing questions and opening up new dimensions of a text are as fruitful an enterprise as the traditional critical approach of seeking answers as if answers were objectively verifiable. Like psychoanalysis, psychoanalytical criticism is neither extern-

---

11. Clines (1990: 67-84).
12. So Vawter (1977: 245); Miscall (1983: 32); Clines (1990: 75-76).

ally verifiable nor falsifiable. We can only follow it, as Freud says about analysis, to see where it will lead,[13] and, in the process, hope to illuminate a hitherto uncharted textual level, the narrative unconscious. My approach appeals to the multiple levels on which stories function; like dreams, they are overdetermined. As Freud points out in comparing texts to dreams, which, he argues, require over-interpretation in order to be fully understood, 'All genuinely creative writings are the product of more than a single motive and more than a single impulse in the poet's mind, and are open to more than a single interpretation'.[14]

To anticipate my argument: a psychoanalytic-literary approach takes as its point of departure the assumption that the story in Genesis 12, 20, and 26 encodes unthinkable and unacknowledged sexual fantasies. Because there is something fearful and attractive to the (male) narrator about the idea of the wife being taken by another man, a situation that invites the woman's seizure is repeated three times. The tale would thus appear to illustrate Freud's *Wiederholungszwang*, the repetition compulsion—the impulse to work over an experience in the mind until one becomes the master of it— whose locus, according to Freud, is the unconscious repressed.[15] The text is a symptom of the narrator's intrapsychic conflict. But whereas the repetition compulsion is neurotic and an obstacle to awareness, telling the story of the patriarch's repetitive behavior offers the occasion for a 'working out' of the neurosis.

> Repetition is both an obstacle to analysis—since the analysand must eventually be led to renunciation of the attempt to reproduce the past—and the principal dynamic of the cure, since only by way of its symbolic enactment in the present can

13. Freud (1961: 4).
14. Freud (1965: 299). I see little difference in my suggesting below that Abraham behaves as he does because of fear and desire that his wife gain sexual knowledge of another man and, say, Westermann's contention (1985: 164) that Abraham behaves this way because of insufficient trust in the divine promises. For insightful remarks about the way traditional scholarship disguises its subjectivity, see Miscall (1983: 40-42).
15. Freud (1961: 16-25 *passim*.)

the history of past desire, its objects and scenarios of fulfillment, be made known, become manifest in the present discourse.[16]

Repeating the story, working over the conflict until it is resolved, provides a semiotic cure for the neurosis. By the charmed third time the cure is effected; that is to say, it is believed.

In approaching the text from a psychoanalytic-literary perspective, I am not proposing to psychoanalyze the characters. Rather than treat characters in a story as if they were real people with real neuroses, I want to examine the world view these literary creations represent. Taking a cue from psychoanalytical theory and building upon the similarities between interpreting dreams and interpreting texts, I shall consider all the characters in the text as split-off parts of the narrator. When a dream is analyzed in psychoanalysis, the analysand is brought to recognize aspects of herself or himself in the various characters of the dream. In our thrice-told tale we will consider the characters in the story as aspects of the narrative consciousness. Thus not just the female characters but the male characters also are expressions of male fantasies, anxieties, etc. When I say, 'Abraham fears for his life', I refer to Abraham not as if he were a real human being but rather as a vehicle for the androcentric values and the androcentric world view of the biblical narrative. It bears pointing out that I am not proposing to psychoanalyze the author either, in the sense that the author, any more than Abraham, is a real person. I assume, with most biblical scholars, that these ancient texts are a communal product, and, further, I assume they received their final redaction at the hands of men. The narrative thus does not reflect an individual's unconscious fantasies, but, rather, we might say it owes its creation to a kind of collective androcentric unconscious, whose spokesperson I shall call simply 'the narrator'.

16. Brooks (1987: 10).

*Features Obscure and Obscuring*

In a recent study of the Abraham traditions, Joel Rosenberg remarks that 'the "wife-sister" motif, considered as an item of history and tradition, is an obscure and suggestive theme whose full meaning will probably continue to elude us'.[17] As my epigraph from Lacan indicates, I want to look for illumination in what at first glance seems to obscure matters.[18] The tales exhibit many puzzling features. Why, for example, does the patriarch fear that he will be killed for his wife? Why doesn't he consider the possibility that she might simply be taken from him? He could be overpowered and robbed of his wife, or sent away without her, or an attempt could be made to buy him off. He assumes, however, a moral code according to which the foreign men in question will *not* commit adultery but they *will* commit murder. And when he says, in Gen. 12.12 and 20.11, '*they* will kill me', does he imagine that they would all attack him at once (and if so, who would get the woman)? Or, by assuming many men will want his wife, is he simply accepting in advance that there is nothing he can do to save both his wife and his life? He is not concerned about what might happen to his wife in another man's harem, and clearly not interested in protecting her. In fact, by claiming that the beautiful woman is his (unmarried) sister, the patriarch guarantees that his wife *will* be taken.

Having taken the woman (in Gen. 12 and 20), the foreign ruler, upon learning that she is Abraham's wife, gives her back to her husband. He does not kill Abraham, as Abraham had feared, even though now he has good reason, since Abraham's lie about Sarah's status has both placed him in an unacceptable position and brought trouble upon his land (plagues in Gen. 12 and barrenness in Gen. 20). In Genesis 26, Abimelech is incensed at what *might have happened* and takes measures to ensure that it will not happen in the future. What the patriarch seems to fear, and says explicitly

17.  Rosenberg (1986: 77).
18.  Lacan (1988: 41).

that he fears in Gen. 20.11—lack of morality ('there is surely no fear of God in this place')—is proved by events to be not the case. Moreover, he already attributes a certain morality to the foreign men when he assumes they will kill him rather than commit adultery with a married woman. The crucial question is, Why does the patriarch—twice as Abraham and once as Isaac—repeat his mistakes? Why does he need to set things up so that another man will seize his wife not once, but three times? To answer that the threefold repetition is the result of three different pentateuchal sources or of three variants in the oral tradition behind the text is to beg the question.[19] As recent literary criticism of the Bible recognizes, the final form of the text is not a haphazard product but rather the result of complex and meaningful redactional patterning. If the androcentric tradition keeps repeating this story, we can assume that the story fills some need.

### *The Repetition Compulsion*

We begin with what is apparent. The story is about fear and desire: desire of the beautiful woman and fear of death because of her. In all three versions the patriarch considers his wife desirable to other men, and in the first two, he is right: the woman is desired, as is witnessed by the fact that she is taken as a wife by another man. In all three instances, the matriarch's desirability makes the patriarch afraid for his life, though his fear turns out to be unjustified. In assessing the patriarch's behavior in response to the perceived threat, Clines remarks that 'the danger is all in the patriarch's mind to begin with'.[20] This being the case, a psychoanalytical approach should prove especially useful. But it is not just what might or might not be going on in the patriarch's mind that will concern us. As I have indicated, all the characters in

19. Indeed, one of the early arguments of source criticism for multiple authorship of the Pentateuch was the fact that the patriarch, and his son after him, would hardly have been so foolish as to repeat the ruse three times.
20. Clines (1990: 68).

this repeated story are vehicles for the narrative neurosis. Each of the stories, the primal scene and its repetitions, is preoccupied with the *same unconscious fantasy*: that the wife have sex with another man. Psychoanalysis tells us that this must be the unconscious desire because this is precisely what the patriarch sets up to happen. It is important to keep in mind that the desire is unconscious; what Freud says about Oedipus's desire is applicable here: in reality it would likely cause him to recoil in horror.[21] What is unconsciously desired is also unconsciously feared; as I hope to show, the story is repeated in an effort to envision and simultaneously to deny the possibility of such a sexual encounter taking place between the wife and another man. Psychoanalysis draws attention to the close relationship between desires and fears. Am I afraid of heights because unconsciously I desire to jump? Is homophobia in reality a fear of one's own repressed sexual urges? Fear in Genesis 12, 20, and 26 is conscious but displaced. The patriarch fears for his life, the assumption being that the foreign man will want the woman all to himself. Abraham is willing to let the other man have her, since the woman must belong to one man or the other but cannot be shared; she cannot belong to both. This is the familiar double standard, according to which men may have sexual relations with more than one woman, but a woman cannot have sexual knowledge of a man other than her husband. The remarkable thing about the patriarch's ruse is that it ensures that his wife *will* gain sexual knowledge of another man. Certainty is better, more controllable, than doubt.

Since we are dealing with a text, and not with an analysand who can contribute actively to the psychoanalytical process, we can only speculate about what lies behind the fear and desire. It could be the need to have the woman's erotic value confirmed by other men, what René Girard describes as the mechanism of triangular desire.[22] Having

---

21. Freud, Letter to Wilhelm Fliess of Oct. 15, 1897, cited by Felman (1983: 1022).
22. See Girard (1965: esp. 1-52).

chosen a particular woman as the object of his desire, the man needs other men's desire to validate his choice, and even to increase his desire. Or, losing the woman to another man is desirable because he will be free of the woman and the responsibility she entails. This is the male fantasy of sex without commitment; he will be free to have other women, unhampered by the domesticity that the wife represents. There may be deeper, more distressing, desires as well. The same object (originally, according to much psychoanalytical theory, the mother's body) evokes both reverence and hostility. Thus the fascination with the notion of the woman being taken by another man may mask a fear and hatred of woman that desires her humiliation (it is beyond question that the story objectifies the woman). Other explanations might be sought in what Freud calls 'the mysterious masochistic trends of the ego'.[23] Losing the woman to another man is also threatening, because sexual knowledge of another man would provide the woman with experience for comparison. Other men might be 'better', or know some things about sex he does not know, and perhaps she will enjoy with them what she does not experience with him. This takes us back to the patriarch's displaced fear. His fear for his life at the hands of other men disguises the fact that it is really the woman's sexual knowledge that is life-threatening for him. It is 'safer' for him to fear other men than to acknowledge his fear of the woman's sexuality.

### Patriarchy's Talking Cure

The fabula in which the wife is, in effect, offered to the other man is repeated until the conflict revolving around the woman's feared and desired sexual knowledge has been resolved. By managing fear and desire within an ordered discourse, the narrative functions as a textual working-out of unconscious fantasies, a semiotic cure for the neurosis.

Let us consider first the fundamental similarities between

23. Freud (1961: 12). We might also keep in mind that the repetition complex is related to the desire for death and the delaying of it, which is reflected in the patriarch's fear of death because of the woman.

the three tales. All three raise the possibility that the matriarch will have sex with a man other than her husband. The patriarch is not only willing for his wife to commit adultery; he invites it. The foreign ruler, on the other hand, will not willingly commit adultery. The patriarch might thus be viewed as a cipher for the unconscious desire, the foreign ruler as the embodiment of fear, and the story as the locus of the tension. The *difference* in the three tales is significant for resolving the conflict. In the first, Sarah is taken into the royal harem, and restored when the pharaoh learns that she is already another man's wife. But did she have sexual relations with the pharaoh? We cannot be sure, for this version of the story does not satisfactorily resolve the issue. It must, therefore, be repeated. The second time around, matters are different. In Genesis 20, Sarah is again taken, but Abimelech does not lay a hand on her. It is no doubt reassuring that what is unconsciously desired and feared does not take place, but the situation remains potentially threatening as long as the woman is allowed to enter another man's household. In the third version, Genesis 26, the possibility of what is both desired and feared taking place is ruled out from the start: Rebekah is not even taken into Abimelech's house.

In the working out of the neurosis, the realization of the fantasy is precluded. To describe this process as it is actualized in the narrative, I shall borrow some terms from Freud, without applying them in a strictly Freudian sense.[24] Instead I shall use a fundamental Freudian concept as a metaphor in order to clarify the contradictory impulses in the text. The foreign ruler, who expresses moral outrage at the deception Abraham has perpetrated, is a kind of super-ego, an enforcing, prohibiting agency, to Abraham's id, unconscious desire ready to give over the woman. In other words, the positions occupied in Freudian theory by the super-ego and the id, i.e.

24. I am offering neither a Freudian reading nor suggesting the superiority, or even validity, of Freudian analysis (in recent years there have been numerous important feminist critiques of Freudian theory). For basic distinctions between the ego, the id, and the super-ego, see Freud (1960); Freud used these terms differently and sometimes indiscriminately, and he changed his usage over time.

the self-observing, self-critical agency in the ego and the libidinous unconscious desire, are fantasized as characters in the story. The text is metaphorically in the position of the ego, where these contradictory impulses are finally resolved. In the first version, the pharaoh is upset, but his response does not crystallize the moral issue; the super-ego is not yet highly developed.

> What is this you have done to me? Why did you not tell me that she was your wife? Why did you say, 'She is my sister', so that I took her for my wife? (Gen. 12.18-19).

In the second version, in contrast, we find a virtual obsession with issues of sin and guilt, all signs of a highly active conscience. The pharaoh's 'What is this you have done to me?' becomes Abimelech's

> What have you done to us? How have I *sinned* against you that you have brought on me and my kingdom a great *sin*? *Deeds that are not done* you have done to me (Gen. 20.9).

This super-ego, however, needs external moral support, and thus the narrative begins with a lengthy dialogue between Abimelech and God in a dream.[25] God, as symbol and overseer of the moral order, passes judgment: 'You are a dead man because of the woman you have taken; she is another man's wife' (v. 3). With continued emphasis on the issue of innocence versus guilt, Abimelech protests his innocence before the law, appealing to his ignorance of Sarah's status:

> Lord, would you slay a *righteous* people? Did he himself not say to me, 'She is my sister'? And she herself said, 'He is my brother'. In the *integrity* of my intentions and the *innocence* of my hands I have done this.

Abimelech is 'innocent' because God, the moral law, pre-

---

25. On the legal character of the dialogue, see Westermann (1985: 322-23). Interestingly, the locus for dealing with the conflict here is a dream. Freud saw dreams as fulfillments of unconscious wishes. Even anxiety dreams and punishment dreams, such as this one, perform this function, 'for they merely replace the forbidden wish-fulfillment by the appropriate punishment for it; that is to say, they fulfill the wish of the sense of guilt which is the reaction to the repudiated impulse' (Freud 1961: 37).

vented him from 'sinning': 'It was I who kept you from sinning against me; therefore I did not let you touch her' (v. 6). Fear of punishment provides powerful motivation for adherence to the law: 'If you do not return her, know that you shall surely die, you and all that is yours' (v. 7). This ethical rationalization is carried through on every level of the narrative in Genesis 20. Just as Abimelech (in the position of super-ego) justifies himself to God (external moral law), so also Abraham (in the position of the id, the unconscious desire) justifies his deceit to Abimelech (super-ego):

> It was because I thought, There is surely no fear of God in this place, and they will kill me because of my wife. Besides she is indeed my sister, the daughter of my father but not the daughter of my mother; so she could be my wife.

Subtly he tries to shift the blame by implicating God:

> When God caused me to wander from my father's house, I said to her, 'This is the kindness you must do me: at every place to which we come, say of me, "He is my brother"'.

Abraham's protestations of innocence are like psychoanalytical negations: if he were innocent he would not need to protest so much. He undermines his defense—that he feared the lack of morality 'in this place'—by adding that he told Sarah to claim he was her brother 'at every place to which we come', indicating compulsive behavior and not a single aberration. This 'Freudian slip' is a sign of a guilty conscience, the need to be caught in the lie—and commentators have caught him.[26] The libido still feels the need to be held in check against its own powerful impulses.

By the third time (Gen. 26), the super-ego functions independently of external restraints; it rejects the very notion of the woman having sex with another man. The moral issue is generalized. 'One of the people', not the Self who no longer feels threatened, 'might have lain with your wife'—but nothing happens. We are informed in v. 7 that

26. E.g. Miscall (1983: 15); Westermann (1985: 326); Coats (1983: 150).

the men of Gerar asked Isaac about Rebekah, so we know they have noticed her. We are also told (v. 8) that Isaac and Rebekah were in Gerar for a long period of time, so we also know they are not interested. The fascination with the fantasy has been abandoned. As on the previous occasions, the id is held accountable to the super-ego, but it is no longer viewed as threatening: 'You'—the fascination with the woman's desired and feared sexual knowledge—'would have brought guilt upon us', Abimelech tells Isaac (v. 10), but (so the implication) I—the admonitory, judgmental agency in the ego—prevented it. In this version, the super-ego does not need God, the external source of morality, to tell it what to do. It makes its own law: 'Whoever touches[27] this man or his wife shall be put to death' (*mot yumat*). In the Bible, this kind of apodictic formulation appears in the legal material. In psychoanalysis, the ability to internalize moral standards is a sign of maturity.

It can hardly be fortuitous that once the story ceases to entertain the fantasy of another man having the woman, the patriarch is pictured enjoying the woman sexually, and the other man witnesses it. Abimelech looks out his window and sees Isaac 'fondling' (NRSV) or 'caressing' (Westermann) Rebekah. Whatever the precise meaning of the verb *metsaheq*, a pun on Isaac's name, it has to refer to some form of sexual intimacy, since, on the basis of this activity, Abimelech recognizes that Isaac and Rebekah must be man and wife. In this final version of the tale, the fantasy of the woman's having sex with another man is rejected in favor of the (also fantasized) assurance that her sexuality belongs exclusively to the patriarch.

And what of the other man's watching? According to Girard's theory of triangular desire, the relation between the rivals in an erotic triangle is as important as their relation-

---

27. The verb *ng'* was used of approaching the woman sexually in 20.6. Here it has a double meaning, since it is also applied to the man in its more general sense of harming. The inclusion of 'this man' in the edict may be taken as a sign of acceptance of the dangerous impulses as no longer capable of jeopardizing the Self.

ship to the object of desire.[28] Using the Girardian triangle as
a model, I suggested above that the desiring subject (the
position occupied in our narratives by the patriarch) needs
the desire of other men to confirm the excellence of his sexual choice. The patriarch sees the matriarch as an object of
beauty, and thus an object of desire ('I know that you are a
beautiful woman', 12.11; cf. 26.7), but he needs to know that
other men desire her too; so he sets up a situation that will
elicit their desire: he presents her as an available woman.[29]
The prestige of his rival only serves to affirm that the
woman he has selected is worthy of desire.[30] The rival who
takes the matriarch has the ultimate social prestige—he is
the pharaoh or the king—and he has sexual prestige because
he has a harem; he can have any woman he likes, and one
assumes he chooses only the best. He is also willing to pay a
high price for the woman, either to possess her (12.16) or as
restitution (20.14, 16)—further testimony to her value.
Girard examines stories, like ours, where the hero appears to
offer the beloved wife to the rival, and concludes, 'He
pushes the loved woman into the mediator's arms in order
to arouse his desire and then triumph over the rival
desire'.[31] Having Abimelech, the rival, witness his sexual

28. Girard (1965) proposes that our desire for something does not
really come from ourselves, nor does it lie in some kind of intrinsic
worth in the object of our desire; rather it is based on looking at what
other people find desirable. Other people become our models,
'mediators of desire' in his theory, whose desire we copy. The positions in Girard's metaphorical triangle are: the desiring subject; the
mediator of desire, who defines the subject's desire for him or her; and
the object of the desire.
29. White (1991: 180-83) makes a similar point about the beautiful
woman as an object of desire in Gen. 12, but he evaluates Abraham's
desire differently, as different from and superior to that of his rivals.
30. Girard (1965: 50).
31. Girard (1965: 50). Girard also argues that 'the impulse toward
the object is ultimately an impulse toward the mediator' (p. 10) and
that the desiring subject wants to become his mediator/rival (p. 54).
The patriarch becomes like his wealthy, powerful rival when he
becomes wealthy at the foreign ruler's expense (12.16, 20; 20.14, 16; cf.
26.12-14, where the envy theme is continued), and when the ruler
recognizes him as more powerful—for example, as a prophet who can

activity with the matriarch is the patriarch's ultimate turn-on, his incontestable victory over rival desire. In this version of the fantasy, the roles are reversed. The patriarch is no longer in the position of the fearing/desiring subject; the other man is. Fear of the woman's knowledge of other men is transformed into other men's envy of him.

## Not a Woman's Story

I have argued that Genesis 12, 20, and 26 deal with an unacknowledged and unthinkable male fantasy. In the patriarch–matriarch–foreign ruler triangle, the matriarch never becomes a narrative presence. Though addressed by men—Abraham says, 'Say you are my sister' (12.13); Abimelech says, 'Look, I have given your brother a thousand pieces of silver; it is your vindication... ' (20.16)—the matriarch never speaks and only once is she reported to have spoken (20.5). The woman has no voice in determining her sexual status and no control over how her sexuality is perceived or used. Susan Niditch calls Sarah in Genesis 12 a 'tacit accomplice'.[32] Sharon Pace Jeansonne considers her less an accomplice than a silent object.[33] In my reading, she is both accomplice and object because she, like the other characters, is a creation of the narrative unconscious. The male fantasy that created her character is not interested in the woman's point of view—her reaction to Abraham's suggestion, her willingness to be exchanged for her husband's well-being, or her experience in the harem of a strange man. The question of force versus consent, crucial for constructing

pray for him, or simply as 'much mightier than we are' (26.16).
    32. Niditch (1987: 59).
    33. Jeansonne (1990: 17). Jeansonne maintains that Sarah's silence is not evidence of complicity but rather a sign of her powerlessness; similarly Rashkow (1992). This is quite literally an argument from silence, and it too easily leads us into the victim–victimizer dichotomy (discussed above in Chapter 1) that ignores women's complicity in patriarchy. On this point I agree with Niditch (1987: 59), but for a different reason: Sarah is an accomplice because her character is the creation of an androcentric narrator. Sarah is not, as White (1991: 185), would have it, an 'innocent victim', because she is complicit.

the woman's perspective, is not raised.[34]

The woman is only an object in a story about male fears and desires. The possibility of the wife's having sex with another man is taken out of the control of the woman and made solely an affair between men. This is the only way androcentric ideology can conceive of it, unless, as in the case of Potiphar's wife, the woman is a 'bad woman',[35] which, of course, the matriarch cannot be or else she would not qualify to be the matriarch. As it is posed in Genesis 12, 20, and 26, the question is not, Will the woman commit adultery, but, Will the other man commit adultery? The patriarch thinks not: he thinks the other man will kill him rather than commit adultery with a married woman. The foreign ruler also rejects the thought of adultery. The result is a kind of gentlemen's agreement about the other man's property, which reflects the biblical understanding of adultery as less a matter of sex than a violation of another man's property rights.[36] Legislating the husband's exclusive sexual rights to his wife is an effective way of controlling women's feared and desired sexuality. That the patriarch, the foreign ruler, and God all recognize the seriousness of adultery with a married woman is crucial to the ideology of all three versions (what the woman thinks is irrelevant).

### 'She Is Indeed My Sister'

Scholars generally deal with Abraham's claim that Sarah really is his half-sister in Gen. 20.12 by asking whether or not it is a lie. Clines and Miscall think Abraham is lying;[37] Westermann, von Rad, Speiser, and Skinner think he is

---

34. This is also the case with Hagar in Gen. 16; see above; see also Chapter 6 below.

35. See Bach (1993).

36. See Westbrook (1990). For an interpretation of Gen. 12 that sees the taboo against sex with a married woman exploited by Abraham to set up the pharaoh, see White (1991: 174-86). For an anthropological perspective, see Pitt-Rivers (1977: 159), who suggests the stories are about 'sexual hospitality', where women are used to establish relations among groups of men; see pp. 113-70.

37. Clines (1990: 76); Miscall (1983: 14-15).

telling the truth.[38] Some apologists call Abraham's claim that Sarah is his sister a 'white lie'.[39] Regardless of whether or not Sarah and Abraham are sister and brother, we know it is not true of Isaac and Rebekah. From a psychoanalytic-literary perspective, the important issue is not the veracity of Abraham's claim but the fact that in all three versions the brother–sister relationship is imagined. All three accounts raise the issue of consanguinity simply by having the patriarch tell the foreigners that the matriarch is his sister. Might we not see in this latent incest fantasy a desire to achieve unity with the other? In the Song of Songs, for example, the man uses the epithet 'sister, bride' to refer to the woman as sign of intimacy. Clearly the matriarch's kinship ties to the patriarch are important to these stories in Genesis 12–36; she must come from his own people, his own kind.[40] As a sibling, the matriarch is more 'self' than 'other'—more like the patriarch than different. Fantasizing her as his sister may represent a narcissistic striving toward completeness or wholeness, whose realization can only be imagined in his mirror-image from the opposite sex (she is what he would be if he were a woman). Oedipal desire, of which, according to Eve Kosofsky Sedgwick, the Girardian triangle is a schematization,[41] may be at work here as well. As his close female relative, the sister is a stand-in for the mother as object of desire (and Sarah is the arch-mother). In this case, Abraham will have married a girl as much like the girl who married dear ol' dad as possible. Fear of the father's wrath

38. Westermann (1985: 326); von Rad (1961: 222); Speiser (1964: 92); Skinner (1910: 318).

39. Anderson, annotations to the RSV; Fox (1989: 32).

40. For anthropological readings of the three accounts as representing a movement from incest to the preferred form of marriage, see Pitt-Rivers (1977: 154-55); Donaldson (1981). Pitt-Rivers offers a suggestive reading of these accounts in relation to the story of the rape of Dinah, Gen. 34; see 1985: 151-71.

41. Sedgwick (1985: 22). See her discussion (1985: 21-27), which, in contrast to Girard, takes gender into account as a constituent factor. Interestingly, Freud saw the repetition complex as going back to some period of infantile sexual life, to the Oedipus complex; see Freud (1961: 19).

may explain his willingness to give her back, symbolically, to the father—the subject position held in our tale by the powerful, foreign ruler–authority figure. In the end, his relationship to his mother-substitute is legitimized by the father. This is the significance of the fact that Abimelech *sees* Isaac and Rebekah engaged in sexual play: it represents the father's acknowledgment that this woman rightfully belongs to the 'son' and the father's permission for him to have sex with her.

### Who's Afraid of 'The Endangered Ancestress'?

We have looked at the thrice-told tale in Genesis 12, 20, and 26 as symptoms of the narrative's intra-psychic conflict, a conflict between the unconscious desire that the wife gain sexual knowledge of another man and the fear that this could happen. The conflict appears in disguised and distorted form: the patriarch fears for his life because of his beautiful wife, and passes her off as his sister, thereby allowing another man to take her into his harem. In reality, the fear is of the woman's sexuality, which is desired as well as feared. There is a compulsive need to repeat the story until the conflict is resolved. In Genesis 12, the super-ego (the pharaoh) is subject to the id (Abraham); he takes the woman. In Genesis 20, the super-ego (Abimelech) has external moral support (God). He is subject to the id (Abraham) in that he takes the woman, but subject to external law (God) in that he does not touch her. But morality based on external authority is not the best solution for the patriarchal neurosis. In the third version (Gen. 26), the moral code is internalized; the fascination with the woman's desired and feared sexuality no longer poses a threat; the neurosis is cured; the cure is believed.[42]

---

42. Later retellings of these stories continue the process of filling gaps, thereby resolving some of the anxiety-provoking ambiguities (for example, Did Abraham lie about Sarah's being his sister? What happened to Sarah in the harem? Did Abraham know what happened in the harem?) and some give Sarah a greater role (for example, Sarah prays for protection, and the ruler is afflicted 'because of the word of

In the children's refrain, 'Who's afraid of the big bad wolf, the big bad wolf, the big bad wolf?', we find a denial of fear that, as such, is also a recognition of fear. The thrice-told tale in Genesis 12, 20, and 26 functions similarly. It says, in effect, 'Who's afraid of the woman's sexual knowledge?' And it answers by reassuring the patriarch that there is no need to fear. But it betrays itself, for, like the ditty about the big bad wolf, it acknowledges that there is something to be feared. If the danger in these three stories is woman's sexuality and woman's sexual knowledge, who or what is in danger? To the question, 'Who or what is afraid of the woman's sexual knowledge?', the answer is, 'Patriarchy'.

Sarai' ['*al debar sarai*, Gen. 12.17]). On later versions of the tale in Jewish and Islamic sources, see Firestone (1991).

# Chapter 6

## RAPED BY THE PEN

In the last war we lost a lover.

A.B. Yehoshua, *The Lover*

Male domination of the female body is the basic material reality of women's lives; and all struggle for dignity and self-determination is rooted in the struggle for actual control of one's own body, especially control over physical access to one's own body.

Andrea Dworkin

Raped by the pen is not the same as raped by the penis. There is no sense in which the damage that can be done by a literary text is comparable to actual violence as experienced by women in the real world, to the trauma and pain inflicted on the body through an act of sexual aggression and hatred. This is obvious, but it needs to be stated, since in speaking of rape by the pen I am applying the language of bodily experience to literary representation.[1] In this chapter, I am not dealing with real violence against women, but rather with violence against women as it takes place in biblical narrative. I take this violence seriously, though I do not take it literally, for like pornography—though not so blatantly—these literary rapes perpetuate ways of looking at women that encourage objectification and violence. I want to consider certain features common to two very different kinds of textual rape: rape that is recounted in a narrative, and rape that takes place by means of a narrative (obviously, I am using the word 'rape' metaphorically in this instance). My primary interest in the comparison is to see how women are por-

---

1. On the complex relationship of embodiment and voice, pain and acts of imagining and creative work, see Scarry (1985).

trayed in texts where they are the object of sexual aggression and to inquire how women's bodies are focalized in these texts; that is, to investigate women as the object of male gaze.

The narrated rape is perhaps the most gruesome and violent tale in the Bible, the gang rape of the unnamed wife of an unnamed Levite by unnamed members of a mob of ruffians recounted in chapter 19 of the book of Judges. Against that horrible story, which some people are shocked to discover is in the Bible, I propose to juxtapose a well-known story of named rather than anonymous characters: the story of David and Bathsheba, which has long held a place in popular imagination both as a tale of unbridled lust and also, curiously, as a famous 'love story'. Bathsheba, the wife of Uriah, is 'sent for' by King David, who has sex with her in a moment of passion that unleashes a chain of disaster upon his house. It is not my intention to make David's exploitation of Bathsheba into a rape, though I will explore its potential for such an interpretation below. The rape of Bathsheba is something that takes place not so much in the story as by means of the story. When I refer to the 'rape of Bathsheba' in what follows, I use it as a metaphor to describe Bathsheba's treatment at the hands of the androcentric biblical narrator, whose violation of her character consists both in depriving her of voice and in portraying her in an ambiguous light that leaves her vulnerable, not simply to assault by characters in the story but also by later commentators on the story.

Throughout this study, I have taken the position that women in the biblical narrative are male constructs. I do not assume, therefore, that these stories report actual events. If there was a historical Bathsheba, I do not believe incidents from her life can be reconstructed from the story we have about her. And, because the violence against the woman in Judges 19 is so brutally excessive and offensive, I prefer to think that she is a literary creation. I do, however, take these stories to be realistic: they represent a society and its values. They show us a society's norms, and they show us how that society responds to the violation of those norms. Moreover, by presenting models of acceptable and unacceptable behav-

ior for men and women—by encoding messages to men and
women about sexual transgressions and sexual limits—they
shape and perpetuate gender roles and expectations. For this
reason, a feminist response to them is needed, particularly in
view of the enduring cultural influence they have exerted
because of their presence in the Bible. Let us consider, then,
ways in which these stories reflect androcentric ideas about
women and promote androcentric interests.

### The 'Rape' of Bathsheba

In what sense is Bathsheba raped? The account is remark-
ably brief:

> David sent messengers and took her. She came to him and he
> lay with her, while she was purifying herself from her unclean-
> ness. Then she returned to her house (2 Sam. 11.4).

The encounter takes place in a context of aggression and
violence—war with Ammon during which David stays at
home. Given the long-standing and integral association of
war with rape—to which the other text under discussion
here, Judges 21, bears witness—is the embeddedness of this
account in that of the Ammonite war a hint that force is used
here?[2] The text seems ambivalent on the matter. 'Sent' and
'took' indicate aggression on David's part; on the other
hand, the two verbs of which Bathsheba is the subject,
'came' and 'returned', are not what one would expect if
resistance were involved. The king sends for a subject and
she obeys. His position of power gives him an advantage: he

---

2. The association of war and rape is well documented; see, e.g.,
Brownmiller (1975: 31-113). To be sure, in 2 Sam. 11, David is not a
soldier on the battlefield and Bathsheba is not among the 'spoils of
war'. I am speaking here only of the fact that war and rape are connected in fact and as literary tropes; cf., e.g., the representation of war
and rape in Kleist's *The Marquise of O* discussed by Winnett (1991); see
also Fokkelman (1981: 41-70), and Bal (1987: 10-36), who discuss the
significance of the combination of war, sexuality, and violence in
2 Sam. 11. In Judg. 21, the rape precedes, and in fact is presented as
resulting in, the war. Cf. Num. 31.6-18; Deut. 21.10-14; Amos 7.17; Hos.
2.9-13 [Heb. 11-15]; Isa. 3.16–4.4; Jer. 38.22-23.

'takes'. Does she know for what purpose she is summoned? Sexual extortion can take many forms, and coercion can be exerted subtly, making women feel they must agree to sex. Is it, then, against her will that David has sex with Bathsheba? Whereas some commentators recognize Bathsheba's status as passive object,[3] rare is the commentator who would go so far as to describe this encounter as rape.[4] Can it be because most commentators are men, and men are uneasy accusing other men of rape, even in an ancient text?[5] In what sense is Bathsheba raped? The question is not whether or not she could have resisted. We cannot subject a literary creation to cross-examination. The point is not what Bathsheba might have done or felt; the point is we are not allowed access to her point of view. There is no attempted seduction recounted, which would give the woman a role, even if one in which she is manipulated.[6] The denial of subjectivity is an important factor in rape, where the victim is objectified and, indeed, the aim is to destroy her subjectivity. The issue of force versus consent is crucial for constructing the woman's point of view, and it is never raised. By denying her subjectivity, the narrator symbolically rapes

3. E.g. Fokkelman (1981: 53). The withholding of information about Bathsheba in 2 Sam. 11 leads Berlin (1983: 27) to conclude that she is 'not even a minor character, but simply part of the plot'.
4. Bal (1987: 11) and Yee (1988: 243) raise the question of rape.
5. On this point and the tendency among classical scholars to downplay, and even to romanticize, rape, see Curran (1984). I witnessed a similar reaction on the part of biblical scholars at the 1991 Society of Biblical Literature International Meeting in Rome, when Azila Reisenberger, of the University of Cape Town, read a paper on rape cases in the Bible (she dealt with legal texts and four narrative examples: Dinah, Tamar, Lot's daughters in Gen. 19, and the women in Judg. 19). Men in the audience were quick to challenge Reisenberger's use of the word 'rape' on the grounds that what we today consider rape may not have been considered rape in ancient times. What struck me about their response was not the content or even the cogency of their arguments, but the intensity of emotion and vehemence of their objections. What in this situation evoked such an angry protest? The fact that a woman called a rape a rape?
6. On the difficulty with the rape/seduction opposition, see Rooney (1991: 92-99). She notes: 'A feminine subject who can act only to consent or refuse to consent is in fact denied subjectivity' (p. 92).

Bathsheba, and by withholding her point of view, he presents an ambiguous portrayal that leaves her vulnerable to the charge of seduction. 'We must, however', says H.W. Hertzberg, 'ask whether Bathsheba did not count on this possibility [being seen bathing]'.[7] Why must we? In the story, David, not Bathsheba, is the offender (we shall investigate below the exact nature of his guilt). Should we blame Bathsheba for appearing on the scene naked, when it is the narrator who has chosen to portray her this way? The narrator who disrobes Bathsheba and depicts her as the object of David's lust is the real perpetrator of the crime against Bathsheba, and commentators like Hertzberg, who imply Bathsheba may have desired the king's attentions, perpetuate the crime.

We also are forced to participate. By introducing Bathsheba to us through David's eyes, the narrator puts us in the position of voyeurs:

> ... he saw from the roof a woman bathing, and the woman was very beautiful (v. 2).

The narrator controls our gaze; we cannot look away from the bathing woman but must consider her appearance: 'very beautiful'. And we presume she is naked, or nearly so; at any rate, we are forced to think about it, to disrobe or partially robe her mentally. Is not this gaze a violation, an invasion of her person as well as her privacy? Nakedness makes her more vulnerable, and being observed in such a private, intimate activity as bathing, attending to the body, accentuates the body's vulnerability to David's and our shared gaze. A woman is touching herself and a man is watching. The viewing is one-sided, giving him the advantage and the position of power: he sees her but she does not see him.

---

7. Hertzberg (1964: 309). Hertzberg also speaks of 'the honour of having attracted the king' (p. 310). Cf. Nicol (1988: 360): 'It cannot be doubted that Bathsheba's action in bathing so close to the king's residence was provocative, nor can the possibility that the provocation was deliberate be discounted. Even if it was not deliberate, Bathsheba's bathing in a place so clearly open to the king's palace can hardly indicate less than a contributory negligence on her part.'

Looking at the female body is both a cultural preoccupation and an accepted expression of male sexuality. Art, film, and pornography provide constant reminders that men are aroused by watching a woman touch herself. And if Bathsheba is purifying herself after her menstrual period, we can guess where she is touching. Readers of this text are watching a man watching a woman touch herself, and I suspect male and female readers react differently to the scene. For my part, I am uncomfortable being put in the position of voyeur, watching a naked woman being watched.

Nor are we and David the only voyeurs: 'Is this not Bathsheba, the daughter of Eliam, the wife of Uriah the Hittite?' (v. 3). It is not clear who says these words, whether David[8] or an attendant,[9] but, in any event, 'Is this not Bathsheba?' suggests that someone else is looking too.

I said that the encounter is brief. This is no love story. David and Bathsheba do not have sex again until after she has become his wife. Nor is there any evidence to suggest that David wanted Bathsheba for himself. On the contrary, the text makes clear that he would prefer to have Uriah assume paternity of the child. David has Uriah killed and then marries Bathsheba only because his ploy to get Uriah to 'go down to his house'—that is, to have sex with his wife (11.11)—fails. Indeed, the narrative necessity to establish paternity accounts for the one circumstantial clause in the controlled description of the encounter between David and Bathsheba: 'while she was purifying herself from her uncleanness' makes it clear that, when Bathsheba becomes pregnant, it is with David's child. Otherwise the scene is the biblical equivalent of 'wham bam, thank you, ma'am': he sent, he took, she came, he lay, she returned.

If force is played down in 2 Sam. 11.4, it is not entirely edited out: 'he took her', the text says. Not only the larger context—the position of the story in the middle of the account of the Ammonite war—but also the aftermath of the encounter suggests force. When David's children reenact his

8. So, convincingly, Bailey (1990: 85).
9. So most commentators and most translations.

crimes as part of his punishment, David's adultery with Bathsheba is replayed as rape, not once but twice. Following closely upon this scene, Amnon rapes his sister Tamar (2 Sam. 13), who, like Bathsheba, is beautiful (13.1) and, like Bathsheba, is objectified (13.17).[10] And when Absalom does in the sight of the sun and all Israel what David had done in secret, he openly rapes ten of David's wives in a tent pitched for him on the roof—the roof, of course, serving as a reminder that this is where David's crime began (2 Sam. 12.11-12; 16.21-22).

## The Levite's Wife of Secondary Rank

The anonymity of the woman who is gang-raped in Judges 19 encourages readers not to view her as a person in her own right. We can counteract this textual strategy for distancing the reader from the character by giving the woman a name. Mieke Bal, whose work on this story has convinced me of the importance of naming the woman,[11] calls her 'Beth', a name that fits the context of Bal's analysis of the story, where the house (*beth*) plays a central role. But because 'Beth' strikes my ear as odd and somehow modern, I give her a different name, even though I recognize that if every interpreter chooses a name that is right in her own ears, discussion of the story could become complicated. On the analogy of Bath-sheba (daughter of an oath, or daughter of seven), I call her Bath-sheber (daughter of breaking). The Hebrew verb *shabar* means 'to break' or 'to break in pieces'; the noun *sheber* can mean 'breaking', as in the breaking of pottery into pieces (Isa. 30.14), or 'fracture', as in the fracture of a limb (Lev. 21.19; Lev. 24.20); it can also refer to anguish or brokenness of spirit (Isa. 65.14). I choose Bath-sheber as a name for this woman because it can serve to remind us both of what happens to her at the hands of the men of Gibeah and also of her subsequent dismemberment by her husband. I do not want Bath-sheber's name to stand for only the

10. Unlike Bathsheba, Tamar speaks and we see something of her point of view. In particular, she resists.
11. Bal (1988a, 1988c).

horrible things that happen to her. The word *sheber* can refer to interpretation, as in the phrase, 'breaking of a dream' (Judg. 7.15). Like dreams, according to Freud, texts require over-interpretation.[12] Since I propose to over-interpret this text, I intend Bath-sheber's name to signify the role feminist criticism plays in breaking open the text's phallocentric ideology and exposing the buried and encoded messages it gives to women—messages upon which it relies to control women and keep them in their place. Both naming the woman and making her the focus of our inquiry are interpretive moves that restore her to the subject position the androcentric narrative destroys.

Like Bathsheba, Bath-sheber is a married woman; she is a *pilegesh*, a legal wife of secondary rank.[13] The English translation, 'concubine', gives the impression that she is less valued, and probably more expendable than a legitimate wife. Indeed, an odd feature of this story is the absence of a primary wife. According to the Hebrew text, this Levite's wife 'played the harlot against him' (the verb is *zanah*), a reading most English translations acknowledge in a textual note. The translation of *pilegesh* as 'concubine', together with the note about *zanah*, encourages the popular identification of concubine and prostitute, which Bal rightly criticizes. It also, I believe, predisposes readers to view the rape of this nameless 'Levite's concubine' less sympathetically than they might view the rape of a lawful wife, for, as Andrea Dworkin observes, 'a whore cannot be raped, only used'.[14]

---

12. See the discussion in Chapter 5 above.
13. Zakovitch (1981: 38) points out that her relation to the Levite is described in terms of marriage: the technical use of 'to take' (v. 1); the description of the woman's father as the Levite's father-in-law (*hoten*, v. 4); and the fact that the term *pilegesh* is interchangeable with *shiphah* and *'ishshah* in the case of Bilhah (Gen. 35.22; 32.22 [Heb. 23]; 30.4; 37.2). Bal (1988a: 83-86) argues that *pilegesh* designates a wife who remains in her father's house after her marriage (so-called *beena* marriage or *tsadiqah* marriage), but such a meaning does not fit most biblical occurrences. It may well be, as Bal suggests, that the meaning of the word changed over time; clearly further study of the social position of the *pilegesh* is called for.
14. Dworkin (1981: 204).

An understanding of the woman as sexually promiscuous is not promoted by the story, however, which describes not the woman's involvement with other men but only her act of leaving her husband: 'she went away from him to her father's house' (v. 2).[15] As Robert Boling observes, 'It is strange that the woman would become a prostitute and then run home'.[16] Moreover, if she were promiscuous, why would her husband go to such lengths to get her back? In view of such incongruity, it is not surprising that many translations follow the versions in reading that she 'became angry with him'.[17] But what are we to make of the Hebrew text, which clearly has the woman 'zanahing', to coin a word? As Bal points out, the translation of the unique combination, *zanah* + *'al*, as 'play the harlot *against*' implies an ideology according to which women's bodies are the property of men.[18] Bal proposes that originally the verb referred to an act related to a particular type of marriage, specifically to the woman's breach of patrilocal marriage to live with her husband: 'The unfaithfulness—to the father, to the old institution—for the sake of marriage, hence for sex, becomes [through linguistic development] sexual unfaithfulness'.[19] Yair Zakovitch argues that *zanah* refers to what amounts to divorce on the woman's part: 'The verb simply means that she dared to leave her husband, a phenomenon which was frequently connected with immoral behaviour'.[20] Indeed, Zakovitch's argument that Bath-sheber essentially divorced

15. If marital infidelity were meant, one might expect the verb *na'ap*, 'to commit adultery'; on *zanah* and *na'ap*, see Bird (1989: 77).
16. Boling (1975: 273).
17. Cf. LXX[AL], OL.
18. Bal (1988a: 86). The very concept of 'harlot' or 'whore' has meaning only within the ideology of male sexual domination; see Dworkin (1981: 203-209). Only women are harlots or whores; if the terms are applied to males it is only in an extended or figurative sense. This is true in Hebrew as well; see Bird (1989).
19. Bal (1988a: 88).
20. Zakovitch (1981: 39). Zakovitch suggests that perhaps the term *zanah* was applied to women who left their husbands without the possibility of returning to their father's house, and thus had to become prostitutes to support themselves.

her husband and that she had the right to decide whether or
not to take him back is supported by the *Ketib* of v. 3,
according to which the Levite went after her 'to let him
return to her' (most translations follow the *Qere*, 'to bring
her back').[21]

Rather than argue for a specific meaning of *zanah*, I propose to consider how its use promotes the text's androcentric agenda. That the word *zanah*, which commonly refers to
sexual relations outside of marriage,[22] appears here is, in my
opinion, no coincidence. By juxtaposing these two acts—
*zanah*ing and leaving her husband—the text establishes a
connection between them that is critical for what happens
later. Whether the woman acts contrary to patrilocal or virilocal marriage customs (in the first case, by living with her
husband; in the second, by returning to her father), or
whether she divorces her husband, her behavior is a gesture
of sexual autonomy. The issue, as Bal and Zakovitch are
aware, is male ownership of women's bodies, control over
women's sexuality. A woman who asserts her sexual autonomy by leaving her husband—and whether or not she
remains with him is a sexual issue—is guilty of sexual misconduct.[23] This ideology informs the way gender relations
are understood and evaluated in this story. Women give up
autonomy in return for protection by their men from other
men. By daring to act autonomously in the first place, Bath-
sheber puts herself beyond male protection, and for this she
must be punished. The men who ordinarily would be
expected to protect her—her husband and their host—
participate in her punishment because her act is an offense
against the social order; that is, against the patriarchal system itself. In the end, the woman is raped by a mob and

21. Zakovitch (1981: 39).
22. See Bird (1989: 76-79), who notes that the primary usage of the
verb is limited to female subjects, 'since it is only for women that marriage is the primary determinant of legal status and obligation' (p. 77).
*zanah* can refer to premarital sex by a daughter, sex by a levirate-obli-
gated widow, or the activity of a professional prostitute (p. 77).
23. Boling (1975: 274) draws a similar conclusion: 'As Israelite law
did not allow for divorce by the wife, she became an adulteress by
walking out on him'.

dismembered by her own husband. As narrative punishment for her sexual 'misconduct', her sexual 'freedom', she is sexually abused, after which her sexuality is symbolically mutilated.

The woman is raped and tortured all night and released only at daybreak (19.25). Her husband (the text has *'adoneha*, 'her lord') finds her at the doorstep in the morning. He speaks to her but receives no answer. He puts her on his donkey and takes her home, where he divides her body into twelve parts which he sends 'throughout all the territory of Israel' (v. 29). It is not entirely clear at what point the woman died or even that she is dead when he dismembers her, a detail the LXX and Vulgate translators apparently felt the need to clarify by adding 'and she was dead' after 'there was no answer' (v. 28).

Why is this additional act of violence necessary? I am prepared to grant that the dismemberment is a morbid parody of Saul's cutting into pieces a yoke of oxen and sending the parts throughout Israel to muster the people to battle (1 Sam. 11.5-7).[24] There, however, it constituted a threat: 'Whoever does not come out after Saul and Samuel, so shall it be done to his oxen!' Here, commentators are at a loss to explain its symbolic value.[25] This is because they have looked elsewhere than the gender code for its meaning. If we seek the meaning of the act in the gender code, we discover that an implicit message about sexual behavior is

24. Most commentators note the parallel; on the relationship between these two accounts, see Lasine (1984).

25. Niditch (1982: 371) sees the dissected body as a symbol of Israel's 'body politics', its divisions; Lasine (1984) takes it as a sign of perversity in a topsy-turvy world. He comments (p. 42), 'The "message" sent by the Levite by means of the severed body is made more bizarre because he is not quoted as declaring the exact significance of the message, unlike Saul, who makes it clear that the dismembered oxen represent what will happen to the oxen of those who do not rally to his call'. Soggin (1981: 282) offers a typical response: 'However, in this instance the symbolism seems to be missing: the quartered limbs of the concubine are not a summons to arms, nor do they threaten the reluctant; they simply arouse horror. Such a macabre gesture is not only unnecessary for summoning the assembly; it does not even seem to serve a useful purpose.'

being given to women. By leaving her husband the woman makes a gesture of sexual autonomy so threatening to patriarchal ideology that it requires her to be punished sexually in the most extreme form. The symbolic significance of dismembering the woman's body lies in its intent to de-sexualize her. Otherwise the act remains insufficiently motivated. It is not enough that the woman who has offended sexually, by acting as if she and not the man owned her body, is abused sexually, by having her body possessed by many men. An even more radical punishment is called for. Because it has offended, the woman's sexuality must be destroyed and its threat diffused by scattering. 'If the female body offends you, cut it up' might be the motto. Cutting up the woman can be viewed on a psychological level both as an expression of male fear of women's sexuality, which must therefore be destroyed, and as an attempt to discover the secret of woman's sexuality. Because woman is the seductive and dangerous other, her mystery must be opened up by force.[26]

If one man, her husband, cannot possess her, then many men will. But in the end, no one can possess her. What is the husband to do with his damaged goods? He destroys the evidence of the rape in a way that symbolically repeats it, by sharing the woman's body among men, but that at the same time de-sexualizes the female body, by cutting it up and scattering the parts. And we shall see below how he also destroys the evidence of the crime against the woman by giving a different account of what happened when he offers his testimony to the Israelite assembly.

What I am describing here is a gender-motivated subtext, not a conscious misogynistic design on the part of the narrator. It is a subtext motivated by male fear of female sexuality and by the resultant need of patriarchy to control women. In order to illustrate the social and moral disintegration of Israel before the monarchy, the narrator of Judges 19–21 tells

26. I borrow the notion of forcibly opening the woman to reveal her mystery from Showalter (1990), whose discussion has influenced my thinking on this issue; see especially pp. 105-43.

a story in which the threatened abuse of the Levite and the actual treatment of his wife lead to internecine warfare, the near-extinction of an Israelite tribe, and mass rape and murder. All of these events come under narrative censure, with violence against women treated merely as part of a larger social and moral problem—that is, as if the gender of the victims of violence were irrelevant.[27] Yet the fact that the central act in the illustration is the rape and dismemberment of a woman foregrounds the important role gender plays, on a deeper level, in the presentation. Moreover, in the aftermath, women are again the objects of male violence.

Something else could have been chosen to illustrate the depravity of the times. In fact, the narrator offers another possible scenario: the rape of the Levite himself. This is what the men of Gibeah are portrayed as having in mind: 'Bring out the man who came into your house that we may know him' (19.22). Does this mean that all these men of Gibeah are homosexuals? Hardly.[28] Rape is a crime of violence not of passion; homosexual rape forces the male victim into a passive role, into the woman's position. The men of Gibeah want to humiliate the Levite in the most degrading way. But this is, as we know, not what happens. And since it does not happen, it obviously—in terms of narrative poetics, in terms of the story the narrator chose to tell—was not meant to happen. Certainly the threat to rape the man, in violation of ordinary mores and the laws of hospitality, illustrates the baseness of the men of Gibeah, and thus the lawlessness of the times. In terms of the gender politics of the narrative, however, it has the effect of deflecting attention from the woman as the object of a different moral lesson, a warning to women about the consequences of sexual independence, so that the gender issue becomes submerged in issues of concern to men: hospitality and codes of behavior. The success of this narrative ploy in promoting the androcentric agenda is witnessed by the amount of attention commenta-

27. This is still a problem with violence against women; like race and ethnicity, the role of gender in violence should not be ignored.
28. See the discussion in Bal (1988c: 20-21).

tors devote to the issue of hospitality—a host's obligation to his guests in the ancient world—as compared with the treatment of the woman. The de-gendering of male sexual violence that results when the story is interpreted in terms of violation of the rules of hospitality is a displacement. Our unwillingness to look at what is most disturbing about this story prevents us from seeing its buried and coded message to women.[29]

The men want the man; they get a woman. They are offered two women; they get one. Why, since they could obviously overpower the host and his guests, do they settle for only Bath-sheber? I suggest that two impulses are at work here: homosexual rape is too threatening to narrate, and, in terms of the subtext, it would leave the woman unpunished. The narrative possibility of the Levite's rape by the mob is therefore abandoned. 'Do it to women but not to the man' is the androcentric ideology, for which the host is the spokesperson. He offers his virgin daughter to the crowd along with his guest's wife: 'Rape them and do to them whatever you like, but to this man do not do so foul a thing' (19.24). Commentators are often perplexed that although both women are offered, only Bath-sheber is thrown out. It seems, in fact, that her husband, and not the host, is the one who throws her to the licentious mob, though 'the man' who casts her out is not specifically identified—an ambiguity that shields the true culprit and paradoxically exposes the guilt of both men. If we understand Bath-sheber's abuse as her narrative punishment, then the sparing of the virgin

29. I owe both these ways to looking at reactions to the textual violence to Showalter (1990: 152, 142). The coded message to women is also overlooked by readings that see the violence against the woman as the prelude to the 'real problem' of social and moral anarchy in Israel. For example, Fokkelman (1992: 43) reads with the text's ideology when he says, 'After all, and without any underestimation of the woman's experience, the crime of chap. 19 is merely an incident'. Similarly, Niditch (1982: 371): 'The man's insensitivity towards his concubine, his non-communication with her, his selfishness are, in fact, a microcosm of larger community-relationships in Israel'. My reading is very much at odds with that of Penchansky (1992: 83-86), whose speculations about a feminist critique of this story are self-defeating.

daughter makes sense: she is not mistreated because, unlike Bath-sheber, she has not committed a sexual offense against male authority. Decoded, the message the story of Bath-sheber gives to women is that the consequences of sexual autonomy (presented as unfaithfulness or misconduct) are terrible and deadly. Male violence is something every woman fears. The best defense is, stay out of the way; maybe you won't be noticed. The host's daughter illustrates that sometimes this stratagem works.

## Narrative Judgment

I have been speaking about rape—rape *in* a narrative and *by means of* a narrative—and about crimes. But what, exactly, are the crimes that are condemned in these stories? The fact that, in both our examples, judgment occurs *within the story itself* enables us to probe more deeply into the workings of biblical sexual politics. In 2 Samuel 12, God sends the prophet Nathan to condemn David:

> Why have you despised the word of Yhwh to do what is evil in his eyes? Uriah the Hittite you have slain with the sword, and his wife you have taken to be your wife, and him you have killed with the sword of the Ammonites. Now therefore the sword shall never depart from your house.

> Because you have despised me and have taken the wife of Uriah the Hittite to be your wife—thus says Yhwh—I am raising up evil against you out of your own house, and I will take your wives before your eyes and give them to your neighbor, and he shall lie with your wives in the eyes of this sun. For you did it in secret, but I shall do this thing before all Israel and before the sun (2 Sam. 12.9-12).[30]

David's crime is twofold: he had Uriah killed and he took Uriah's wife—both are crimes against Uriah and against God (as the protector of the patriarchal social order). But they are not treated as crimes against Bathsheba, who is defined solely in terms of her relation to Uriah. Having sex-

---

30. Dividing v. 10 with Fokkelman (1981: 83-86), who makes a convincing case against the Masoretic division.

ual intercourse with Bathsheba is a crime because it violates another man's marital rights. Adultery is always a matter of the woman's status: a married woman who has sex with a man other than her husband commits adultery; a married man who has sex with a woman other than his wife commits adultery only if that woman is another man's wife.[31] Indeed, David's punishment—that what he did to another man will be done to him, only more so—shows how irrelevant the woman's perspective is. *David's* punishment for adultery is that *his wives* will be raped. No thought is given to their experience of being publicly raped or to their treatment after the rape. In effect, they are punished for having been raped:

> And David came to his house at Jerusalem, and the king took the ten wives whom he had left to care for the house and put them in a house under guard, and provided for them, but did not go in to them. So they were shut up until the day of their death, living as if in widowhood (2 Sam. 20.3).

In Judges 19–21, the narrator presents a graphic picture of moral depravity in Gibeah of Benjamin. A strange feature of these chapters is the disparity between the information given to us about events at Gibeah and the information given to the assembly of Israelite tribes, on the basis of which they go to war against the Benjaminites, who refuse to hand over the evil men for punishment. This is the account the tribes hear from the Levite:

> To Gibeah that belongs to Benjamin I came, I and my wife, to spend the night. The men of Gibeah rose against me and surrounded the house against me by night. Me they meant to kill and my wife they raped, and she died. I took my wife and cut her in pieces and sent her throughout all the country of the inheritance of Israel, for they have committed abomination and wantonness in Israel (Judg. 20.4-6).

31. On adultery in ancient Near Eastern law, see Westbrook (1990), and the references cited there. There are obvious similarities between the David–Bathsheba–Uriah triangle and the patriarch–matriarch–foreign ruler triangle discussed above in Chapter 5; for a comparison of the stories, see Miscall (1979; 1983: 27-40). In Chapter 5, I spoke of the Genesis stories in terms of Girard's theory of triangular desire; for a Girardian reading of 2 Sam. 11–12, see Jensen (1992: 44-54).

The Levite stresses the threat to himself: the men 'rose against *me*'; they 'surrounded the house against *me*'; '*me* [in first place for emphasis] they meant to kill'. In his version of the events, his life is at stake, and he does not mention the humiliating threat of homosexual rape. Indeed, it sounds as if the mob set out to kill him and only incidentally did it come about that they raped his wife. He neglects to mention that he and his host remained in the safety of the house while the woman was thrown out to the crowd to be raped all night. His statement, 'and she died' (*wattamot*), implies that her death resulted from the mob's abuse, whereas in the earlier version whether she died from the rape or later was left somewhat ambiguous. His act of dismembering a human being, his own wife, he describes matter-of-factly, while accusing the men of Gibeah of committing lewdness.

By placing in the Levite's mouth an account so self-serving and so unlike the events described to us in ch. 19, the narrator reveals the Levite's baseness. Indeed, the narrator's sympathy does not lie with the Levite. He represents him as too irresolute to leave on his journey home at a reasonable hour and then too stubborn to remain another night at his father-in-law's house (19.5-10). Had he left early in the morning with his wife and servant as intended, they would not have needed to stop in Gibeah and the outrage might have been avoided. Moreover, it is surely a callous man who, upon finding his raped and battered wife lying at the door, can say, 'Get up; let's go' (v. 28).[32] But even though the Levite is a disreputable character, it is nonetheless the Levite's version of events to which the tribes respond. They go to war with Benjamin to avenge the threatened crime against the Levite and the actual abuse of his wife. As in David's case, where the crimes of adultery and murder are crimes against the husband and not the wife, here also the threat of murder and the rape are crimes against the husband.[33] Is it, then, the case that Bath-sheber's mistreatment

---

32. On the negative narrative evaluation of the Levite, see Trible (1984); Lasine (1984); Exum (1990).

33. It is not clear to me what Fokkelman (1992: 43) means when he asserts: 'What the Levite is concerned with is the sexual crime, not a

by the mob is as irrelevant for the narrative judgment as Bathsheba's exploitation by David?

There seems, indeed, to be some lingering guilt on the narrator's part about the treatment of the woman. After the Levite dismembers Bath-sheber and sends the parts of her body throughout Israelite territory, we read:

> All who saw it said, 'Such a thing has never happened or been seen from the day that the people of Israel came up out of the land of Egypt until this day; consider it, take counsel, and speak' (Judg. 19.30).

What is this thing (*kazo't*) that has never happened or been seen before? Unless we assume that some explanation accompanied the body parts, in its context 'such a thing' can only refer to the dismemberment and parceling out of the woman's body, since only later do the tribes learn from the Levite what happened at Gibeah.[34] When they assemble at Mizpah, they ask the Levite: 'Tell us, how did this evil come to pass?' (20.4). Here, too, the only obvious referent for 'this evil' is the dismemberment.

We have, then, in Judges 19–21 a situation in which the narrator *tells* us that the tribes go to war to avenge what are certainly crimes against a man and his property. But he *shows* us horrible crimes against the woman, both the gang rape and the dismemberment. When, in the story, judgment is executed upon the guilty, the Benjaminites are punished for their role; that is, for siding with the rapists and would-be murderers (though later the tribes will have 'compassion

---

case of mere loss of property'. This seems to me a false dichotomy, since both sex and property are involved: the wife is a special kind of property who, if used by another for sex, cannot be returned in the same state as she was taken. If, for example, she had been kidnapped but not sexually abused, it seems to me she could have been restored to him; cf. 1 Sam. 30, where David's wives and the other women taken as spoil by the Amalekites are recaptured. As I suggest here, the mistreatment of Bath-sheber is problematic; similarly, Bal (1987: 20-36) exposes the problem the narrator of 2 Sam. 11 has with the treatment of Bathsheba.

34. The differences in LXX do not resolve the problems posed by v. 30.

for Benjamin, their brother'; 21.6; cf. also v. 15). The mutilation of the woman's body by the Levite, in contrast, is
neither redressed nor explicitly censured. This does not
mean that the mutilation is unproblematic, however. The
narrative disjunction that allows the Israelites' strongly negative reaction to 'such a thing' and 'this evil' to be read as a
response to the dismemberment may be regarded as a
symptom of the narrator's discomfort and guilt about the
crime against Bath-sheber.

### She Asked for It

It is well known that in cases of rape the issue of the woman's responsibility is often raised. Why was she dressed like
that? What was she doing alone at night in that neighbor-
hood? Consider simply how the 'stories' of these women
begin: Bathsheba is bathing; Bath-sheber is '*zanah*ing'.
Gender is an important factor here; a man bathing or behaving in a sexually autonomous way would not raise the same
questions about provocativeness because what is being pro-
voked is *male* desire. Bathing or *zanah*ing is sexually suggestive in our respective stories because a woman is doing it
and because a man is affected. On a different occasion,
David exposes himself, at least partially, when he dances
before the ark of Yhwh (2 Sam. 6). The sight arouses a woman's anger, not her desire. But unlike Bathsheba, who is the
passive object of the voyeuristic gaze, David displays himself publicly, and when Michal criticizes him for his exhibitionism ('How the king of Israel has honored himself today,
exposing himself today in the eyes of his subjects' women
servants!'), he revels in the attention focused on him
('among the women servants of whom you have spoken,
among them I shall be held in honor'). Freud saw voyeurism
as the passive counterpart to exhibitionism.[35] It doesn't take
David long to make the transition from exhibitionist, with
wife Michal watching from the window as the subject, to
voyeur, with wife-to-be Bathsheba as the object whom he

---

35. Freud (1962: 33); I owe this reference to Bal (1993: 4-6).

watches from his subject position on the roof.[36]

Biblical style typically suggests a causal connection by means of simple juxtaposition:[37] because Bathsheba was seen bathing, she was sent for. It is thus the woman's fault that the man's desire is aroused. To be desirable means being desirable in someone's eyes, which introduces the voyeur or rapist perspective. Bathsheba is guilty of being desired, but the text hints that she asked for it: she *allows* herself to be seen. Bath-sheber asks for it too, the text implies. Had she stayed in her place, under her husband's authority where she belonged, she would not have ended up at the wrong place—Gibeah of Benjamin—at the wrong time. By insinuating that women, either by the way they let themselves be seen by men or by the way they behave, are responsible for male sexual behavior, our two texts rely on a fundamental patriarchal strategy for exercising social control over women. Using women's fear of male violence as a means of regulating female behavior is one of patriarchy's most powerful weapons. And it remains effective. As Peggy Sanday observes:[38]

> By blaming the victim for provoking their own sexual aggression, men control and define acceptable and unacceptable female sexual behavior through the agency of fear. A woman who does not guard her behavior becomes the target of male sexual aggression.

36. Male display of sexuality is active (David is dancing) and public (he is in control; he lets himself be seen by many women, as well as men) and (as the dispute between David and Michal shows) nothing to be ashamed of. Female 'display' of sexuality is passive and private (Bathsheba is bathing and observed). In both accounts, fertility is a related issue: Michal sees and objects to David's nakedness and she has no children; Bathsheba is seen naked and it leads to her pregnancy (I thank Martha Morrison for drawing my attention to the fertility aspect). For detailed comparison of the two scenes, see Bach (forthcoming). For a compelling analysis of the male as glorified nude and the female as shamefully naked in the art of the Christian West, see Miles (1989).

37. As, for example, the verse about Michal's childlessness (2 Sam. 6.23), discussed in Chapter 1 above.

38. Sanday (1990: 13). On gang rape as a means of social control, see also Brownmiller (1975: 284-89, 397-400).

If the message to women encoded in the story of Jephthah's daughter was: yield to the paternal word and you will be remembered and celebrated for generations to come; and that of Michal's story was: a woman who does not remain in her place courts disaster; the message in our two 'rape' stories is a cautionary one: since the way men perceive you determines the way they treat you, do not do anything that might arouse male sexual aggression.

## Corpus delicti

The woman who is gang-raped in Judges 19 has no name and no voice. After the initial identification of the bathing woman in 2 Samuel 11 as 'Bathsheba the daughter of Eliam, the wife of Uriah the Hittite', Bathsheba becomes nameless. Throughout the events that follow, she is referred to as either Uriah's wife or 'the woman'. Only when the child born of the adulterous union is dead do we again hear her name: 'then David comforted his wife Bathsheba' (12.24).[39] In the crucial scene, the initial brief sexual encounter with David, Bathsheba has no voice (nor does David, for that matter).

In the absence of voice, can the body speak? And can the speaking body provide evidence that a crime has occurred? Bathsheba's body 'speaks' in an obvious way, giving her voice: 'I am pregnant' (11.5). David, throughout the narrative, is shown exercising power, controlling people's movements like pawns on a chessboard: he *sends* and inquires about Bathsheba and *sends* messengers to take her. He *sends* word to Joab to *send* him Uriah, and he *sends* Uriah's death letter to Joab by Uriah's own hand. The speaking body gives Bathsheba power over David; she *sends* word to David, informing him of her condition. The king must act because

---

39. The infant's death is presented as *David's* punishment for his crime of adultery and considerable attention is given to David's reaction to the child's illness and death (2 Sam. 12.16-23). We see David's mourning, but except for being 'comforted', Bathsheba's perspective is ignored.

he cannot ignore the witness her body provides against him. Earlier the female body was exposed to his voyeuristic gaze; now he risks exposure by that same body because it makes visible a crime that otherwise would have remained hidden. Surely Bath-sheber's body is the speaking body *par excellence*. Her body, dismembered and scattered, is used semiotically to call a full-scale assembly of the Israelite tribes. At this tribal gathering, however, Bath-sheber's body is not allowed to speak; rather, the Levite gives his testimony.[40] We have seen how he distorts the evidence of the crime and also how his dismemberment of the evidence symbolically repeats the crime. Although Bath-sheber's body does not convict the Levite of a crime, as Bathsheba's body convicts David, the narrator casts suspicion upon the Levite, and thus himself, by dropping a clue: by providing no clear referent for 'such a thing' (19.30) and 'this evil' (20.4) other than the dismemberment itself, he has failed to provide the Levite with an alibi. Paradoxically, in destroying the evidence of the crime by dismembering the body, the Levite brings to light the evidence against himself, so that all who see it ask how such an evil could come to pass. Betrayed by a guilty narrative conscience, the text in this instance criticizes its own ideology.

As we saw above, the dismemberment functions to desexualize Bath-sheber by violently opening up the mystery of woman and diffusing her threat by scattering the parts. Through pregnancy, Bathsheba, the sensual woman, is desexualized in a different way: by being transformed into a mother. In the discussions of Samson's mother, as well as of Michal, Jephthah's daughter, and the matriarchs, we observed how patriarchy severs the relationship between eroticism and procreation in order to render non-threatening the mother's sexuality. In the phallocentric economy, when women become mothers, their desire is denied and they become less desirable.[41] Pregnancy 'redeems' Bathsheba for

40. For an analysis of speech-acts and 'the scandal of the speaking body' in this account, see Bal (1988c).
41. Like all generalizations, this one is subject to exceptions. There is, for example, a pornography of pregnancy; see Dworkin (1981: 218-

patriarchy; though her first child dies for David's sins, immediately thereafter she conceives a second son, Solomon, who will be king. She takes on the role of mother, which patriarchy values so highly, and recedes into the harem not to be heard from again until her son has grown to adulthood, ready to become king, and she is called upon to play a role in furthering his interests (1 Kgs 1–2). The pregnant body of Bathsheba and the body of Bath-sheber, whose sexuality has been mutilated, bear witness in different ways to male attraction to and fear of female sexuality, ambivalence that in both cases results in crimes against women. And the two stories—the one in which rape takes place and the one by means of which a woman is violated—represent two different responses to women's powerful and dangerous sexuality: the one destroys the threat; the other incorporates and transforms female sexuality into something more manageable.

## The Spiral of Violence

Feminist critics have argued that woman occupies a position at the border of the patriarchal symbolic order. She is the seductive and dangerous other. This view of women relates to the tendency on the part of phallocentric texts like ours to attribute the introduction of disorder to women, as, for example, when the Genesis narrator holds Eve responsible for the expulsion from Eden. In both our 'rape' stories, episodes involving women seem to trigger a chain of violence, as if the women had disrupted things. Bathsheba's bath, because it is viewed by David, sets off a series of disasters for David and his house. When Bath-sheber leaves her husband and returns to her father's house, she, too, sets in motion a sequence of fateful events: because her husband goes after her to bring her back, and because they begin their journey late in the evening, they end up in Gibeah, where their presence invites assault. In both stories violence escalates as male aggression is replayed on an ever larger

23).

scale. David's sins are reenacted by his children. Rapes within the Davidic house, echoing the Bathsheba episode (Tamar's by Amnon and ten of David's wives by Absalom), are only part of the evil that God promised to raise up against David from within his house as a consequence of his transgression. God also said, 'The sword shall never depart from your house', and, one by one, David's sons fall by the sword—first Amnon, then Absalom, and finally Adonijah.[42]

Nor does the violence stop with the Davidic house. The whole kingdom is torn apart by strife: no sooner is Absalom's revolt against his father put down than Sheba calls the northern tribes to revolt. When David Gunn, following the lead of Joseph Blenkinsopp, identifies one of the traditional motifs in the story of King David as 'the woman who brings death', he is both expressing and reinscribing the text's androcentric ideology.[43] It is men in this story who bring death and who shift the blame onto women through an encoded message that holds women responsible for male aggression.

Like Bathsheba's story, Bath-sheber's story culminates in full-scale war, and here, too, the Israelite men end up fighting among themselves. Just as the taking of Bathsheba and the murder of Uriah are replayed in various permutations in David's house and kingdom, so too the rape and murder of Bath-sheber are reenacted in mass rape and murder. When the Israelites realize that they have almost destroyed the tribe of Benjamin, they have a change of heart. In order for Benjamin to continue to exist as a tribe, the surviving Benjaminites need wives. But because the other Israelites have sworn not to give their daughters to the Benjaminites as wives, they procure wives for Benjamin by carrying out the ban against Jabesh-gilead, sparing only four hundred virgins. To punish the violence threatened against a man and committed against his property, Israelite men kill many innocent women. Women from Benjamin are obviously

---

42. On the disruptive events within the Davidic house, see the discussion in Exum (1992: 127-49).
43. Gunn (1978: 43); Blenkinsopp (1966).

killed in the destruction of Benjaminite cities, and women from Jabesh-gilead who are not virgins die also. Nor does the sexual violence end with the abduction of the four hundred virgins from Jabesh: because yet more wives are needed for the Benjaminites, the Israelites instruct the Benjaminite men to lie in wait and capture wives from the dancers in the yearly festival at Shiloh. Male violence reinscribes the story of female violation, as Israelite men repeat on a mass scale the crimes of the men of Gibeah.

Blaming women for violence of which they are the victims is one of the ways patriarchy seeks to avoid facing and having to deal with its own violent legacy. Dworkin argues that men become advocates of violence in order to master their fear of violence. They *do* violence in order not to be victimized by it; in other words, to prove their manhood by distinguishing themselves from women, who are victims by definition.[44] Exposing the strategy of scapegoating women in our texts allows us to look beneath it and see that male violence begets male violence; it needs no women to give it birth.

## Behold, the Woman

Let us consider a point in each narrative where the woman is focalized through the male gaze and ask, What is seen and what is the response of the one who sees? And we may also ask, What is our response, and our responsibility? What is seen in both cases is the female body, 'before and after sex', we might say; that is, before sexual intercourse takes place and after repeated acts of sexual brutality.

> ... and he saw a woman bathing, and the woman was very beautiful (2 Sam. 11.2).

> ... behold [*hinneh*], the woman, his wife, fallen at the door of the house, with her hands on the threshold (Judg. 19.27).

How do the men in our stories, through whose eyes we see the women's bodies, react to what they see? The sight of

44. Dworkin (1981: 51-53).

Bathsheba's body arouses David's desire, and he acts on it: he sends for her and has sex with her. Voyeurism, which is passive and one-sided, leads in this case to involvement on the part of the voyeur. Lustful looking is the prelude to possessing. The story thus raises the question of the relationship between looking, desiring, and acting on the basis of desire.[45] For women who may be raped, this relationship is serious and dangerous. Fortunately, not every voyeur acts on his lustful impulses. The text condemns David for doing so, but only because the woman is another man's property. The voyeuristic gaze at the female body that can lead to appropriation is permanently inscribed in the text, and we have already considered the ways readers are implicated in it. With all this looking, it is little wonder Bathsheba has become the quintessential object of the gaze in literature and art through the ages. Her 'punishment' for being desired is to be forever visualized as the sensual woman who enflames male lust.

Unlike David, the Levite is not spying on the woman. Quite the contrary, he is portrayed as though he were casually leaving his host's house the next morning to go on his way and as if he practically stumbles over the woman at the door: 'Her husband rose up in the morning and opened the door of the house. He went out to go on his way, and there was [*hinneh*] the woman, his wife, lying at the door ...' (Judg. 19.27). The particle *hinneh*, often translated 'behold', alerts us to the fact that we are looking at the body from the Levite's point of view. What he sees is not the desire-arousing female body. Rapish desire originally directed toward him has been satisfied on the female body, and he is looking at the result of it. How does the sight of his wife's ravished body affect him? His attention, and thus ours, focuses on one part of the body: the hands. The hands, grasping the threshold of the house that harbors the men who sacrificed her to the mob, accuse him of denying her asylum. His response is shocking. He shows no respect for the dead, or nearly-dead, woman; he makes no gesture to

45. See Bal's discussion of this relationship (1993).

cover or otherwise tend to her injured body. Instead, he commits further violence against it:

> He said to her, 'Get up so we can go', but there was no answer. He *put* her upon the donkey and he *went at once* to his place. When he *came* to his house, he *took* the knife and he *seized* his wife and he *cut her up*, limb by limb, into twelve pieces, and he *sent* her throughout all the territory of Israel (Judg. 19.28-29).

How should we visualize these events? They are graphic and brutal: a woman's body is the object of mutilation by the man who gave it over to sexual abuse by a mob. If this scene and the gang rape that precedes it were portrayed in film today, we would label it pornographic. We see the woman fall down at the door after an entire night of sexual abuse. The focus on one part of the body, the accusing hands, is a prelude to the division of the body into parts. From the brusque command to get up to the rough handling and then methodical dismemberment of the body, the Levite's behavior is scandalous. In pornographic literature and in actual cases, rape and other violent crimes against women are frequently accompanied by bodily mutilation, a chilling attestation to the intensity of the fear and hatred of women that lie behind them.[46]

The nature of the relation between voyeurism and pornography, both of which involve looking or visualizing, needs to be considered in comparing these literary rapes.[47] Since meaning is constructed through interaction between text and reader, readers will make their own judgments as to whether or not they are called upon to be voyeurs or pornography viewers. Some readers will resist the phallocentric premises of these texts more than others. The story of David and Bathsheba, for example, invites a kind of voyeuristic complicity between the narrator and his assumed or ideal male readers. The narrator does more than control our

---

46.  See Gubar (1989); Brownmiller (1975: 194-209); Dworkin (1981: 129-98).

47.  My discussion of this relationship is influenced by Bal's analysis of the story of Susanna (1993). For a sensitive analysis of the way pornography affects all our lives, see Griffin (1981).

gaze at the naked, or partially naked, female body; he excuses it by letting us look without any blame being attached—which is more than he does for David. The text insinuates that David has no business looking: he should be at war, leading his troops, instead of at home napping indolently until late afternoon. Moreover, we know that looking leads him to sin against man (Uriah) and God. By setting it up so that what we see through David's eyes becomes part of our judgment against David, the narrator gives us the moral high ground. This makes it possible for readers to gaze upon the naked woman without embarrassment, or at least without feeling guilty about it. Furthermore, to the extent that the narrator implies culpability on Bathsheba's part, he is being hypocritical—morally condemning her for the nakedness he has depicted for his pleasure, David's, and that of his ideal readers.[48] This narrative strategy—allowing us to look guiltlessly and, if we wish, to blame the woman at the same time—is what I call Bathsheba's rape by the pen.

Similarly, by portraying the men of Gibeah as depraved and the Levite as base and insensitive, the narrator of Judges 19 allows us to feel moral outrage at their behavior—and this is, I think, his goal: to present his audience with a compelling illustration of the depravity of the times. But his illustration is also typical of the way violence against women is presented, as if gender bias were not an issue. Here, too, if we choose, we can look without guilt; that is, without thinking of ourselves as viewers of pornography. Indeed, we are given the opportunity to follow the fast pace of the consecutive verbs used to describe the mutilation, so that we need not dwell on the explicit details. We are

48. Berger (1972: 51) makes this point about visual art, but it applies as well to narrative: 'You painted a naked woman because you enjoyed looking at her, you put a mirror in her hand and you called the painting *Vanity*, thus morally condemning the woman whose nakedness you had depicted for your own pleasure'. David could have, for example, seen Bathsheba in a way similar to Samson's seeing the Timnite: 'David went out in Jerusalem and he saw a woman who was the right one in his eyes'.

encouraged, but we are not, as Lasine concludes, 'forced to view the scene with detachment'.[49] We can pause, and if we do, we are likely to stumble over the pornographic element in the account. The Levite nearly stumbles over the woman's body, but it is there and he cannot avoid dealing with it. If we take the gender message of this tale seriously, neither can we.

## Bathsheba's Reappearance

There is a major difference between Bathsheba's story and Bath-sheber's: Bathsheba reappears at a later point in the biblical narrative (1 Kgs 1–2). Like so many other biblical women, her story is fragmented. Like another of David's wives, Michal, Bathsheba has two 'big scenes' in the larger story of David, pivotal for the future of the Davidic house and separated by a period of time during which we hear nothing about her. Throughout the vicissitudes of David's troubled reign (2 Sam. 13–24), Bathsheba is out of sight; even when David abandons Jerusalem to Absalom, leaving only ten wives behind to keep his house, the text is silent about Bathsheba. She appears again as David is approaching death, in a scene that can only be described as an ironic parody of her first appearance in 'David's story': the once lustful and virile monarch is now old and senile, and a young, 'very beautiful' woman is brought to his bed to warm him. But the man who seized the moment with Bathsheba is unable to take advantage of this opportunity: 'the king knew her not', says the text euphemistically. Bathsheba enters the king's chambers as Abishag is ministering to him (1 Kgs 1.15).[50] She has been sent by Nathan to induce David to proclaim Solomon king, and it is possible that Bathsheba and Nathan dupe the king into believing he had promised the

49. Lasine (1984: 45).
50. Berlin's discussion of Bathsheba's jealousy of Abishag (1983: 28-29) assumes she at some point shared David's passion and reflects modern notions of romantic love. Bathsheba is part of a royal harem, and we do not know her feelings toward David or her co-wives, since we never get her point of view.

throne to Solomon, since nowhere does the text record such a promise.

Is Bathsheba no more than a pawn manipulated by Nathan or does she play a genuine role in persuading David to make Solomon king? Nathan tells her what to say: 'Did you not, my lord the king, swear to your maidservant, saying, "Solomon your son shall reign after me, and he shall sit upon my throne"? Why then is Adonijah king?' (1 Kgs 1.13). But she elaborates upon this speech quite persuasively, changing Nathan's rhetorical question to a statement that allows David no room to disagree, and introducing the issue of the threat to herself and her son Solomon should Adonijah become king (vv. 17-21). After Solomon's accession and David's death, Bathsheba appears again, this time to convey to Solomon Adonijah's request that Solomon give him Abishag as a wife (1 Kgs 2.13-23). Why does she intercede on Adonijah's behalf?[51] Does she fail to perceive the threat Adonijah poses to Solomon's kingship? Is she merely 'a good-natured, rather stupid woman' as Whybray would have it?[52] Or is she cunning, recognizing that Solomon will take the request as a claim to the throne and thus use the opportunity to rid himself of his rival? She readily agrees to take Adonijah's request to Solomon and she presents it straightforwardly. Typically, the narrator withholds from us Bathsheba's point of view, and the result in this case is the implication she may not be rationally motivated; women, after all, do not need to act logically or consistently. Bathsheba is metaphorically raped again in these chapters: once again her subjectivity is denied and she is an object exploited by men. She is the quintessential manipulable woman, always acted upon by men—taken by David, used by Nathan, and imposed upon by Adonijah. Though she has voice this time around, there is a real question whether or not she has a voice of her own. Nathan's words, then Adonijah's, are placed in her mouth.

51.  See the discussion of this question by Berlin (1983: 29).
52.  Whybray (1968: 40). Whybray notes how Bathsheba is always acted upon by men. For interesting observations about the principle of 'measure for measure' in the account, see Marcus (1986b).

One might conclude that by taking advantage of David's apparent senility in order to obtain the throne for her son Solomon, Bathsheba gets her literary revenge against David for taking advantage of her. In Adonijah's case, by doing exactly what a man asks, she brings about his ruin, making him pay with his life for his intended appropriation of a woman in a kind of displaced revenge.[53] The one who benefits is Bathsheba's son. With the help of his mother, Solomon first gets the kingship willingly bestowed upon him by David and then eliminates his elder brother who is his rival for the throne. In the patriarchal scheme of things, a mother's most important contribution lies in obtaining advantages for her son(s), as we saw in the case of the matriarchs. Bathsheba's 'reward' is to be queen mother—no small achievement in this royal house (recall only the fates of co-wives Michal, who is literarily murdered, and Abigail, who simply drops out of the picture after becoming David's wife, perhaps because she is too powerful a figure for the biblical narrators to handle).[54]

*Was It Rape?*

As narrative punishment for claiming sexual autonomy, Bath-sheber is gang-raped and her sexuality is symbolically mutilated. She is the ultimate fragmented woman of this book. In Bathsheba's case, in contrast, there is no rape recounted in the narrative—at least, not one we can be sure of. Bathsheba's sexuality is brought under patriarchal control by means of literary rape. Rape in texts and by texts is different from the real thing, as I said at the beginning of this Chapter. But like actual cases of rape, literary rape is difficult to prove. Proving it depends upon taking the woman's word for it. Often the question of rape involves the issue of

53. The parallel is interesting: David takes another man's wife, but he does not pay with his life; his son dies instead. Adonijah wants a woman, who may only symbolically be another man's, but he cannot take her and he pays for his desire with his life.
54. For the threat posed by a powerful woman like Abigail, see Bach (1989).

perception. What a woman experiences as a rape may be viewed as something else by a man.[55] So, too, in the case of literary rape. I do not suggest that the biblical narrators set out to violate the female characters they created, and, indeed, there may be many critics who will come to their defense. In calling these stories literary rape, the woman critic attempts to give voice to biblical women whose experience has been suppressed and distorted by androcentric texts. Readers will judge for themselves whether or not the literary representation of the woman in each of our stories constitutes a rape by the pen.

Patriarchal texts can neither fully nor successfully ignore or suppress women's experience. Like the rapist in my example, they can only have a different perspective from that of the women whose stories they represent—one they impose on the women, presenting it as *the story*, and one the feminist critic resists, challenging their version and its motivation. By piecing together the scattered evidence of Bathsheba's and Bath-sheber's fragmented stories—as well as, in the preceding Chapters, those of Michal, Jephthah's daughter, Samson's mother, Samson's Timnite wife, Delilah, and the matriarchs—I have sought in this book to subvert the dominant male voice or phallocentric ideology of these biblical narratives and, thereby, to offer alternative ways of reading these women's stories. My first step has been to claim that a crime has been committed. Proving it depends upon taking the woman's word for it. And taking the woman's word for it is crucial for recovering women's experience in patriarchal literature.

55. See the discussion in Higgins and Silver (1991). As they point out, 'Who gets to tell the story and whose story counts as "truth" determine the definition of what rape *is*' (p. 1, italics theirs).

# BIBLIOGRAPHY

Abou-Zeid, Ahmed
    1966        'Honor and Shame among the Bedouins of Egypt.'
                In *Honour and Shame: The Values of Mediterranean*
                *Society*, ed. J.G. Peristiany, pp. 243-59. Chicago: Uni-
                versity of Chicago Press.

Ahlström, G.W.
    1978        '*krkr* and *ṭpd*.' *Vetus Testamentum* 28: 100-101.

Alexander, T.D.
    1992        'Are the Wife/Sister Incidents of Genesis Literary
                Compositional Variants?' *Vetus Testamentum* 42:
                145-53.

Alter, Robert
    1981        *The Art of Biblical Narrative*. New York: Basic Books.
    1983        'How Convention Helps Us Read: The Case of the
                Bible's Annunciation Type-Scene.' *Prooftexts* 3: 115-
                30.

Amihai, Miri, George W. Coats, and Anne M. Solomon, eds.
    1989        *Narrative Research on the Hebrew Bible. Semeia* 46.
                Atlanta: Scholars Press.

Andriolo, Karin R.
    1973        'A Structural Analysis of Genealogy and World-
                view in the Old Testament.' *American Anthropologist*
                75: 1657-69.

Aschkenasy, Nehama
    1986        *Eve's Journey: Feminine Images in Hebraic Literary*
                *Tradition*. Philadelphia: University of Pennsylvania
                Press.

Avishur, Y.
    1976        'KRKR in Biblical Hebrew and Ugaritic.' *Vetus Tes-*
                *tamentum* 26: 256-61.

Bach, Alice
    1989        'The Pleasure of Her Text.' *Union Seminary Quarterly*
                *Review* 43: 41-58 [= *The Pleasure of Her Text: Feminist*
                *Readings of Biblical and Historical Texts*, ed. A. Bach,
                pp. 25-44. Philadelphia: Trinity Press International,
                1990].
    1993        'Breaking Free of the Pentateuchal Frame-up: Un-
                covering the Woman in Genesis 39.' In *A Feminist*
                *Companion to Genesis*, ed. A. Brenner, pp. 318-42.

The Feminist Companion to the Bible, 2. Sheffield: JSOT Press.

forthcoming    'Signs of the Flesh.' In *Characterization in Biblical Literature*, ed. E. Struthers Malbon and A. Berlin. *Semeia.* Atlanta: Scholars Press.

Bailey, Randall C.
1990    *David in Love and War: The Pursuit of Power in 2 Samuel 10–12.* Journal for the Study of the Old Testament Supplement Series, 75. Sheffield: JSOT Press.

Bal, Mieke
1987    *Lethal Love: Feminist Literary Readings of Biblical Love Stories.* Bloomington: Indiana University Press.
1988a    *Death and Dissymmetry: The Politics of Coherence in the Book of Judges.* Chicago: University of Chicago Press.
1988b    'Tricky Thematics.' In Exum and Bos 1988: 133-55.
1988c    'The Rape of Narrative and the Narrative of Rape: Speech Acts and Body Language in Judges.' In *Literature and the Body: Essays on Populations and Persons*, ed. E. Scarry, pp. 1-32. Baltimore: Johns Hopkins University Press.
1988d    'How Does an Author Become the Author of a Crime?' Paper read at the 1988 Annual Meeting of the Society of Biblical Literature.
1993    'The Elders and Susanna.' *Biblical Interpretation* 1: 1-19.

Berger, John
1972    *Ways of Seeing.* London: Penguin Books.

Berlin, Adele
1983    *Poetics and Interpretation of Biblical Narrative.* Sheffield: Almond Press.

Berlinerblau, Jacques
1991    'The Israelite Vow: Distress or Daily Life?' *Biblica* 72: 548-55.

Bettelheim, Bruno
1976    *The Uses of Enchantment: The Meaning and Importance of Fairy Tales.* New York: Vintage Books.

Biddle, Mark E.
1990    'The "Endangered Ancestress" and Blessing for the Nations.' *Journal of Biblical Literature* 109: 599-611.

Bird, Phyllis
1974    'Images of Women in the Old Testament.' In *Religion and Sexism*, ed. R.R. Ruether, pp. 41-88. New York: Simon and Schuster.
1989    '"To Play the Harlot": An Inquiry into an Old Testament Metaphor.' In Day 1989: 75-94.

Blenkinsopp, Joseph
1963        'Structure and Style in Judges 13–16.' *Journal of Bibli-cal Literature* 82: 65-76.
1966        'Theme and Motif in the Succession History (2 Sam. xi 2ff.) and the Yahwist Corpus.' *Vetus Testamentum Supplements* 15: 44-57.
Boling, Robert G.
1975        *Judges*. Anchor Bible, 6A. Garden City, NY: Double-day.
Brenner, Athalya
1985        *The Israelite Woman: Social Role and Literary Type in Biblical Narrative*. The Biblical Seminar, 1. Sheffield: JSOT Press.
1986        'Female Social Behaviour: Two Descriptive Patterns within the "Birth of the Hero" Paradigm.' *Vetus Tes-tamentum* 36: 257-73.
Brenner, Athalya and Fokkelien van Dijk-Hemmes
1993        *On Gendering Texts: Female and Male Voices in the Hebrew Bible*. Biblical Interpretation Series, 1. Lei-den: Brill.
Brooks, Peter
1987        'The Idea of a Psychoanalytic Literary Criticism.' In *Discourse in Psychoanalysis and Literature*, ed. S. Rimmon-Kenan, pp. 1-18.
Brownmiller, Susan
1975        *Against Our Will: Men, Women and Rape*. New York: Simon and Schuster.
Burney, C.F.
1970        *The Book of Judges*. New York: Ktav. Originally pub-lished 1903.
Camp, Claudia V.
1988        'Wise and Strange: An Interpretation of the Female Imagery in Proverbs in Light of Trickster Mytho-logy.' In Exum and Bos 1988: 14-36.
Camp, Claudia V. and Carole R. Fontaine
1990        'The Words of the Wise and Their Riddles.' In *Text and Tradition: The Hebrew Bible and Folklore*, ed. S. Niditch, pp. 127-51. Atlanta: Scholars Press.
Cartledge, Tony W.
1992        *Vows in the Hebrew Bible and the Ancient Near East*. Journal for the Study of the Old Testament Supple-ment Series, 147. Sheffield: JSOT Press.
Cassuto, Umberto
1964        *Commentary on the Book of Genesis*. Vol. 2. Jerusalem: Magnes Press.
Cixous, Hélène and Catherine Clément
1986        *The Newly Born Women*. Trans. B. Wing.

Minneapolis: University of Minnesota Press.

Clines, David J.A.
1972        'X, X *ben* Y, *ben* Y: Personal Names in Hebrew Nar-
            rative Style.' *Vetus Testamentum* 22: 266-87.
1978        *The Theme of the Pentateuch.* Journal for the Study of
            the Old Testament Supplement Series, 10. Sheffield:
            JSOT Press.
1990        *What Does Eve Do to Help? and Other Readerly Ques-
            tions to the Old Testament.* Journal for the Study of
            the Old Testament Supplement Series, 94. Sheffield:
            JSOT Press.
1991        'The Story of Michal, Wife of David, in Its Sequen-
            tial Unfolding.' In Clines and Eskenazi 1991: 129-40.
Clines, David J.A. and Tamara C. Eskenazi, eds.
1991        *Telling Queen Michal's Story: An Experiment in Com-
            parative Interpretation.* Journal for the Study of the
            Old Testament Supplement Series, 119. Sheffield:
            JSOT Press.
Coats, George W.
1983        *Genesis, with an Introduction to Narrative Literature.*
            The Forms of the Old Testament Literature, 1.
            Grand Rapids: Eerdmans.
Collins, Adela Yarbro, ed.
1985        *Feminist Perspectives on Biblical Scholarship.* Chico,
            CA: Scholars Press.
Coogan, Michael David
            'The Woman at the Window: An Artistic and Liter-
            ary Motif.' Unpublished paper.
Crenshaw, James L.
1974        'The Samson Saga: Filial Devotion or Erotic
            Attachment?' *Zeitschrift für die alttestamentliche Wis-
            senschaft* 86: 470-504.
1978        *Samson: A Secret Betrayed, a Vow Ignored.* Atlanta:
            John Knox.
Cross, Frank Moore, Jr, and David Noel Freedman
1975        *Studies in Ancient Yahwistic Poetry.* SBL Dissertation
            Series, 21. Missoula, MT: Scholars Press.
Crüsemann, Frank
1980        'Zwei alttestamentliche Witze: I Sam 21: 11-15 und
            II Sam 6: 16. 20-23 als Beispiele einer biblischen Gat-
            tung.' *Zeitschrift für die alttestamentliche Wissenschaft*
            92: 215-27.
Culley, Robert C.
1976        *Studies in the Structure of Hebrew Narrative.* Semeia
            Supplements. Philadelphia: Fortress Press; Mis-
            soula, MT: Scholars Press.

Curran, Leo C.
1984        'Rape and Rape Victims in the Metamorphoses.' In
            *Women in the Ancient World: The Arethusa Papers*, ed.
            J. Peradotto and J.P. Sullivan, pp. 263-86.

Damrosch, David
1987        *The Narrative Covenant: Transformations of Genre in
            the Growth of Biblical Literature*. San Francisco:
            Harper and Row.

Daube, David
1969        *Studies in Biblical Law*. New York: Ktav.

Day, Peggy L.
1989        'From the Child Is Born the Woman: The Story of
            Jephthah's Daughter.' In Day 1989: 58-74.

Day, Peggy L., ed.
1989        *Gender and Difference in Ancient Israel*. Minneapolis:
            Fortress Press.

Donaldson, Mara E.
1981        'Kinship Theory in the Patriarchal Narratives: The
            Case of the Barren Wife.' *Journal of the American
            Academy of Religion* 49: 77-87.

Douglas, Mary
1966        *Purity and Danger: An Analysis of the Concepts of Pol-
            lution and Taboo*. London: Routlege & Kegan Paul.

Dworkin, Andrea
1981        *Pornography: Men Possessing Women*. New York:
            Plume.

Edelman, Diana Vikander
1991        *King Saul in the Historiography of Judah*. Journal for
            the Study of the Old Testament Supplement Series,
            121. Sheffield: JSOT Press.

Eilberg-Schwartz, Howard
1990        *The Savage in Judaism: An Anthropology of Israelite
            Religion and Ancient Judaism*. Bloomington: Indiana
            University Press.
1991        'People of the Body: The Problem of the Body for
            the People of the Book.' *Journal of the History of Sex-
            uality* 2: 1-24.

Eissfeldt, Otto
1910        'Die Rätsel in Jdc 14.' *Zeitschrift für die alttesta-
            mentliche Wissenschaft* 30: 132-35.

Exum, J. Cheryl
1980        'Promise and Fulfillment: Narrative Art in Judges
            13.' *Journal of Biblical Literature* 99: 43-59.
1981        'Aspects of Symmetry and Balance in the Samson
            Saga.' *Journal for the Study of the Old Testament* 19: 3-
            29. Errata in *JSOT* 20: 90.

1983        'The Theological Dimension of the Samson Saga.'
            *Vetus Testamentum* 33: 30-45.
1985        '"Mother in Israel": A Familiar Figure Recon-
            sidered.' In *Feminist Interpretation of the Bible*, ed.
            L.M. Russell, pp. 73-85. Philadelphia: Westminster.
1989        'Murder They Wrote: Ideology and the Manipula-
            tion of Female Presence in Biblical Narrative.' *Union
            Seminary Quarterly Review* 43: 19-39 [= *The Pleasure of
            Her Text: Feminist Readings of Biblical and Historical
            Texts*, ed. A. Bach, pp. 45-67. Philadelphia: Trinity
            Press International, 1990].
1990        'The Centre Cannot Hold: Thematic and Textual
            Instabilities in Judges.' *Catholic Biblical Quarterly* 52:
            410-31.
1992        *Tragedy and Biblical Narrative: Arrows of the Almighty.*
            Cambridge: Cambridge University Press.

Exum, J. Cheryl and J. William Whedbee
1984        'Isaac, Samson, and Saul: Reflections on the Comic
            and Tragic Visions.' In *Tragedy and Comedy in the
            Bible*, ed. J.C. Exum. *Semeia* 32: 5-40.

Exum, J. Cheryl and Johanna W.H. Bos, eds.
1988        *Reasoning with the Foxes: Female Wit in a World of
            Male Power. Semeia* 42. Atlanta: Scholars Press.

Fagles, Robert, trans.
1990        *Homer: The Iliad.* New York: Viking.

Felman, Shoshana
1983        'Beyond Oedipus: The Specimen Story of Psycho-
            analysis.' In *Lacan and Narration: The Psychoanalytic
            Difference in Narrative Theory*, ed. R. Con Davis,
            pp. 1021-53. Baltimore: Johns Hopkins University
            Press.

Fewell, Danna Nolan, ed.
1992        *Reading between Texts: Intertextuality and the Hebrew
            Bible.* Louisville: Westminster/John Knox.

Firestone, Reuven
1991        'Difficulties in Keeping a Beautiful Wife: The
            Legend of Abraham and Sarah in Jewish and
            Islamic Tradition.' *Journal of Jewish Studies* 42: 196-
            214.

Fishbane, Michael
1979        *Text and Texture: Close Readings of Selected Biblical
            Texts.* New York: Schocken Books.

Flanagan, James W.
1983        'Succession and Genealogy in the Davidic Dynasty.'
            In *The Quest for the Kingdom of God*, ed. H.B. Huff-
            mon, F.A. Spina, and A.R.W. Green, pp. 35-55.
            Winona Lake: Eisenbrauns.

Fokkelman, J.P.
1975        *Narrative Art in Genesis.* Assen: van Gorcum.
1981        *Narrative Art and Poetry in the Books of Samuel.* I. *King David.* Assen: van Gorcum.
1986        *Narrative Art and Poetry in the Books of Samuel.* II. *The Crossing Fates.* Assen: van Gorcum.
1990        *Narrative Art and Poetry in the Books of Samuel.* III. *Throne and City.* Assen: van Gorcum.
1992        'Structural Remarks on Judges 9 and 19.' In *Sha'arei Talmon: Studies in the Bible, Qumran, and the Ancient Near East Presented to Shemaryahu Talmon,* ed. M. Fishbane and E. Tov with W.W. Fields, pp. 33-45. Winona Lake: Eisenbrauns.

Fox, Everett
1989        'Can Genesis Be Read as a Book?' In Amihai, Coats, and Solomon 1989: 31-40.

Freedman, David Noel
1972        'The Refrain in David's Lament over Saul and Jonathan.' In *Ex Orbe Religionum,* ed. C.J. Bleeker, S.G.F. Brandon, and M. Simon, pp. 115-26. Studies in the History of Religions, 21. Leiden: Brill.

Freud, Sigmund
1960        *The Ego and the Id.* Trans. Joan Riviere. Rev. and ed., James Strachey. New York: W.W. Norton & Company.
1961        *Beyond the Pleasure Principle.* Trans. and ed., James Strachey. New York: W.W. Norton & Company.
1962        *Three Essays on the Theory of Sexuality.* Trans. and rev. by James Strachey, with a New Introduction by Steven Marcus. New York: Basic Books.
1965        *The Interpretation of Dreams.* Trans. and ed., James Strachey. New York: Avon Books.

Frymer-Kensky, Tikva
1981        'Patriarchal Family Relationships and Near Eastern Law.' *Biblical Archaeologist* 44: 209-14.

Fuchs, Esther
1985a       'The Literary Characterization of Mothers and Sexual Politics in the Hebrew Bible.' In Collins 1985: 117-36.
1985b       'Who Is Hiding the Truth? Deceptive Women and Biblical Androcentrism.' In Collins 1985: 137-44.
1988        '"For I Have the Way of Women": Deception, Gender, and Ideology in Biblical Narrative.' In Exum and Bos 1988: 68-83.
1989        'Marginalization, Ambiguity, Silencing: The Story of Jephthah's Daughter.' *Journal of Feminist Studies in Religion* 5: 35-45.

Furman, Nelly
1985        'His Story versus Her Story: Male Genealogy and
            Female Strategy in the Jacob Cycle.' In Collins 1985:
            107-16.
Gaster, Theodor H.
1981        *Myth, Legend, and Custom in the Old Testament*, vol. 2.
            Gloucester, MA: Peter Smith.
Gennep, Arnold van
1960        *The Rites of Passage*. Trans. B. Vizedom and G.L.
            Caffee. Chicago: University of Chicago Press.
Girard, René
1965        *Deceit, Desire, and the Novel: Self and Other in Literary
            Structure*. Trans. Y. Freccero. Baltimore: Johns
            Hopkins University Press.
1977        *Violence and the Sacred*. Trans. Patrick Gregory. Bal-
            timore: Johns Hopkins University Press.
Goitein, S.D.
1988        'Women as Creators of Biblical Genres.' *Prooftexts* 8:
            1-33.
Gottwald, Norman K.
1979        *The Tribes of Yahweh: A Sociology of the Religion of Lib-
            erated Israel, 1250–1050 B.C.E.* Maryknoll, NY: Orbis
            Books.
Green, Alberto R.W.
1975        *The Role of Human Sacrifice in the Ancient Near East*.
            ASOR Dissertation Series, 1. Missoula, MT: Scholars
            Press.
Greenberg, Moshe
1962        'Another Look at Rachel's Theft of the Teraphim.'
            *Journal of Biblical Literature* 81: 239-48.
Greenstein, Edward L.
1981        'The Riddle of Samson.' *Prooftexts* 1: 237-60.
Gressmann, Hugo
1922        *Die Anfänge Israels*. 2. Aufl. Die Schriften des Alten
            Testaments, II/3. Göttingen: Vandenhoeck &
            Ruprecht.
Griffin, Susan
1981        *Pornography and Silence: Culture's Revenge against
            Nature*. New York: Harper & Row.
Gubar, Susan
1989        'Representing Pornography: Feminism, Criticism,
            and Depictions of Female Violation.' In *For Adult
            Users Only: The Dilemma of Violent Pornography*, ed.
            S. Gubar and J. Hoff, pp. 47-67. Bloomington:
            Indiana University Press.
Gunkel, Hermann
1913        'Simson.' In *Reden und Aufsätze*, pp. 38-64.

Göttingen: Vandenhoeck & Ruprecht.
Gunn, David M.
1978        *The Story of King David: Genre and Interpretation.*
            Journal for the Study of the Old Testament Supple-
            ment Series, 6. Sheffield: JSOT Press.
1992        'Samson of Sorrows: An Isaianic Gloss on Judges
            13–16.' In Fewell 1992: 225-53.
Hackett, Jo Ann
1985        'In the Days of Jael: Reclaiming the History of
            Women in Ancient Israel.' In *Immaculate and Power-
            ful: The Female in Sacred Image and Social Reality,* ed.
            C.W. Atkinson, C.H. Buchanan, and M.R. Miles, pp.
            15-38. Boston: Beacon Press.
Hare-Mustin, Rachel T. and Jeanne Marecek
1990        'On Making a Difference.' In *Making a Difference:
            Psychology and the Construction of Gender,* ed. R.T.
            Hare-Mustin and J. Marecek, pp. 1-21. New Haven:
            Yale University Press.
Hertzberg, H.W.
1964        *I and II Samuel.* The Old Testament Library. Trans.
            J.S. Bowden. Philadelphia: Westminster.
Higgins, Lynn A. and Brenda R. Silver
1991        'Introduction: Rereading Rape.' In Higgins and Sil-
            ver 1991: 1-11.
Higgins, Lynn A. and Brenda R. Silver, eds.
1991        *Rape and Representation.* New York: Columbia Uni-
            versity Press.
Holladay, William L.
1970        'Form and Word-Play in David's Lament over Saul
            and Jonathan.' *Vetus Testamentum* 20: 153-89.
Huehnergard, John
1985        'Biblical Notes on Some New Akkadian Texts from
            Emar (Syria).' *Catholic Biblical Quarterly* 47: 428-31.
Huston, Nancy
1986        'The Matrix of War: Mothers and Heroes.' In
            Suleiman 1986: 119-36.
Jay, Nancy
1985        'Sacrifice as Remedy for Having Been Born of
            Woman.' In *Immaculate and Powerful: The Female in
            Sacred Image and Social Reality,* ed. C.W. Atkinson,
            C.H. Buchanan, and M.R. Miles, pp. 283-309.
            Boston: Beacon Press.
1988        'Sacrifice, Descent and the Patriarchs.' *Vetus Testa-
            mentum* 38: 52-70.
1992        *Throughout Your Generations Forever: Sacrifice, Reli-
            gion, and Paternity.* Chicago: University of Chicago
            Press.

Jeansonne, Sharon Pace
1990            *The Women of Genesis: From Sarah to Potiphar's Wife.*
                Minneapolis: Fortress Press.
Jensen, Hans J.L.
1992            'Desire, Rivalry and Collective Violence in the
                "Succession Narrative".' *Journal for the Study of the
                Old Testament* 55: 39-59.
Jobling, David
1978            *The Sense of Biblical Narrative: Structural Analyses in
                the Hebrew Bible,* I. Journal for the Study of the Old
                Testament Supplement Series, 7. Sheffield: JSOT
                Press.
Keller, Carl A.
1954            '"Die Gefährdung der Ahnfrau." Ein Beitrag zur
                gattungs- und motivgeschichtlichen Erforschung
                alttestamentlicher Erzählungen.' *Zeitschrift für die
                alttestamentliche Wissenschaft* 66: 181-91.
Keukens, Karlheinz H.
1982            'Richter 11,37f.: Rite de passage und Übersetzungs-
                probleme.' *Biblische Notizen* 19: 41-42.
King, Philip J.
1988            *Amos, Hosea, Micah: An Archaeological Commentary.*
                Philadelphia: Westminster.
Koch, Klaus
1969            *The Growth of the Biblical Tradition: The Form-Critical
                Method.* Trans. S.M. Cupitt. New York: Charles
                Scribner's Sons.
Kristeva, Julia
1980            *Desire in Language: A Semiotic Approach to Literature
                and Art.* Ed. L.S. Roudiez. Trans. T. Gora, A. Jardine,
                and L.S. Roudiez. New York: Columbia University
                Press.
1982            *Powers of Horror: An Essay on Abjection.* Trans. L.S.
                Roudiez. New York: Columbia University Press.
1986a           *About Chinese Women.* Trans. A. Barrows. New York:
                Marion Boyars.
1986b           'Stabat Mater.' In Suleiman 1986: 99-118.
Lacan, Jacques
1988            'Seminar on "The Purloined Letter".' Trans.
                J. Mehlman. In *The Purloined Poe: Lacan, Derrida and
                Psychoanalytic Reading,* ed. J.P. Muller and W.J.
                Richardson, pp. 28-54. Baltimore: Johns Hopkins
                University Press.
Lamphere, Louise
1974            'Strategies, Cooperation, and Conflict among
                Women in Domestic Groups.' In Rosaldo and Lam-
                phere 1974: 97-112.

Landy, Francis
1984            'Are We in the Place of Averroes? Response to the
               Articles of Exum and Whedbee, Buss, Gottwald,
               and Good.' In *Tragedy and Comedy in the Bible*, ed.
               J.C. Exum. *Semeia* 32: 131-48.
1989           'Narrative Techniques and Symbolic Transactions
               in the Akedah.' In *Signs and Wonders: Biblical Texts
               in Literary Focus*, ed. J.C. Exum, pp. 1-40. Semeia
               Studies. Decatur, GA: Scholars Press.
Lasine, Stuart
1984           'Guest and Host in Judges 19: Lot's Hospitality in
               an Inverted World.' *Journal for the Study of the Old
               Testament* 29: 37-59.
Leach, Edmund R.
1966           'The Legitimacy of Solomon: Some Structural
               Aspects of Old Testament History.' *Archives
               européennes de sociologie/European Journal of Sociology*
               7: 58-101 [= 1969: 25-83].
1967           'Magical Hair.' In *Myth and Cosmos: Readings in
               Mythology and Symbolism*, ed. J. Middleton, pp. 77-
               108. Garden City, NY: The Natural History Press.
1969           *Genesis as Myth and Other Essays*. London: Jonathan
               Cape.
Lerner, Gerda
1986           *The Creation of Patriarchy*. New York: Oxford Uni-
               versity Press.
Lévi-Strauss, Claude
1966           *The Savage Mind*. Chicago: University of Chicago
               Press.
1973           *From Honey to Ashes*. Trans J. and D. Weightman.
               New York: Harper & Row.
1978           *The Origin of Table Manners*. Trans. J. and D. Weight-
               man. Chicago: University of Chicago Press.
Levy, Ludwig
1916           'Sexualsymbolik in der Simsonsage.' *Zeitschrift für
               Sexualwissenschaft* 3: 256-71 [= *Psychoanalytische
               Interpretationen biblischer Texte*, ed. Y. Spiegel, pp.
               75-93. Munich: Kaiser, 1972].
Loraux, Nicole
1987           *Tragic Ways of Killing a Woman*. Cambridge, MA:
               Harvard University Press.
Marcus, David
1986a          *Jephthah and His Vow*. Lubbock, TX: Texas Tech
               Press.
1986b          'David the Deceiver and David the Dupe.' *Prooftexts*
               6: 163-71.

McCarter, P. Kyle, Jr
1980a 'The Apology of David.' *Journal of Biblical Literature* 99: 489-504.
1980b *I Samuel*. Anchor Bible, 8. Garden City, NY: Doubleday.
1984 *II Samuel*. Anchor Bible, 9. Garden City, NY: Doubleday.

Meyers, Carol
1988 *Discovering Eve: Ancient Israelite Women in Context*. New York: Oxford University Press.
1991 '"To Her Mother's House": Considering a Counterpart to the Israelite *Bêt āb*.' In *The Bible and the Politics of Exegesis: Essays in Honor of Norman K. Gottwald on His Sixty-fifth Birthday*, ed. D. Jobling, P.L. Day and G.T. Sheppard, pp. 39-51. Cleveland: Pilgrim Press.

Miles, Margaret R.
1989 *Carnal Knowing: Female Nakedness and Religious Meaning in the Christian West*. New York: Vintage Books.

Miscall, Peter D.
1979 'Literary Unity in Old Testament Narrative.' In *Perspectives on Old Testament Narratives*, ed. R.C. Culley. *Semeia* 15:27-44.
1983 *The Workings of Old Testament Narrative*. Semeia Studies. Philadelphia: Fortress Press; Chico, CA: Scholars Press.

Moi, Toril
1985 *Sexual/Textual Politics: Feminist Literary Theory*. London: Methuen.

Morrison, Martha A.
1983 'The Jacob and Laban Narrative in Light of Near Eastern Sources.' *Biblical Archaeologist* 46: 155-64.

Newsom, Carol A.
1989 'Woman and the Discourse of Patriarchal Wisdom: A Study of Proverbs 1–9.' In Day 1989: 142-60.

Nicol, George G.
1988 'Bathsheba, a Clever Woman?' *Expository Times* 99: 360-63.

Niditch, Susan
1982 'The "Sodomite" Theme in Judges 19–20: Family, Community, and Social Disintegration.' *Catholic Biblical Quarterly* 44: 365-78.
1987 *Underdogs and Tricksters: A Prelude to Biblical Folklore*. San Francisco: Harper & Row.
1990 'Samson as Culture Hero, Trickster, and Bandit: The Empowerment of the Weak.' *Catholic Biblical*

Noth, Martin
  *Quarterly* 52: 608-24.

1972        *A History of Pentateuchal Traditions*. Trans. Bernhard
            W. Anderson. Englewood Cliffs, NJ: Prentice–Hall.

Oden, Robert A.
1983        'Jacob as Father, Husband, and Nephew: Kinship
            Studies and the Patriarchal Narratives.' *Journal of
            Biblical Literature* 102: 189-205.

Ortner, Sherry B.
1974        'Is Female to Male as Nature Is to Culture?' In Ros-
            aldo and Lamphere 1974: 67-87.

Pardes, Ilana
1992        *Countertraditions in the Bible: A Feminist Approach*.
            Cambridge, MA: Harvard University Press.

Parker, Simon B.
1979        'The Vow in Ugaritic and Israelite Literature.'
            *Ugarit-Forschungen* 11: 693-700.
1989        *The Pre-Biblical Narrative Tradition*. SBL Sources for
            Biblical Study, 24. Atlanta: Scholars Press.

Penchansky, David
1992        'Staying the Night: Intertextuality in Genesis and
            Judges.' In Fewell 1992: 77-88.

Petersen, David L.
1973        'A Thrice-Told Tale: Genre, Theme, and Motif.' *Bib-
            lical Research* 18: 30-43.

Pitt-Rivers, Julian
1977        *The Fate of Shechem or the Politics of Sex*. Cambridge:
            Cambridge University Press.

Polzin, Robert
1975        ' "The Ancestress of Israel in Danger" in Danger.' In
            *Classical Hebrew Narrative*, ed. R.C. Culley. *Semeia* 3:
            81-98.
1980        *Moses and the Deuteronomist. A Literary Study of the
            Deuteronomic History, Part 1*. New York: Seabury.

Prewitt, Terry J.
1981        'Kinship Structures and the Genesis Genealogies.'
            *Journal of Near Eastern Studies* 40: 87-98.

Rad, Gerhard von
1961        *Genesis*. Trans. J.H. Marks. Philadelphia: Westmin-
            ster.

Rashkow, Ilona N.
1992        'Intertextuality, Transference, and the Reader in/of
            Genesis 12 and 20.' In Fewell 1992: 57-73.

Reinhartz, Adele
1992          'Samson's Mother: An Unnamed Protagonist.' *Journal for the Study of the Old Testament* 55: 25-37.
Rich, Adrienne
1979          'Motherhood: The Contemporary Emergency and the Quantum Leap (1978).' In *On Lies, Secrets, and Silence: Selected Prose 1966–1978*. New York: W.W. Norton & Co.
Rooney, Ellen
1991          ' "A Little More than Persuading": Tess and the Subject of Sexual Violence.' In Higgins and Silver 1991: 87-114.
Rosaldo, Michelle Zimbalist
1974          'Woman, Culture, and Society: A Theoretical Overview.' In Rosaldo and Lamphere 1974: 97-112.
Rosaldo, Michelle Zimbalist and Louise Lamphere, eds.
1974          *Woman, Culture, and Society*. Stanford: Stanford University Press.
Rosenberg, Joel
1986          *King and Kin: Political Allegory in the Hebrew Bible*. Bloomington: Indiana University Press.
Sanday, Peggy Reeves
1990          *Fraternity Gang Rape: Sex, Brotherhood, and Privilege on Campus*. New York: New York University Press.
Sasson, Jack M.
1988          'Who Cut Samson's Hair? (And Other Trifling Issues Raised by Judges 16).' *Prooftexts* 8: 333-39.
Scarry, Elaine
1985          *The Body in Pain: The Making and Unmaking of the World*. New York: Oxford University Press.
Sedgwick, Eve Kosofsky
1985          *Between Men: English Literature and Male Homosocial Desire*. New York: Columbia University Press.
Shea, William H.
1986          'Chiasmus and the Structure of David's Lament.' *Journal of Biblical Literature* 105: 13-25.
Sherwood, Stephen K.
1990          *'Had God Not Been on My Side': An Examination of the Narrative Technique of the Story of Jacob and Laban*. European University Studies, Series 23, Vol. 400. Frankfurt am Main: Peter Lang.
Showalter, Elaine
1990          *Sexual Anarchy: Gender and Culture at the Fin de Siècle*. New York: Penguin Books.
Skinner, John
1910          *A Critical and Exegetical Commentary on Genesis*. International Critical Commentary. Edinburgh: T. &

T. Clark.

Soggin, J. Alberto
1981    *Judges*. The Old Testament Library. Trans. J.S. Bowden. Philadelphia: Westminster.

Speiser, E.A.
1964    *Genesis*. Anchor Bible, 1. Garden City, NY: Doubleday.

Stade, B.
1884    'Miscellen: 4. Ri. 14.' *Zeitschrift für die alttestamentliche Wissenschaft* 4: 250-56.

Steinberg, Naomi
1984    'Gender Roles in the Rebekah Cycle.' *Union Seminary Quarterly Review* 39: 175-88.
1989    'The Genealogical Framework of the Family Stories in Genesis.' In Amihai, Coats, and Solomon 1989: 41-50.
1991    'Alliance or Descent? The Function of Marriage in Genesis.' *Journal for the Study of the Old Testament* 51: 45-55.

Suleiman, Susan Rubin, ed.
1986    *The Female Body in Western Culture: Contemporary Perspectives*. Cambridge, MA: Harvard University Press.

Thiselton, Anthony C.
1974    'The Supposed Power of Words in the Biblical Writings.' *Journal of Theological Studies* NS 25: 283-99.

Thompson, J.A.
1974    'The Significance of the Verb *Love* in the David–Jonathan Narratives in 1 Samuel.' *Vetus Testamentum* 24: 334-38.

Thompson, Thomas L.
1974    *The Historicity of the Patriarchal Narratives: The Quest for the Historical Abraham*. Beihefte zur Zeitschrift für die alttestamentliche Wissenschaft, 133. Berlin: de Gruyter.

Tiger, Lionel
1984    *Men in Groups*. New York: Marion Boyers.

Toorn, K. van der
1986    'Judges xvi 21 in the Light of the Akkadian Sources.' *Vetus Testamentum* 36: 248-51.

Torczyner [Tur Sinai], Harry
1924    'The Riddle in the Bible.' *Hebrew Union College Annual* 1: 125-49.

Trible, Phyllis
1984    *Texts of Terror: Literary-Feminist Readings of Biblical Narratives*. Philadelphia: Fortress Press.

Tsevat, Matitiahu
1975      'b^ethûlāh; b^ethûlîm.' In *Theological Dictionary of the Old Testament*, II, ed. G.J. Botterweck and H. Ringgren, pp. 340-43. Trans. J.T. Willis. Grand Rapids: Eerdmans.

Turner, Victor
1967      *The Forest of Symbols: Aspects of Ndembu Ritual.* Ithaca: Cornell University Press.
1977      *The Ritual Process: Structure and Anti-Structure.* New York: Aldine Publishing Company.

Van Seters, John
1975      *Abraham in History and Tradition.* New Haven: Yale University Press.

Vawter, Bruce
1977      *On Genesis: A New Reading.* Garden City, NY: Doubleday.

Wander, Nathaniel
1981      'Structure, Contradiction, and "Resolution" in Mythology: Father's Brother's Daughter Marriage and the Treatment of Women in Genesis 11–50.' *Journal of the Ancient Near Eastern Society* 13: 75-99.

Wenham, G.J.
1972      '*Betulah* "A Girl of Marriageable Age".' *Vetus Testamentum* 22: 326-48.
1983      'Why Does Sexual Intercourse Defile (Lev 15: 18)?' *Zeitschrift für die alttestamentliche Wissenschaft* 95: 432-34.

Westbrook, Raymond
1990      'Adultery in Ancient Near Eastern Law.' *Revue Biblique* 97: 542-80.
1991      *Property and the Family in Biblical Law.* Journal for the Study of the Old Testament Supplement Series, 113. Sheffield: JSOT Press.

Westermann, Claus
1980      *The Promises to the Fathers: Studies on the Patriarchal Narratives.* Trans. David E. Green. Philadelphia: Fortress Press.
1985      *Genesis 12–36.* Trans. J.J. Scullion. Minneapolis: Augsburg Press.

Wharton, James A.
1973      'The Secret of Yahweh: Story and Affirmation in Judges 13–16.' *Interpretation* 27: 48-65.

White, Hugh C.
1991      *Narration and Discourse in the Book of Genesis.* Cambridge: Cambridge University Press.

Whybray, R.N.
1968      *The Succession Narrative: A Study of II Sam. 9–20 and I*

*Kings 1 and 2.* Studies in Biblical Theology, Second Series, 9. Naperville, IL: Alec R. Allenson.

Williams, James G.
1982       *Women Recounted: Narrative Thinking and the God of Israel.* Sheffield: Almond Press.

Wilson, Robert R.
1977       *Genealogy and History in the Biblical World.* New Haven: Yale University Press.

Winnett, Susan
1991       'The Marquise's "O" and the Mad Dash of Narrative.' In Higgins and Silver 1991: 67-86.

Yee, Gale A.
1988       '"Fraught with Background": Literary Ambiguity in II Samuel 11.' *Interpretation* 42: 240-53.

Zakovitch, Yair
1981       'The Woman's Rights in the Biblical Law of Divorce.' *The Jewish Law Annual* 4: 28-46.

1993       'Through the Looking Glass: Reflections of Genesis Stories in the Bible.' *Biblical Interpretation* 1: 139-52.

# INDEX OF BIBLICAL REFERENCES

# INDEX OF AUTHORS